DEVELOPMENTAL INNOVATION:
EMERGING WORLDVIEWS
AND INDIVIDUAL
LEARNING

TOM CHRISTENSEN, EDITOR

INTEGRAL PUBLISHERS
TUCSON, AZ

Integral Publishers
4845 E. 2nd St.
Tucson, AZ 85711

ISBN: 978-1-4951-5909-1

Cover by QTPunque.

DEDICATION

Feeling gratitude and not expressing it is like wrapping a present and not giving it.

William Arthur Ward

Thank you Professor Clare W. Graves.

The efforts of the many brilliant and skilled professionals documented in these volumes would not be here if it were not for the diligent and long term efforts of the first Gravesian, Professor Clare W. Graves (1914 – 1986). As the classic metaphor says, these authors would not have risen to this level of competence and visibility without the broad and tall shoulders of Professor Graves to stand upon.

There are a few who knew "Clare" personally, and all reports indicate he was a personable, caring, and artful researcher, theorist, educator, family man and friend. This would be legacy enough for many of us. Graves, however, left us with even more; he embodied the leading edge of human development that he discovered. He was captured by a vision of how all the apparently limited perspectives on a healthy psychology could be lined up so as to address the contexts they pertain to. His approach was not constrained by either/or thinking, but had the scope to integrate truths into a larger vision where all well-founded truths had their place.

Graves' level of cognitive complexity could not be served by linear thinking or models. He had to reach to what is still the most complex template for organizing information, General Systems Theory, in order to be able to account for feedback loops between capacity and context. Systems Theory was necessary to describe the emergence of more complex and unpredictable measures out of the less complex and predictable; to give theoretical consistency to the levels of maturation he noted as deriving from changes of equilibrium and disequilibrium; to account for change occasioned by perturbations from excessive energy deriving from solved challenges; to include the relevance of an array of subsystems, including human biology, physiology, neurology, as well as culture, education and management. If you had any trouble comprehending those past few sentences, then you have gotten a sense of how complex Grave's cognition might have been and what understanding may yet lie ahead for you.

Graves was a path finder. He struggled with the concepts of his time and left us with a map that resolved many of the developmental conundrums of his time; a map that may well drive creative thinking about humans and human systems for ages to come. For those whose curiosity about human nature is insatiable, Graves has provided answers, directions, milestones, insights, and nudges towards what is still unknown. From the stories that follow, it should be clear that we now have new degrees of freedom for engaging humanity's problems.

At the leading edge of Graves' model, we find a humanity that has left selfish behavior behind, that cares for planetary well-being as its own well-being, that has integrated love and compassion, and gone beyond this with artful, collaborative, action. For all the effort, enjoyment, records, ideas, and trail-making that Graves left behind, gratitude is a natural, as well as deserved response. For his vision of what else is possible for humanity, he deserves much more than gratitude. Perhaps living his highest vision for humanity is what comes after gratitude. May he be honored in such a way... until what is beyond even this appears.

TABLE OF CONTENTS

PERSONAL PSYCHOLOGY AND THE JOURNEY OF EMERGENCE

GRAVES—CONTEXTUALIZATIONS 284

THE BOOKS SPEAK 288

INDEX 290

PUBLISHERS PREFACE

The chapters in the book, *Innovative Development: Emerging Worldviews and Systems Change,* and in its companion, *Developmental Innovation: Emerging Worldviews and Individual Learning,* represent the conjunction of many streams of thought and practice. Each chapter is influenced by one or more of the following conceptual frameworks.

First is adult development psychology. This is a young field with several frameworks and approaches to understanding how we develop as individuals. Theorists and researchers such as Clare W. Graves, Michael Commons, Michael Basseches, Jane Loevenger, William Perry, Jean Gebser, Susann Cook-Greuter, Robert Kegan, Bill Torbert and others have laid foundations for better understanding how we as individuals develop and evolve cognitively, emotionally, psychologically and even spiritually.

Another is integral theory. This is based on the work of theorists such as Ervin Laszlo and Ken Wilber. While not all authors or all of their offerings give attention to integral theory, the relationship between adult development psychology and integral theory is an interesting one in that it provides a way of understanding how our development as individuals cannot be fully understood without attention to our psychology and our biology. In addition, we cannot understand our development without attention to the cultural and systemic Life Conditions we have encountered and created. Integral theory supports the integration of monological views of individual psychology in which the focus is on the internal dynamics of each individual with a dialogical view. The dialogical approach requires that we understand individual psychology in terms of the interactive processes of individuals with their contexts and Life Conditions.

A central concern of both adult development psychology and integral theory is how we create meaning and make sense of ourselves and our world. We cannot achieve that by focusing on individuals and their human relationships. We also need to attend to the cultures, systems, technologies, structures, processes, and artifacts of that world, those contexts. In the case of the chapters found in these two books, this contextual perspective is underscored by Clare Graves' attention to the importance of Life Conditions to the worldview we bring to making sense and meaning out of our selves and our world. As a growing interest in transdisciplinarity suggests, we are recognizing that we cannot effectively address the complex and critical challenges we face with simplistic solutions. Science and spirituality are in need of integration. This requires the integration of diverse worldviews and ways of making meaning. The authors in these volumes have been influenced by many elements of this diversity.

In these volumes we will find work that seeks to integrate our understandings from the labors of Clare W. Graves and the extension of his research by others, particularly Don E. Beck and his colleagues and students, with theories and models drawn from systems theory, cognitive science, cultural theory, organization development, learning theory and a myriad of other influences. These two volumes represent a step along the path toward more transdisciplinary engagement with the development of human systems and of individuals. The editor, Tom Christensen, has organized this material around the two themes of systems, on the one hand, and individuals, on the other. Keep in mind that this separation is an organizing device. It would be a mistake to think of these as two independent domains.

The reader is encouraged to review the material in both volumes as a way to build an appreciation of the depth and scope of the work of Clare W. Graves and his followers, as well as promoting an integration of how we make sense and meaning out of the complex dynamics facing us in the world, today. The fourth dimension of time is playing a more and more limiting role on the choices we make and how we go about implementing them. Until we can more effectively integrate our individual learning and development with how we develop and evolve our systems and relationships with cultural and developmental diversity in the world we will likely continue down a path that seems to be leading to the destruction of the world as we know it.

This is a time in which it is increasingly difficult to muster up a sense of optimism for the world and our selves. We require a critical mass of individuals around the world building the capacity for engaging with diversity and realigning our systems to embrace that diversity in ways that help us build more constructive allocation of resources and addressing the critical challenges of our day. There are not many signs for optimism in this era of the clash of civilizations, the leveraging of technology to build and to destroy, the inequities that exist not just in the distribution of wealth within developed nations, but between nations and within cultures that span national boundaries. The construction of boundaries in all aspects of human being in the world underlies much of our sense of identity, as well as the ways in which we engage with each other – and seek to destroy each other.

Daily headlines expose us to barbarism and destruction as individuals seek to protect these boundaries designed to defend the status quo, the distribution of resources, the growing economic and political power of the oligarchies, the freedoms enjoyed by the military-industrial complex at the expense of millions of human lives, the aggressive defense of the past by religious fanatics, the barbaric destruction of human life and cultural artifacts by those seeking to dominate in the face of power vacuums and inequities, the ongoing destruction of the environment, the loss of species due to greed and environmental degradation, and so on.

It seems an overwhelming challenge to find a path that will lead us out of this self-destructive chaos. Today, as I write this in my office in Tucson, Arizona the world seems peaceful and delightful. We have been blessed with cooler than usual temperatures for a few days. Birds are chirping – I can see sparrows, desert doves, woodpeckers and blackbirds taking turns enjoying the water filled birdbath outside my office window. For this rare moment – a period of ongoing challenges in our lives – peace and contentment seem possible. But I know this is just a moment in an ongoing process of development and destruction. I can enjoy this moment of peace and personal contentment, yet the threats of our collective challenges in the world are all around me.

While I may find it difficult to see generative paths ahead, I am convinced that it is the work of people like the authors in these two volumes that holds out hope for the development of such paths. Theirs are not quick fixes, nor simplistic solutions. Instead, their work helps us understand the necessity to shift our ways of meaning making so that our views are less static, are open to seeing dynamic processes of being and living and creating. It is my intention that bringing these two volumes to you will contribute to the design and implementation of a generative path for us, individually and collectively, in support of life on this planet for the natural evolution of species and systems.

Russ Volckmann, PhD
Publisher, Integral Publishers
May 25, 2015

FOREWARD

Laura Frey Horn

More than sixty years ago, Dr. Clare W. Graves began his research and quest to develop a fuller, more complex understanding and theory of human development, or as he described it "the psychology of the mature human being." He continued his work until his death in 1986. With the work of others, including initially Dr. Don E. Beck and those in this book, Graves' work lives on.

Dr. Graves was keenly aware of the limitations of other theories of adult development. His research was carried out over decades. My understanding was that he conducted research within organizations in addition to his research at the individual levels of development. He was also extremely well versed in all of the current and past theories of adult development and current scientific, sociological and other research that could impact human development. However, an area of research of which I am certain I was a part that did occur at Union and involved students was the assignment in one of the upper class courses he taught. One major paper was to address our own theory of adult development. My later understanding (from Don E. Beck in one of our many conversations about Clare) was that this was a part of his research.

Dr. Graves was, in my opinion, a constant observer. On one of my trips to Union's Library and the special archives, I found pages of his notes where he had made observations about different individuals' behaviors, actions, comments or words. At the top of pages, he would denote a level (i.e. D-Q, F-S, G-T, etc.). It was clear that comments had been added over time and the comments could have been made by different individuals.

As Graves moved more deeply into his research, he recognized that all aspects of human development needed to include our understanding of whole systems. His research focused on the complete spectrum of the adult human being, including the psychological, sociological, physical, cultural, biological and developmental impacts of systems changes in the development of human beings. Although other psychologists had developed hierarchal developmental models and theories, Graves' work was the first to include a holistic or whole systems approach.

Gravesian theory is deeply and widely complex simply because human development is deeply and widely complex. The deeper Graves' research took him, the more he found connections to complementary systems that impacted the psychology of the mature human being. Graves also uncovered how individuals' collective growth and development could impact sociological systems at the tribal, community, organizational and cultural levels. Graves identified the significant impact of open and closed systems as well as effective/ineffective (healthy/unhealthy) traits or behaviors. Hence, Gravesian theory was known, at least for a time at Union College, as the Gravesian "Bio-Psycho-Social-Double Helix Model of Emergent Adult Development". (I believe that it went through several name changes over time.) Dr. Graves had recognized that the levels of human development he had been researching also applied to organizational levels of adult psychology. He recognized that biology, psychology, sociology and other areas – including culture – impacted human development. He was the first psychologist to acknowledge the critical importance of all of these parameters. And, yet, many of his peers did not understand his theory and its importance.

By the time I arrived at Union College in the early 1970s (the second class of women admitted to the college), Graves had already spent two decades of his life extensively researching and developing his theory. Clare Graves was an iconic figure on Union College's campus. He was tall, strong and rarely spoke to students when he strode across campus. (I do believe that he had already experienced health issues by the time I came to Union, but doubt many students knew.) He was admired, but certainly misunderstood by many students.

There were certainly many students, including psychology majors at Union, who resisted taking Graves' courses because they knew the theory was challenging and difficult to follow. I often wondered if other psychologists resisted or resented his work because his theory was difficult to understand. Dr. Don E. Beck once told me that Clare held off publishing results of his studies until he felt his research was incontrovertible because his colleague, Abraham Maslow, warned him that he would be attacked for such a remarkably different theory of human development, as had been Maslow's experience in presenting his theory of motivation.

It was well known that Dr. Graves had a "ranch" outside the town of Schenectady, New York where he trained and rode horses. The rumor was that he "broke wild stallions with his bare hands" in his spare time – when he wasn't teaching or doing his research. The role of "stallion tamer" only added to his reputation. And, the fact that he was developing a complex, new theory that few, including psychology majors, could understand created an image even larger than life. I think Clare knew that many students were reticent to talk to him and he used it to his advantage. I also often thought that he used it as a test, even as a piece of his own research. In fact, it seemed many students were afraid of him. He was a legend on and off campus. If the man could "break" wild stallions, what would he do if you challenged that gruff demeanor?

I learned just how strong this iconic image of Dr. Graves was within the first days of arrival at Union. During Freshman Orientation, the few women (fewer than 100 women in the 1500 student body) were offered considerable guidance by the upperclassmen. A senior psychology major offered to provide a tour of the Psychology Department and building, with a complete run down of my advisor and the other professors. When told my advisor was Dr. Clare W. Graves, he immediately said, "Oh no! Tomorrow morning, first thing you MUST go to the registrar's office and request a new advisor. Tell the registrar anything! Just tell her you have got to have a different advisor! I mean it! First thing, before anyone else puts in their request!" There was fear in his voice. I don't scare easily, so I asked, "Really? How bad can SHE be?!" Needless to say, I did not request a change. Graves' deep voice and focus on his research may have contributed to the sense that he seemed aloof and hard to reach to those who didn't know him well. In fact, more than a large number of students were wary of him and willing to avoid him. I think Dr. Graves was quite aware of his reputation and probably found it humorous.

When I first met him I was exposed to his gruff persona. As my advisor, Dr. Graves had to approve and sign off on my course selection. He also required that students come to him in person for the sign off, while many advisors were delighted to have students leave the form under the door.

Dr. Graves only taught upper class courses, but as his advisee, I had the opportunity to meet him as a freshman. Although most faculty members – especially full professors like Dr. Graves – chose the more spacious offices on the second floor of the "Psych Department" building, he chose the quieter, smaller third floor "attic" office. Although I don't scare easily, I did hear and heed the legendary stories of Dr. Clare W. Graves, and proceeded with caution. When I reached his office, he was deep in thought and writing. I paused outside his office for a moment and waited. I knew he had heard and seen me, but there was no response. Finally, I said quietly, "Dr. Graves?" "YES!" with a bit of a BOOM! I was a bit taken aback and considered the options – run or stay. Before I could decide, I noticed it… the small square of beautiful blue sky behind Dr. Graves! There, behind him, the legend, the man who "…breaks wild stallions with his bare hands…" sitting in a tiny office… with boxes surrounding him and a pile of papers on his desk! Shouldn't he be outside right this moment on a horse… racing across the mountains?!

"Dr. Graves, WHAT are you doing inside right now?! It is so beautiful outside! Shouldn't you be outside now?" With that Dr. Graves startled and looked at me. Oh no, I am really in for it now!

"WELL, IF YOU DAMN STUDENTS DIDN'T GIVE US DAMN PROFESSORS SO MUCH DAMN WORK, I COULD BE OUTSIDE!"

And, a glare. Do I stay or run… Hmmph… Two can play this game! "Well (A TINY bit more quietly than his BOOM), IF YOU DAMN PROFESSORS DIDN'T GIVE US DAMN STUDENTS SO DAMN MUCH WORK, YOU COULD BE OUTSIDE RIGHT NOW! (Quick now, SMILE!! BIG SMILE!)

Then, suddenly a huge smile from Dr. Graves, "What can I do for you, Teri?" He knew my family/friend nickname! That was the start of Dr. Graves truly becoming my professor, my advisor, and whether he ever realized it or not my mentor. I was fortunate to work in the Psychology Department the rest of my time at Union in addition to my full time jobs. It allowed more time for short conversations for me and for my dog, Dutch, to visit Dr. Graves in his office.

Dr. Graves had his softer side, too. When I was taking his classes it was not uncommon for students to bring their dogs onto campus and into classrooms. This I did with Dutch. He would go to Dr. Graves' classes with me and lie down under the table next to where Dr. Graves was lecturing.

Dr. Graves had much to say, and sometime lectured a bit longer than the allotted class time. One day the class went way past the end time. Dutch got up, strode to the door, turned around, sat down and quizzically looked at Dr. Graves. Some of my fellow students became nervous. Students might challenge other professors, but never Dr. Graves. Dr. Graves finally looked up and noticed Dutch at the door. As students looked my way and wondered what wrath would befall my pet and me, Dr. Graves looked at Dutch and said in his gruff voice, "I guess Dutch thinks class must be over! And it is." As I was leaving, Dr. Graves gave me a brief smile.

He knew I had figured out that his gruff persona was a ruse and that I kept his secret.

Dr. Graves, as a full professor, was able to spend most of his time at Union focused on his research. He taught two courses for upper class students. I remember the titles as "Theories of Personalities" and "Organizational Psychology." The first half of the course, "Theories of Personalities" was similar to the college textbook I had read years before coming to Union. It was the reason I wanted to become a psychologist. However, in Graves' course, only the first half of the course covered the theories the textbook covered, while the second half of the course covered Gravesian theory. I knew then I was exactly where I belonged. The second of Clare Graves' courses, "Organizational Psychology" was pure application of Gravesian theory in organizations. From our first encounter, when I called his bluff on gruffness, I knew I was at Union to meet and learn from him. From the moment I stepped into his first class session, I knew this was the critically important theory missing from the textbook I had read years earlier. Between the two courses, Gravesian theory not only became easily applicable, but I could immediately see the relevance in everyday life – in my work, studies, and social encounters.

When I was his student and he was my mentor and advisor, Clare Graves never told me what to do. He might ask me a question or two, but would then indicate that I would know just what needed to be done. And, he was right! In fact, our conversations were always short. (Probably surprising for those who know me and not at all surprising for those who knew Clare.) He gave me advice only once and then only after I had returned to Union —more than a year after graduating—for a stint as an administrator. He welcomed me and asked about events since we had last seen each other. He then told me not to stay too long. I promised I would not. He smiled and told me he knew I wouldn't. And, when I called him "Dr. Graves," he acknowledged my new position and reminded me, "It's Clare now, Laura." It was the last time we had the opportunity to speak.

Dr. Clare W. Graves was probably at least 40 years ahead of his time. He told our mutual dear friend, Dr. Don E. Beck, that he should continue to develop the theory, which Don has continued to do with Spiral Dynamics & Spiral Dynamics Integral. I have used Gravesian and Spiral Dynamics Integral in all areas of my life and work. I believe that my beloved mentor and professor would be thrilled that this book is filled with examples of applications by authors who are actively using Gravesian theory in their work. Several of the authors in this volume are dear friends and colleagues whose work I know and admire. There are others whose work I do not yet know. May they all shine as well in honoring Dr. Clare W. Graves with their works.

INTRODUCTION

This book is intended for:

1) Those who are hungry. Worms, mold, and other micro organisms will turn it into healthy soil, which grows healthy food.

2) Those two leggeds who need a physical embodiment of sacred wisdom, a book that sits in a sacred place, silently guides one's clan, and holds the sacred stories of those who were possessed by its special spirit.

3) Those who want power over people, places and things and can use the knowledge herein to establish their territories of unquestionable expertise.

4) Those who are looking for THE answers, and know learning them will, one day, provide a reward that fulfills the purpose of human life.

5) Those who wish to be more effective in their efforts, who have a vision of personal goals, and are doing all they can to achieve these ends.

6) Those who know nothing will work until everyone is included, understood, cared for and about.

7) Those who have found loving fully is not enough to fix the world. Artful action is required. Resources, capacities and abilities must be aligned to satisfy the existential needs of all of those in categories 1–6.

8) Those who have realized their integral presence in the collective of all of life, and live so as to foster the health and wellbeing of the whole planet.

The reader who can see themselves in all these categories will find the most value in this book. Consider one ideal situation: A person recognizes they are a system of many systems (8), and sees that artful action is necessary to foster healthy living in all their systems (7), they respect all points of view (6), have personal goals they are striving to achieve (5), know the conventional purpose and rules of life (4), have a territory where their presence is respected (3), appreciate the magical in their lives (2), and make sure their basic survival needs are reliably addressed. This could very well describe you, dear reader. And the fact that one frame of reference could suggest the life story of any reader here, is a measure of the value of the work of Professor Clare W. Graves, who first created this framework from the years of research data he had collected.

What you will read in the following chapters is a reiteration of the 8 perspectives above, framed in a multiple of contexts. There are nuances you will find in the reports to follow, and there are individual spins on the body of Gravesian knowledge represented here. But all the stories told here are built around the same developmental trajectory, the same path of maturation, the same line of increasing cognitive complexity.

We all begin with a need to resolve the demands of survival. If we transcend and include our survival needs we enter the path of increasing cognitive complexity. We don't all mature to the maximum available to humans. Sometimes capacity is not there for further maturation. Sometimes Life Conditions argue against further maturation. The end of this maturation line is unknown. Graves noted this ever unfolding human nature as the "Never ending Quest."

What the following advises is that there is a path of existential development; it is knowable; knowing it can reduce suffering and foster health and well-being. Some of you will note this is not a unique claim. What follows, however, is a unique formulation, perhaps retold in an idiom perfect for our time.

Orienting Details

Graves, being the research scientist that he was, designated the developmental levels he asserted, with a two letter indicator. The first letter pertains to individual capacity, the second to context, showing that any level is a combination of these two. Thus Graves would call the first level, A-N, the second B-O, and so on. Don Beck, who has done more than anyone to popularize Graves' work, has provided a nomenclature for these levels based on colors (Beck & Cowan, *Spiral Dynamics.* (1996) Blackwell. Malden, MA, USA). AN is Beige. BO is Purple. CP is Red. DQ is Blue. ER is Orange. FS is Green. GT is Yellow. HU is Turquoise.

Cowan has since presented his work as "Spiral Dynamics". Beck presents his work as "Spiral Dynamics Integral" (SDi) All the authors in each Volume we are preparing have studied in the lineage of Don Beck, and thus you will find the Beck and Cowan colors, and "SDi" used throughout… except for academic researcher and author John Cook, who uses the alpha nomenclature in his chapter.

This book presumes a basic knowledge of SDi, such as that available in the following: *Spiral Dynamics, The Never Ending Quest,* or your editor's Second Tier tutorial here http://www.academia.edu/6716201/An_Introduction_To_and_Tutorial_For_Spiral_Dynamics_Integral_SDi_. Most of the SDi related books noted in Appendix 1 have excellent introductory material in them. Both Beck and Cowan, separately, continue to market their versions of Graves' work through their own trainings, and you may find attending these periodic offerings of value. If you are a newbie to Graves' work, there is sufficient content and context provided in the chapters ahead that you will soon get a grasp of the framework.

What follows are reports from the field, the complement to the theory sources mentioned above. Volume 1 is focused on professional practitioners' experiences with larger scale systems. Volume 2 focuses on reports from people who apply Graves' insights to themselves, their relationships, and to others thru self-study, therapy, counseling and coaching. In short we can say that Volume 1 focuses on Ken Wilber's lower right quadrant, while Volume 2 focuses either on the introjection of the theory, the upper left quadrant, or relationships, the lower left quadrant (Wilber, *Integral Psychology*, 2000). Together the two volumes present a foundation for understanding the wide range of application of Graves' work.

The chapters presented here are, in sum, the voices of Third Generation Gravesians. There could be no third without a second and that debt is honored by all here.

Thank you to my parents, Harry and Gladys, and wife Stephanie. Without them these volumes would not have occurred.

Tom Christensen, Editor

SDi AND INTERPERSONAL RELATIONS

Joyce Kilmartin

Have you ever wondered why some people seem to push your buttons every time you encounter them? It's obvious that you don't see things alike. You can't understand how they reason or why they make the decisions they do. The problem may be one of divergent worldview, the set of ethics, values, and purposes a person holds. SDi the theory that evolved from Clare W. Graves's *"Emergent Cyclical Double-Helix Model"* (Cowan & Todorovic, pp. 159-197), provides very reasonable and satisfying explanations for many of the difficulties in interpersonal relations that are so commonplace and which often feel intractable. Not only does it help to explain problems; it shows how to avoid them and even to overcome them.

The SDi lens can help one to understand people in the context of associations, including romantic partnerships, parent/child relationships, friendships, civic and workplace relationships, and commercial interactions, among others. SDi provides a framework for understanding, relating to, and communicating with individuals who operate from differing worldviews. It also enables one to recognize the influence of one's own worldview, including the subconscious biases that may color one's perceptions of others.

One of the very best things about SDi is that the theory is elegant, simple to understand, and practically applicable in nearly every interpersonal situation. For anyone new to the theory, applying the system to relationships is a good way to familiarize oneself with the concepts. In fact, once the stages of the Spiral and their complementary value systems or vMemes (Beck & Cowan, p. 31) are understood, it is almost impossible not to begin analyzing people in order to identify which vMemes are driving their behaviors. In the beginning, it can seem like a game of "spot-the-vMemes" in operation among all you meet, including yourself.

In order to illustrate how SDi can be used to understand how value systems affect motivation, behavior, and change, I will present a case study using the main characters of a popular movie and their relationships as a proxy for a real-life scenario. Once you see how the analysis works, you will have a good idea of how to apply the concepts to yourself and the people in your life. I have chosen to use the year 2000 film, *Chocolat*, adapted from the novel of the same name, written by Joanne Harris and starring Johnny Depp, Juliette Binoche, and Judi Dench, among others.

The aspects of the SDi theory to be highlighted in this chapter include:

1) The value systems at each stage of development and their exposition at entering, peak/nodal, and exiting phases.

2) Express-self versus deny-self manifestations of values.

3) Healthy and unhealthy expression of vMemes.

4) Meme stacks within an individual.

5) Progression and regression along the Spiral.

6) Meshworks.

7) Spiral Wizardry.

8) Superordinate goals as a means of bringing diverse people together.

Before getting into the Spiral analysis, let's begin with a short synopsis of the film's main action and characters. The movie opens with Vianne, a beautiful single mother, and her six year old daughter making their way on foot into a traditional old village in France, seemingly being blown in by a strong wind. The year is 1959. Vianne carries with her the cremated remains of her peripatetic mother, whose legacy Vianne is perpetuating with her own daughter.

It is the Lenten season and mother and daughter arrive at the door of a run-down apartment that they have leased right across the square from the Roman Catholic church. The villagers are devoutly religious, and their behavior is further administered by the Comte (Count) Paul de Renaud, the Mayor of the village. The Comte is rigid in his belief in abstinence, penitence, authority, responsibility, and maintaining appearances. His family has advanced and enforced these values in the village for centuries and the pressure on the Comte to continue is self-imposed.

Vianne's warm and accepting demeanor almost immediately collides with the Comte's authoritarian ways. The Comte sees Vianne's plans to open a decadent chocolaterie during Lent as a sacrilegious act bound to tempt the villagers and plummet them inexorably into sin. The way Vianne dresses and her comfort in her own body seem to offend the Mayor, as well.

Vianne's landlady is an exquisitely independent-thinking older woman named Armande. She appears bitter and cantankerous and keeps to herself. We learn that Armande's daughter, Caroline, who has recently lost her husband, wants to place her mother in a nursing home because Armande has diabetes and is in pain. Armande refuses to go, insisting on making her own decisions, even unhealthy ones, almost in defiance of her daughter. Caroline keeps her young son from his grandmother, whom Caroline says is a bad influence. However, one also can see that Caroline uses her son as a pawn to punish Armande for her obstinacy.

There is another key figure in the village, a battered wife named Josephine. Her husband, Serge, who is something of a simpleton and an alcoholic to boot, owns the village bar/café and treats Josephine as his property. Josephine is caught between what she knows is wrong in her marriage and the demands of the village's rigid moral values. Josephine is so nervous and scared that she talks to herself and has become something of a kleptomaniac. The villagers think she is crazy. Vianne befriends Josephine almost immediately, speaks to her candidly about Serge, and eventually takes Josephine in, giving her a job in the chocolaterie that helps stabilize her life and restore her confidence.

Most of the story revolves around the Comte's attempts to undermine Vianne and her small business. He wields control over the village by spreading rumors about Vianne's "illegitimate" daughter. Vianne perseveres despite the Comte's efforts and makes a few friends in the village. She has a seemingly magic ability to guess a person's favorite chocolate, which is really a metaphor for her ability to intuit their relational needs.

The Comte fights Vianne's progress among the villagers by taking on Serge's moral reformation as a personal project. He is convinced that, with the proper retraining, Josephine can be convinced to return to Serge, upholding the sanctity of their marriage vows and restoring the natural order.

The Comte is further disturbed by the arrival of a riverboat company of free-spirited gypsies led by a man named Roux. Roux is accustomed to being maligned and shunned wherever he goes because his open lifestyle does not comport with the traditional values of towns he visits. True to form, the Comte initiates a "boycott against immorality" throughout the village so that the gypsies are not allowed to sell wares in the village or even to earn honest income doing odd jobs. Vianne, however, befriends Roux and his company as fellow outsiders in a mostly inhospitable community.

Cognizant that he has been losing ground to Vianne in their war of wills, the Comte sees the arrival of the gypsies as yet another challenge to his authority. One night Serge sees his estranged wife, Josephine, dancing on the gypsies' boat, and complains of her depravity to the Comte. The Comte concurs that "Something must be done," meaning the wantonness of such behavior during Lent. However, Serge takes the comment as a literal command and torches the boat later that evening.

The fire is very destructive but fortunately all escape unharmed. However, when the Comte learns that Serge acted on the Comte's "orders," he banishes Serge from the village. This is the Comte's first inkling that his long-standing strategies for dealing with life's problems have lost their efficacy.

The gypsies continue down the river after the fire, cutting short a budding love affair between their leader and Vianne. Demoralized, she decides that it's time to move on herself, despite the fact that it is the night before Easter, the day of her long-planned-for chocolate festival. Her daughter, however, objects to being uprooted yet again. Vianne packs their bags and tries to leave, but the young girl resists and cries. During the struggle, one of their suitcases flies open and Vianne's mother's ashes spill out. Despite the shock of this event, Vianne still plans to leave in the morning.

While Vianne and her daughter rest, however, Josephine rallies all of the friends that Vianne has made in the little village. They come to the chocolaterie and work through the night to finish preparing all of the treats for the festival, with Josephine teaching and leading them. When Vianne awakens and sees what is going on, she is amazed and touched.

Meanwhile, the Comte notices the villagers going happily in and out of the chocolaterie on the eve of Easter. All his efforts have been for naught. In despair, the Comte prays for God to tell him what to do. He looks down and spies a knife. The Comte takes it and heads for the chocolaterie. After breaking into the shop, he goes to the front window and begins to destroy Vianne's elaborate chocolate display. By chance, a piece of chocolate touches his lips. The Comte finally surrenders to temptation, gorges himself on the sweets, eventually falling asleep in the shop window.

Early on Easter morning the village priest discovers the Comte passed out in the chocolaterie window, his faced smeared with chocolate. He rouses Vianne who, rather than condemning the Comte, helps him clean up and vows to protect his honor. It is the beginning of a rapprochement and a clear moment of growth for both of them.

The movie ends on Easter morning. The Comte sits quietly in the back of the church instead of up front in his usual position of prominence. The young priest abandons the moralizing sermon which the Comte had prepared for him. Instead, he implores the parishioners to define themselves by who they let in and what they create, not by whom they exclude and what they deny. Apropos to the religious season, one can feel the village being reborn in that moment.

In the end, a new breeze blows in. Although it exerts its usual mystic pull on Vianne, this time she does not respond. She releases her mother's ashes into the wind and finally decides to settle down in the village with her daughter.

SDi offers us a vocabulary to describe the characters in the film and to explain their behaviors and decisions. According to SDi, Life Conditions create patterns of thinking, i.e., a framework for structuring reality. So far, eight levels of consciousness/thinking have been identified. As individuals attain each level, they acquire a progressive capacity for organizing and interpreting what they experience. The levels are holonic and increasingly complex. As one progresses to a new level, however, the wisdom of the previous levels is subsumed within the higher level. Thus, the vMemes are stacked upon each other, so to speak.

Problems can sometimes arise in interactions between persons of differing dominant worldviews. The more complex thinker is aware of the reasoning framework of the less complex thinker, but the inverse is not true. Many of the conflicts which drive the action of the film can be understood in terms of such "clashes" in worldview.

In SDi terms, most of the villagers, and most definitely the Comte, are operating within a Blue, sacrifice-self system. Per the narration which opens the film, "If you lived in this village you understood what was expected of you . . . You knew your place in the scheme of things." The Comte himself epitomizes this value system, not solely for his own aggrandizement but because he believes that, without these values, chaos would ensue.

But our analysis should not end with the classification of dominant vMemes at work in the village. SDi describes each level as having entering, nodal, and exiting phases. This means that each stage's values ebb and flow like a wave. First, the emergent way of thinking gains ground gradually; next, it becomes standard and accepted; finally, it begins to die out and it is overtaken by the successive wave of thinking. The Blue system in the village initially appears to be at peak, with most villagers seemingly content with the status quo. We soon see, however, that there are some cracks beginning to show.

In the absolutist Blue system, the primary moral value is obedience; through self-imposed guilt and community-imposed shaming, obedience is maintained. Individual expression is antithetical to the Blue system. The needs and traditions of the community are paramount. When Vianne arrives in the village, the Comte immediately invites her to worship with the villagers, as the church serves as his community's central instrument for transmission and enforcement of Blue values. To his shock and dismay, Vianne informs the Comte that she does not attend church. When the Comte addresses her as Madame, Vianne corrects him and says she is a Mademoiselle, (i.e., unmarried), and she displays no shame for having a child out of wedlock. Her unapologetic independence and non-conformity are both threatening and incomprehensible to the Comte. In this brief encounter the central tension of the movie is set up. There will be a battle of worldviews. This is not surprising if one looks at the situation with an SDi Lens.

The various levels in the Spiral hierarchy alternate between sacrifice-self and express-self states. The odd-numbered (Beige, Red, Orange, Yellow) levels have the express-self focus and the even numbered levels (Purple, Blue, Green, Turquoise) have the sacrifice-self focus. While all of the odd levels may share a focus, how that focus should be carried out varies by level; the same goes for the even levels. In general, people in the even-numbered levels attempt to control the external world and expand power over it, while those in the odd-numbered levels focus on the inner world and attempt to come to peace with it. The values of the contiguous levels are almost antithetical to the ones that come before and after them. This film shows how various characters act at their respective levels of thinking, but it by no means describes how all people would act. There are manifold ways to enact each value system.

In SDi most individuals do not operate purely from within one value system. The vMemes that one has traversed remain "on call" so that one can still recognize, and when appropriate, utilize, coping strategies commensurate with the problems of the previous levels. In addition, vMemes can find expression in both healthy and unhealthy ways. A healthy expression would be one that is appropriate for the Life Conditions being encountered. That healthy expression would do no harm to people experiencing different conditions. An unhealthy expression is harmful or disrespectful to either the person expressing that behavior or to others. According to Beck and Cowan, the very qualities that the Comte idealizes, such as stability, predictability, and safety are healthy Blue values (Beck & Cowan, pp. 229-243). Indeed, they are values that Vianne could use. Her wandering existence is hard on her and her daughter. Vianne has to repeatedly rebuild her life and her business from the ground up. However, the unhealthy aspects of Blue, such as chauvinism, judgmentalism, over-protectionism, and intimidation, stifle the villagers. Unhealthy value expression often occurs when the value system encounters new or different Life Conditions, but rather than an openness and curiosity about them, the person denies or rejects the new conditions and continues to operate in the same old ways. In the film, this is how the Comte at first reacts.

By contrast, in the relationship between Josephine and her husband, we see a different dynamic. At the beginning of the movie, Josephine seems to be operating within a Beige system. Graves called this state the "Autistic State" and said, "The person who lives at this level lives in a need-satisfying, wish-fulfillment manner. . . is aware only of the presence and absence of tension" (Cowan & Todorovic, p. 200). Josephine, the battered wife, is a perfect example of how one can regress and progress in the Spiral as Life Conditions change. At the start of the film, Josephine's very existence is threatened and she sees no way out, Josephine acts in the way an animal might, i.e., attempting to survive by her wits, by taking what she needs wherever she can get it, and by steering clear of others. We see Josephine with her hair and clothing in disarray, mumbling under her breath, and cowering from Serge. Josephine is so harassed that she really does not even have the energy to worry about consequences. She sits in church, oblivious to the meaning of the service, and steals a makeup compact from the purse of the woman in front of her. She has developed kleptomania as a way for her to satisfy an immediate need. Clearly, Josephine has deteriorated to the Beige level due to the attenuated conditions of her existence.

Alternatively, Josephine exhibits rapid improvement in response to Vianne's kindly overtures. After one extremely violent beating by her husband, Josephine appears at Vianne's door and asks to be taken in. Under Vianne's stewardship Josephine gains a new sense of security; she is able to move up the Spiral once her physical existence is no longer threatened. The next level up from Beige is Purple, the tribalistic stage. According to Beck and Cowan, the healthy aspects of the Purple stage include a sense of safety through bonding with others and a cooperative interdependence and purpose (pp. 215-224). Vianne becomes Josephine's teacher and mentor, imparting to her the secrets of chocolate-making. Josephine becomes an apprentice of sorts, and her work in the chocolaterie and friendship with Vianne give her a new sense of power and joint purpose. So we see that while the Comte becomes stuck in an unhealthy expression of Blue, Josephine is able to fluidly ride the Spiral. As the movie continues, Red, Blue, and Green all get re-activated within Josephine. For example, when Josephine's husband breaks in to Vianne's apartment and tries to force Josephine to come home, Vianne intervenes and is attacked. But in the critical moment, Josephine picks up a frying pan and knocks Serge out. This is an important assertion of her egoic self, which had been trampled upon, a healthy expression of Red.

Most people have multiple vMemes (referred to as meme stacks) active at one time. Although an individual will likely have a center of gravity within one level, he or she may hold multiple worldviews with respect to different aspects of life. In Vianne's life, in addition to Purple, we also see aspects of Orange and Green systems at work. She is a good example of the way multiple vMemes can be stacked within an individual. We learn early in the movie that Vianne is the offspring of a pharmacist father and a mystically-inclined South American tribeswoman. Although Vianne's mother tried to fit into a traditional family, she soon felt smothered by the constraints of her marriage to Vianne's father. She finally ran off with her child and thereafter wandered from town to town, making her living by selling magical

Mayan-inspired potions and cures. These Life Conditions are indicative of the Purple system, which is ritualistic, spiritual, and disposed to magical beliefs. Vianne continues to express these values in her own persistent wanderlust, her bursts of intuitive insight, and her totemic veneration of her mother's ashes. SDi says that when Purple is in play a person feels that her patterns of behavior are in some ways unalterable. In the film, Vianne certainly seems to feel that this is true. She is bound to go where the wind takes her, no matter if she would rather settle down.

The Orange system is an express-self system in which a person rejects authority's prescriptions, instead feeling competent enough to act in one's own self-interest. At this stage, a person sees many ways to accomplish her goals and opts for the best one. Vianne displays a healthy expression of Orange, especially with respect to her business. She is clever, resourceful, and pragmatic. Another aspect of the Orange system is independence. Vianne exemplifies the independent attitude of Orange. She does what needs to be done, such as refurbishing the dingy space to make her shop beautiful; she's not afraid to get her hands dirty.

According to Graves, "At the multiplistic existential level (Orange), interpersonal relations are very tenuous because of trust issues. . . One should go it alone and have absolute self-sufficiency" (p. 314). Over the course of the movie, we see Vianne grow, however. She has been willing to "go it alone" for a long time, but her values seem to be changing toward the end of the movie. Vianne begins to wish for a sense of belongingness with the community. She has made friends who have shown they care for her. Vianne has fallen for Roux and, even though he is a wanderer too, she senses that she could be happy settling down with him. Perhaps most importantly, Vianne's responsibility as a loving and protective mother takes precedence over any other motivations she may have. This change in Vianne, in SDi terms, represents an exiting of the Orange stage into the more affiliative Green stage. Such a development fits nicely within the SDi theory, which describes a "pendulum-like shift between a focus on 'me' concerns [and] 'we,' orientations" (Beck & Cowan, p. 56). The SDi theory posits that when a person encounters new Life Conditions, as Vianne does once people start accepting her, she may progress to the next level of existence. However, such progress is not assured.

Let's compare Vianne's progress to the Comte's. The Comte has been in crisis ever since his wife left him, even though he has attempted to hide that from the villagers. He needs to learn self-sufficiency and not to fear the judgment of the community. Instead, the Comte hides his real problem and projects his insecurity and doubt outward. He deals with his personal situation as a spurned husband by trying to fix Josephine's marriage to Serge. He believes that he has let down his God and must atone for his sins; but he attacks Vianne as the godless one; he struggles with his own temptations but projects licentiousness onto the gypsies. The Comte's carefully ordered universe is imploding, but he tries to gain control by identifying and reforming external "rule-breakers," wherever he finds them. The Comte keeps using the same old techniques of manipulation, gossip, guilt, and shaming that worked in the past to exert his power. However, those techniques are not working anymore. Something has changed in the village, but the Comte is not adapting to change. He is fixated and while in that state his problems escalate.

Graves said, that when change has produced new problems of existence and old ways are no longer adequate to the tasks of living, "feelings of cognitive inadequacy arise as one attempts to solve newly appearing or newly created existential problems by old coping means. . . This is one place in the developmental process where pathology is apt to break out" (p. 180). As we see when the Comte takes off to the chocolaterie with the knife, this is exactly what has happened. The Comte's feeding frenzy in the shop window is the moment when he can no longer keep his need for self-satisfaction at bay. The self-abnegation of Blue suddenly gives way to the ego-orientation of Orange. This is an important step in allowing something different and better to come forward.

As SDi predicts, the emergence of feelings, thoughts, and actions which are simmering just below the surface happens when dissonance is recognized and new insights are allowed to develop. In the film, Caroline, who is the Comte's secretary, reveals that she knows the Comte's wife has left him and she does not judge him poorly for that. In fact, we sense that the whole village has known all along. Graves said that, in order for progress on the Spiral, "There must be a resolution of the existential problems of the level where one is. This is necessary to produce free energy. . . through which change can be ready to occur." (Cowan & Todorovic, p. 170). Once Caroline shows the Comte that he is still respected, regardless of what his wife has done, the problem of having to maintain appearances drops away. This allows the Comte an opportunity to choose a different path. In the film, as in life, relationships are not simply one-to-one. There are many cross-connections. Don Beck uses the term, "Meshworks" (Beck, p. 1) to describe these connections. He says they may be "static and contained . . . designed to hold together elements in some type of relationship" or "crafted to allow the movement or flow of . . . energy, ideas, stages . . . through Spirals" (p. 1)

Simultaneous with the storyline of the Comte and Caroline, is the storyline of Caroline, Armande, and Luc. Their storyline is also instructive when looked at through a Spiral lens. Caroline is fixated just as the Comte has been. Her husband died in an accident at a young age. As a result, Caroline has become over-protective of her son, Luc. She is afraid of losing him too, so she will not let him have the freedom that young boys need, to play freely, have some unsupervised time, to take some risks in order to learn, and so forth. Like most of the villagers, Caroline seems to be at the Blue stage of development, seeing right and wrong in very black and white terms, with no shades of grey; she craves safety and stability. Armande, Caroline's diabetic mother, who seems directed by Orange values, acts in a contradictory fashion. She will eat and drink what she pleases, doctor's orders be damned. In both cases, these are unhealthy expressions of the stages they are at. They are both stuck.

Vianne helps to bridge the impasse between mother and daughter by bringing Luc together with Armande. Once Luc and Armande start interacting, a barrier is breached. This comes to a head when Armande asks Vianne to throw her a "by invitation only" party, to which Luc is invited but his mother is not. Luc sneaks off to his grandmother's party, where most of the invitees are the villagers who have "bucked the system" in some way. When it comes time for dessert, the party guests move from Armande's house down to the river, onto the gypsy riverboat. There they party, sing, and dance, with abandon. When Caroline realizes her son is not in his bed, she searches the village for him. She discovers the abandoned party table at Armande's house and ultimately finds the guests down by the river. There she sees Armande dancing joyfully with Luc, despite her obvious physical limitations and pain. Caroline leaves, shaken, but not before she and her mother share in a moment of unspoken understanding. That night Armande dies, sleeping in her chair. Later, Caroline gets out her husband's bicycle for Luc, which up until then she had forbidden him to use. Caroline has had a breakthrough in thinking. She is moving from an unhealthy expression of Blue to a healthier version. As with the Comte, a crisis has nudged Caroline in a new direction. In Caroline's case she is moving from unhealthy Blue to healthy. In the Comte's case he also is moving to healthier Blue; but additionally, he seems to be opening up to the idea of autonomy which is a characteristic of an entering Orange phase.

A final point in this analysis concerns what Beck and Cowan call "Spiral Wizardry" (pp. 115-142). This ability is evident in Vianne, which means that, at least in some respects, she has emerged into Second Tier thinking at the Yellow stage. Beck describes a Yellow thinker as one who is able to see vertically down through all the previous levels of the Spiral and who looks out for the health of the entire Spiral. "They [seem] not to be driven by status. There [is] a dropping away of fear" (Roemischer, p. 22). I believe the metaphor for this ability is the Mayan plate that Vianne spins that supposedly gives her clairvoyant power. Whenever customers come in, Vianne asks them to look deeply into the plate and to tell her what they see; from their answers she says she discerns their favorite chocolate. I believe that there is no magic in this plate or this ability; Vianne is not psychic. However, she has developed a highly sensitive intuition from dealing with so many different people. Throughout the movie, Vianne is able to help people and solve problems. She cuts through people's defenses with kindness, caring, and authenticity. She is not afraid to put herself on the line to accomplish what she believes is best for others. She does not try to change people, only to help them if they are open to assistance. She is not at all ego-driven. These are all qualities of Second Tier thinking. It was Spiral Wizardry that enabled Vianne to bring Caroline, Armande, and Luc together to resolve their impasse. Likewise, this same ability allowed Vianne to recognize that Josephine could be empowered to leave her husband and reach her full potential. Vianne has a gift for understanding humanity and the links and flows between people and situations. She is a true Spiral Wizard.

What I tried to show through this analysis is that the "encounter with another" is what is responsible for the growth and transformation of the characters in *Chocolat*, just as it is in all of our lives. As the film illustrates, stress, fear, and uncertainty are often what cause people to become stuck or to Spiral backwards to previous levels. For example, Josephine Spirals back due to domestic violence. The Comte Spirals back when he perceives a real threat to his internal stability. Even Vianne Spirals back to Purple after the riverboat fire, as she reverts temporarily to her automatic response in such situations, i.e., to move on under her mother's spell.

On the other hand, people Spiral forward when others give them the space, opportunity, or help to do so. Sometimes what it takes is for the more complex thinker to mirror the healthy qualities of a level for the person who is struggling. For example, Josephine responds to Vianne's respect for and confidence in her. The villagers respond to Vianne's warmth and openness. The Comte responds to Vianne's forgiveness and generosity.

As a Spiral Wizard, Vianne is bringing out the good qualities which these people already have and suggesting possibilities that are just out of reach but not inaccessible. To simplify, I see the pull between the polar opposites of fear and love as the motivation for the backward and forward movement, respectively, on the Spiral. Perhaps we can think of the need for love, respect and kindness as superordinate goals that permeate every level of the Spiral.

Bibliography

Beck, D. (2000). *MeshWORKS: A Second Tier perspective and process.* Retrieved December 28, 2013, *http://www.integratedsociopsychology.net/ meshworks-perspective-process.html*

Beck, D. E., & Cowan, C. C. (2006). *Spiral dynamics: Mastering values, leadership, and change.* Malden, MA: Blackwell.

Cowan, C. C., & Todorovic, N. (Eds.). (2005). *The never ending quest: Clare W. Graves explores human nature.* Santa Barbara, CA: Eclet.

Roemischer, J. (2002, Fall/Winter). The never-ending quest. *What is Enlightenment, 22,* 3-24.

APPLICATION FOR SDi TRAINERS PROGRAM:

By Dan McKinnon

To the SDi Train the Trainer Group, 30 September, 2008.

Thank you for considering me as an applicant. Following are my answers to your questions.

How do you describe your life so far in terms of the Spiral, your key experiences in the stages and your transitions from one stage to another to where you are today? An important philosophical perspective of an SDi trainer/practitioner is the unique, subjective, autobiographical lens of the person. An SDi trainer/practitioner must be acutely and authentically reflexive of the past and present Life Conditions, relationships, experiences and events that constitute who they are as a person. Reflexivity means a person explicitly recognizes that all knowledge claims are first person by nature and inevitably reflect the character, values and worldview of the creator of that knowledge. Each person makes sense of self, others and society by selectively choosing and arranging facts and feelings, from the context and conditions at hand, into a personally constructed, meaningful pattern. Essentially when practicing SDi, as in everyday life, you see as you are.

Key Life Events: Listed below are the key life events that have helped shape and direct my life and which have and are continuing to structure the way I think, feel and act. This format and the chart that follows are based on Marilyn Hamilton's, Journey to Wellness Workbook.

Decade 1 (1953-1963)

Dominant vMeme Development: Purple/Red Transitioning To Blue

Born into a working class family, coal mining and then roofing.

Changing Life Conditions and memetic adaptation in progress:
- Moved twice from small coal mining towns to the city of Calgary.
- During grade school was recommended to "skip" twice, but parents wanted me stay with the stream.
- Began my life-time journey of discovery through reading and musing.
- Achieved self-conscious awareness and commenced my life-time personal development journey.

Decade 2 (1964-1973)

Dominant vMeme Development: Red/Blue Transitioning To Orange

Bullied by others, took up weightlifting and built muscles and established a training mind-set/discipline.

Changing Life Conditions and memetic adaptation in progress:
- The bullying lowered my self-esteem and shocked me into growing up. I adapted by strengthening my body and training my mind, as well as creating a way to earn money, buy cars and go out on dates.
- Had an intense interest in Eastern methods for out of body work and practiced for five years.
- Had an intense interest in psi phenomena and experimented with telepathy and clairvoyance for five years.
- Began working as an independent entrepreneur at 14 years of age. Enjoyed making money.
- My life at this time was about cars, cars, cars, and girls, girls, girls.

Decade 3 (1974-1983)

Dominant vMeme Development: Exited Blue To A Solid Orange Phase

Attended college and university dropped out twice because of shyness.

Changing Life Conditions and memetic adaptation in progress:
- Shyness caused me considerable stress during my early adulthood. I adapted by doing my own thing as an entrepreneur, which gave me the confidence to return to college and practice public speaking.
- Returned to college and obtained a two year diploma in Leisure Education/Community Recreation Leadership, graduated with honors and was valedictorian.
- Met Angela, got married (secretly), owned first home together.
- Fascinated by the philosophy of Ayn Rand, put her objectivist/capitalist ideas into practice.
- Started first company, sales grew from $100,000.00 to $3,500,000.00 within 5 years.
- Became a champion weightlifter for my province.
- Created six companies in four industries, ran into partnership problems, struggled to keep companies afloat.
- Got divorced, Angela has remained life-time friend to this day.

Decade 4 (1984-1993)

Dominant vMeme Development: Orange With Green flashes And Yellow/Turquoise Stirrings

Went bankrupt, mother died, I was grief stricken, and returned to spiritual practices.

Changing Life Conditions and memetic adaptation in progress:
- This was the lowest time of my life. My sadness and fear of failure were overwhelming. I used meditation and mysticism to adapt to my conditions and create a new center of being for myself.
- Studied death and dying, and began two-hour meditative, mystical sunrise walks, four times per week.
- Met second wife, Kay, created a national marketing company, achieved much success.

- Attended courses and became a director of the Calgary Esoteric Philosophy Society for four years.
- Traveled the country as a public speaker, trainer and leader for my national marketing company.
- Became contemplative and philosophical and learned how to mindfully wait-watch with wonder.
- Got Divorced, went broke, started another roofing company, returned to university.
- My dreams of being an entrepreneurial empire-builder were shattered. I used the mentorship and friendship of Ed, a tenured-full professor, to restore my confidence and help me reset my vision as an entrepreneur and possible scholar.
- Ed and I had a deep, almost in-love male friendship, mentored with him in academe.
- Acted as Ed's research assistant at the University of Calgary.
- Co-designed and co-instructed an MBA class, Creativity in Business.
- Met Carol in one of Ed's MBA classes.
- Created an international manufacturing company with Ed and others, realized some big dreams.
- Left manufacturing business partnership, friendship with Ed ended, involved in lawsuits for two years.
- Began living with Carol and Ben (her son) and had my eyes opened about "mother" love.
- Started long-term study (1993 to Present) of Ken Wilber's work – including Phases I-V.
- Started part-time university undergraduate studies in religion and psychology.
- Entered and survived two years of extreme emotional, spiritual and financial strain/stress.
- Losing my assets and close friendship with Ed resulted in feelings that life was meaningless and without purpose. As an adaptive strategy I became a lone entrepreneur and went back to university to get a professional designation so that in the future I would always have a guaranteed fallback position. Essentially I decided to broaden and deepen my skills to overcome my disappointments.

Decade 5 (1994-2003)

Dominant vMeme Development: Receding Orange And Rising Yellow

- Slowly built my roofing company, by end of decade I had attained financial success.
- Completed undergraduate degree in psychology, completed graduate degree in counselling.
- Started playing competitive squash, developed skills to a better than average level.
- Expanded my contemplative (witness) awareness skills and created a settled, still, spacious self.

Changing Life Conditions and memetic adaptation in progress:
- Father died, experienced a new kind of grief and realization about my own dying and mortality.
- This existential confrontation with mortality was deeply despairing and the only way I could adapt was to accept the utter fact of death and change my way of being in the world. Impermanence has become the activating force that teaches me to love life as it is—NOW, and to be grateful for every moment of life, in each moment. I've learned to meet the world as it's coming to be, not as what I think or expect it to be. I've learned to approach the world out of a sense of abundance, trusting in the "ENOUGH".
- Carol and I built a dream home and got married six months later, after living together for 12 years.
- Completed SDi Level One and Level Two—Natural Designs with Don Beck in Vancouver.

Decade 6 (2004-2013)

Dominant vMeme Development: Primarily Yellow Orientation With Orange Highlights

Completed a 1600-hour internship in organizational development psychology with Dr. Joe Lischeron. Joe is an emeritus professor and organizational psychologist/consultant many years my senior who guided me toward redefining my identity as a lifetime entrepreneur who could also be a professional organizational psychologist and executive coach.

- My internship involved behavioral development assessments, client consultations, executive coaching and workshop facilitation. I passed the psychology licensing exams and became a chartered/registered psychologist.

Changing Life Conditions and memetic adaptation in progress:
- My business flourished and the financial success that resulted exceeded all my expectations.
- Entered a doctoral program (2005)—University of Calgary, completed candidacy in the Fall of 2007.
- Completed SDi Level Two—Personal Emergence with Don Beck and Bert Parlee in Boulder, CO.
- Enjoyed continued love, care, and mutual relational development with Carol.
- Completed SDi Level Two—Praxis with Marilyn Hamilton in Calgary.
- Became "Pa" to our grand-daughter, Zefi. What a JOY!!!
- Began noticing that my sixth decade body is different, still athletic, but slower to respond and recover.
- Completed SDi Level Two—Leading in the Integral Age with Marilyn Hamilton in Calgary.
- Finished a Ph.D. in Education. I created an original qualitative research method called *Integral Hermeneutic Biography*. My dissertation was titled: Uncovering and Understanding the Spirituality and Personal Wholeness of School Educators.
- Started practicing organizational development consulting and counselling psychology.
- Incorporated SDi more fully into my life and practice, continuing development as an Elder-in-training.
- I am enjoying the lessons and rewards of making money, having fun and putting something back.

In the following columns, above each decade I have placed an "X" opposite the per cent of Wholeness or Wellness that I think/feel that the life events described above represent in my life.

Dan's Life Event, Wholeness/Wellness Chart (Spring, 2014)

%							
100						XXX	
90					XXX		
80			XXX				
70		XXX					
60							
50							
40	XXX						
30				XXX			
20							
10							
0							
Age:	0–10	11–20	21–30	31–40	41–50	51–60	
Decade:	1	2	3	4	5	6	
Years:	1953 to 1963	1964 to 1973	1974 to 1983	1984 to 1993	1994 to 2003	2004 to 2013	

How did you become aware of SDi? I became aware of SDi in 2001 when I read Ken Wilber's, *Integral Psychology: Consciousness, Spirit, Psychology, Therapy*. In 2003, SDi became an important part of my life when I read Wilber's, *Boomeritis: A Novel That Will Set You Free.*

With whom, and when have you trained? I have completed 5 modules of SDi training. In 2003, I completed Level One—Introductory and Level Two—Natural Designs with Don Beck in Vancouver, BC. In 2005, I completed Level Two—Personal Emergence with Don Beck and Bert Parlee in Boulder, CO. In 2007, I completed Level Two—Praxis with Marilyn Hamilton in Calgary, AB. In 2008, I completed Level Two—Leadership in the Integral Age with Marilyn Hamilton in Calgary, AB.

How have you been applying SDi? I used the principles of SDi during my 1600-hour internship as an organizational development psychologist. Prior to returning to university for my doctoral work in 2005, SDi was central in the assessments and interventions I planned and utilized when I practiced as an organizational development consultant and executive coach to entrepreneurial-oriented ventures and family-based businesses. I have taught SDi principles and integral theory to the Dreamseekers Group that I have been a member of for eighteen years. For the last five years, I have engaged in monthly one-hour SDi and integral practice reviews and consultation discussions with another SDi graduate, Chad Stewart from Japan. The theoretical orientation and the research methodology of my doctoral dissertation uses integral theory.

For details on how I've been applying SDi into my work and personal life please visit my organizational development websites at *www.talkinc. ca and www.getunbroken.com* and my YouTube Channel at *https://www. youtube.com/user/calgarypsychology/playlists.* On the websites and channel are a number of video talks that I have posted for the use of my clients and friends. Each of these talks was filmed in a one-take, no rehearsal, and impromptu manner. Of special interest for this T of T application are the following videos: Evolving Entrepreneurial Existence, The Value of Values and Let Spirit Become You. Also on my Talkinc website, under the coachworks/ SDi/KEEP tab, are descriptions of the executive coaching process I use with my clients as well as the half-day KEEP seminars—Communication, Motivation, Conflict, Stress, Creativity, Everyday Sales and Leadership— that I have co-designed and co-facilitated over the previous five years.

What insights has the application of SDi brought to you? The application of SDi has convinced me that our life on planet Earth is a continually evolving bio/psycho/cultural/social/spiritual process. As a result of this interdependent, evolutionary process the demands of life are calling forward the emergence of broader and deeper human consciousnesses, capacities and capabilities. In this sense, life is living us as much as we are living life. Understanding and using the SDi model has awakened and improved my knowledge of self and others such that by compassionately meeting others where they are in their development, and encouraging them to go where it is that they are going, I am contributing to a healthier and more whole life for all of us on planet Earth, as well as initiating the emergence of new stages of development for myself.

What do you consider is possible in the further application of SDi in Canada? Further application of SDi in Canada will result in improved communication, less conflict and greater compassion within our corporate and government sectors. This work will also support an interdependent, mutual respect in society-at-large for how a dialogue of difference is actually a dialogue of discovery and mutual becoming.

In which sectors/areas will you continue to be practising the application of SDi? My practice will continue to focus on entrepreneurially-oriented ventures, family business settings, faith-based & spiritual organizations, organizational development/consulting, individual counselling/coaching and increasing public awareness.

In what geographic area(s) would you prefer to practise? I will continue to practice in and near Calgary as well as other locations in Alberta, Saskatchewan & Manitoba.

With whom would you consider co-leading SDi events? I would consider co-leading with Marilyn Hamilton, Don Beck and other certified SDi trainers in Canada.

What are your ideas on furthering the adoption of SDi across Canada? My interest is to run more workshops, create public relations initiatives, involve the media in SDi events, create an SDi Canada multi-media website, create an SDi e-learning platform, partner with charitable organizations, and introduce SDi to spiritual communities.

How would you contribute to the global knowledge base of SDi? I am interested in raising the budget for, managing the design of, and implementing the launch of an SDi e-learning platform. I will use my expertise in spirituality and personal wholeness to influence the re-spiritualization of our global community.

Thank you for the opportunity to be a part of the SDi Train-the-Trainer program.

THE USE OF SDi IN PSYCHOTHERAPY

By Keith E. Rice

Spiral Dynamics Integral (SDi) is often thought of as a means of addressing large-scale issues such as inter-racial conflict, socio-economic malaise and global power plays. This is the way Don Beck himself has used the model in the past, to great success in South Africa, and has been using it more recently, with great promise, in the Middle East. However, Beck (2009) himself refers to micro (individual), meso (inter-group) and macro (global) applications of SDi. Thus, there clearly is, in Beck's view, a legitimate application of the model at an individual level. It also needs to be remembered that Clare W Graves, on whose work SDi has been built, was a psychologist, not a sociologist, though he saw the boundary between the two disciplines as unnecessary and artificial (Beck, 2002).

While I've written much on my Blog, *http://integratedsociopsychology. net/blog/,* about social and political applications of SDi, a significant proportion of my work has actually centered on using SDi in psychotherapy with individuals. My approach can be thought as both "integrative" and "eclectic". Using the distinctions of Stephen Palmer & Ray Wolfe (1999), it is perhaps more "integrative" in that I take a combined approach to theory and practice, i.e. everything is aligned, streamed and integrated around a few core models, of which SDi is the most important. However, I would still claim it is "eclectic" in that I feel no compunction about stealing any idea from any concept if it will work in the interests of a client. And, I can usually see how what I "steal" fits within the framework of what I call "Integrated SocioPsychology"!

I often am told that I am one of the few therapists working with SDi at the level of the individual. While I find this hard to believe, the fact that I get therapy clients Skyping with me from afar, including people from other countries, because they can't find a closer SDi-oriented therapist is perhaps indicative of a genuine shortage.

It's About The Health Of vMemes

My first step in consulting with a client is to treat the hypothetical concept of "vMeme" as an unequivocal reality. In my experience, therapy clients are rarely interested in the scientific arguments for and against the reality of a hypothetical concept. Nor are they usually concerned with the quality of the evidence supporting such a concept. They want help and they want to believe that, whatever help the therapist offers, that help will make a positive difference to their lives. As Bruce Sloane et al (1975) identified, trust in the therapist (which ever techniques they favour) is a key element in successful therapy. In other words, being convinced that the therapist knows what they are doing is a critical factor in building the trust essential to successful treatment.

That said, it is undoubtedly helpful to the client if the models applied and the techniques used appear to have "scientific credibility". Although SDi generally has a low profile amongst academics in the behavioural sciences, the fact it can be easily matched to other models, such as Maslow, Loevinger, Kohlberg, Adorno, etc., helps to establish that trust which is critical to successful treatment. It is then possible to show that, although these other models may have a higher profile, they are less intrinsically complete and, therefore, it is advantageous to use SDi as the foremost model.

vMeme	Needs	Stress Factors
A–N Beige	Water, food, shelter, procreative sex	Absence of basic needs
B–O Purple	Safety, belonging, acceptance, assurance	Rejection, loneliness, change, "tribal" dysfunction
C–P Red	Self-expression, power, self-esteen, respect	Shame, impotency, loss of face, constraint, punishment
D–Q Blue	Consistency, clarity of expectation, procedures, certainty	Guilt, non-conformance, lawlessness
E–R Orange	Goals, achievement, status markers	Lack of opportunity/ resources
F–S Green	Equality, fairness, consensus	Discrimination, intra-group disagreement

Figure 1: Needs and stress factors of First Tier vMemes

Getting the client to understand that they have up to 8 motivational systems operating in their psyche/selfplex and that each of these vMemes has different needs, wants and desires is the next step. I was initially surprised to find that clients usually can access a basic understanding of different and sometimes conflicting motivations without a full-blown exposition of SDi. Simple, everyday examples of vMemes working can illustrate the concepts enough for clients to get the basic idea. Of course, it helps enormously if the client already has some idea of SDi, especially if they have already done training with me. Sometimes clients, in wanting to understand their motivations more, have gone on to join one of my workshop programmes. As many people in the UK have studied Abraham Maslow's Hierarchy of Needs at a basic level as part of GCSE Business Studies, SDi can also be presented to them as an extension of Maslow's work. This can help them to understand the role of vMemes as fulfilling Maslow's "needs".

A key part of any therapy I undertake is to consider the health of each vMeme motivational system in terms of its functioning to meet its needs, wants and desires. In the early part of most consultations, I will draw a mind map of the client's life, from as early as they can remember to their current difficulties. Whilst occasionally, a client may have a specific set of current circumstances which they are experiencing difficulty with, in a way that is effectively isolated from the rest of their life, usually the current problems are a reflection of deeper and more pathological issues often initiated in childhood. In this sense, my approach is heavily influenced by the ground-breaking Psychoanalytic work of Sigmund Freud (1900, 1901, 1920, 1923, 1924) whose 3-part mind concept of Id, Ego and Superego is easily assimilated into the 8-part mind concept of SDi.

I usually find that most clients have a core belief about themselves which effectively equates to, "I'm not good enough". Usually, though not always, longstanding pathological issues are to do with childhood insecurity (the Purple vMeme not having its needs met) and/or suppression of being able to express yourself (Red not having its needs met). Since these vMemes are effectively the cognitive foundation of the Spiral, damage to or inability of these vMemes to function properly can throw the development of the entire Spiral off in an individual. In both the case studies offered as appendices to this chapter, the problems are with Purple and Red malfunctioning. In the case of "Susan" (Appendix 1) in particular, it was almost as if, with resolving the issues of Purple and Red, her entire Spiral began to right itself with peak Blue making its first real appearance in her life.

Beliefs Are Linked To vMemes

People tend to treat the beliefs they have as being reality. This is fine if their beliefs work for them positively and at least do not impinge negatively on others. It's not so fine if their beliefs work to their detriment or the detriment of others. Many psychologists and psychiatrists, from Aaron Beck (1972) on, refer to such beliefs as "maladaptive schemas", "maladaptive" meaning "badly learned" or "badly adapted".

While there seems to be some considerable confusion over use of the terms "schema" and "meme", I have found it helpful to differentiate "schema" as being the internalised belief while "meme" serves to describe the idea outside of the individual's head, whether in a book, a film, music or the words and/or actions of another. Thus, the schemas in someone's head are learned or adapted from memes which, in the terminology of the neo-science of Memetics, "infect" to form new schemas or amend existing ones.

The benefit of this approach is that the client can start to see their own often deeply-held beliefs as just schemas which invariably they have developed from memes. The younger they were when the beliefs were formed, the more likely they are to have been developed from interaction with others, especially significant others such as parents and friends. Amongst other researchers, Dale Hay & Jo Ellen Vespo (1988) have reported parents providing young children with direct tuition to produce what George Herbert Mead (1913) calls the "social self". To reflect Mead's concept, I far prefer to use Susan Blackmore's (1999) term, "selfplex", rather than "psyche". Blackmore's term makes it clear that your concept of "yourself" is merely a collection (or confluence) of schemas. Since schemas are just ideas, ideas can change or be changed.

One of the best means I've found of getting clients to realise the arbitrary and sometimes transitory nature of beliefs is the "Falling in Love Meme". The search to find "true love" is one of the Western world's most ubiquitous memes. Thus, people fall in love, applying memes such as "soulmate" to their partner, and base astounding life-changing commitments such as marrying, buying a house and having children on the schema that they are in love with their boyfriend/girlfriend. 10 years later approximately 45% of those people now love someone else and have moved on.

Two questions then arise:

1) Where did your maladaptive schema come from? I.e. who gave it to you? Since, according to many developmentalists such as Ralph Allison (1995), our first real cognitive sense of self (selfplex) forms around 6-8 years of age, it is a legitimate question to ask who (which older persons) influenced the formation of such maladaptive schemas as "I'm no good", "I'm stupid", "I'm annoying", "No one likes me", etc., etc. All too often I've found it's an unwitting parent who has initiated the beginnings of that core belief. Due to cognitive primacy, the tendency to filter incoming memes for evidence to support existing schemas, the memes which tend to get through have a reinforcing effect on what is already there.

2) Which vMeme is related to that maladaptive schema? Since, as Figure 1 shows, each vMeme has its own set of

concerns, the vMeme dominating in the selfplex will be receptive to some incoming memes and not others. For example, Purple will be highly concerned with memes relating to its safety and acceptance, or lack of them. Red will seek to dominate others who are lower in the "power pecking order" while being grudgingly subservient to those with demonstrably greater power. At the same time Red will have little cognisance of the memes of "doing what's right" that Blue puts out and is likely only to obey the rules if those rules are enforced with greater power. Thus, there is a second filtering effect on how we make sense of information coming in from the outside world.

SDi, of course, offers no tools as such, with which to treat maladaptive schemas and repair damaged and/or malfunctioning vMemes. However, as an NLP Master Practitioner, I have found that Neuro-Linguistic Programming offers a number of powerful tools which can help do that. Cognitive Behavioural Therapy (CBT) also provides several techniques which can be used both to facilitate "Spiral diagnosis" and to help someone take affirmative control of their life. For clients with problematic Purple and Red stemming from childhood experiences, I've found the "Inner Child" exercises designed by Penny Parks (1994) very effective in giving back the maladaptive schema to the person who gave it to the client and showing the client how things should have been. Both the case study appendices make reference to using Parks' techniques.

Interaction Between vMemes And The Environment

As well as taking a Maslowian approach to look at the health of the vMemes in an individual's selfplex in terms of their functioning to achieve needs, wants and desires, sometimes it can be critical for the client to gain insight into how they interact with the external environment. For this, I have found it a great help to link SDi to Robert Dilts' (1990) Neurological Levels model. Figure 2 shows a graphic of the relationship between the SDi and Neurological Levels concepts. The basic presupposition of this schematic is that whichever vMemes are dominating in the selfplex strongly influence the formation of "Identity" and "Values & Beliefs" relative to whatever "Life

Conditions" are prevailing in the "Environment". The linking of SDi to Neurological Levels allows the therapist to operate at either what I call the "Nominal Level" (Figure 4) or the "Deeper Level" (Figure 5).

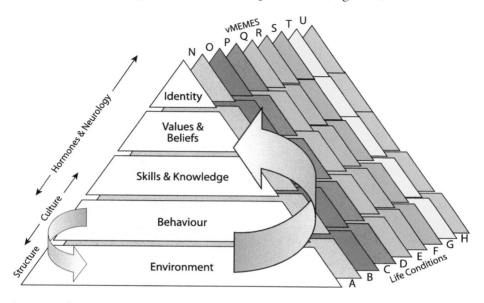

Figure 2: The relationship between vMemes and Identity and Values & Belief and Life Conditions and the Environment presented via the Neurological Levels model.

(Eagle-eyed readers will notice reference is made in the schematic for hormones and neurology, to take into account the internal environment.)

This approach makes use of the original (pre-SDi) Graves coding of A-H for Life Conditions and N-U for vMemes, as shown in basic terms in Figure 3. This enables consideration of whether the vMemes dominating in the selfplex are appropriate to the Life Conditions being experienced in the Environment. Thus, a major change in the Life Conditions being experienced should, in a healthy individual, produce a matching vMeme response to enable the individual to cope in the changed Life Conditions. (This is why vMemes are sometimes described as "coping mechanisms".) In Graves' terminology, an "existential state" is in place when vMeme is matched to Life Conditions.

LIFE CONDITION

COPING SYSTEM

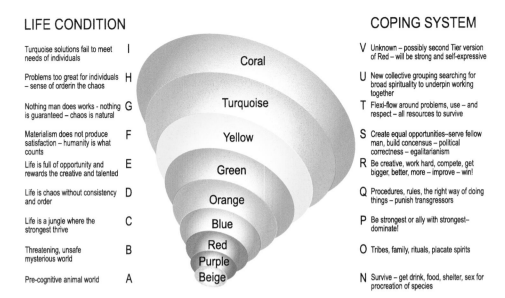

| Turquoise solutions fail to meet needs of individuals | I | | V | Unknown – possibly second Tier version of Red – will be strong and self-expressive |

Turquoise solutions fail to meet needs of individuals — I

Problems too great for individuals – sense of order in the chaos — H

Nothing man does works - nothing is guaranteed – chaos is natural — G

Materialism does not produce satisfaction – humanity is what counts — F

Life is full of opportunity and rewards the creative and talented — E

Life is chaos without consistency and order — D

Life is a jungle where the strongest thrive — C

Threatening, unsafe mysterious world — B

Pre-cognitive animal world — A

Coral
Turquoise
Yellow
Green
Orange
Blue
Red
Purple
Beige

V — Unknown – possibly second Tier version of Red – will be strong and self-expressive

U — New collective grouping searching for broad spirituality to underpin working together

T — Flexi-flow around problems, use – and respect – all resources to survive

S — Create equal opportunities–serve fellow man, build consensus – political correctness – egalitarianism

R — Be creative, work hard, compete, get bigger, better, more – improve – win!

Q — Procedures, rules, the right way of doing things – punish transgressors

P — Be strongest or ally with strongest– dominate!

O — Tribes, family, rituals, placate spirits

N — Survive – get drink, food, shelter, sex for procreation of species

Figure 3: vMemes (coping mechanisms N–V) matched to the appropriate Life Conditions (A–I)

Working at the Nominal Level essentially involves what Dilts intended, namely that therapists work with clients to ensure that their neurological levels are aligned for healthy mental functioning. So, for example, a teenager needs the Identity of "student" in the Environment of school; but, if he lives in the Environment of a rough and violent neighbourhood, he'd better change his Identity to "street tough" if he wants to survive on the proverbial "mean streets". This level of change is what Gregory Bateson (1972) called Level 1 Learning and Don Beck & Chris Cowan (1996) termed First Order Change. It does involve change but within the existing set of paradigms. The change, in fact, can be considerable; but the Identity/Environment matches such as student/school and street tough/rough neighbourhood are well-established.

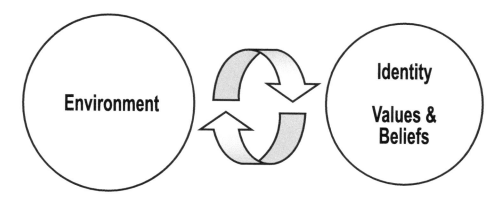

Figure 4: Nominal Level Adaptation

The Deeper Level may well involve paradigm change because now we look at what is actually going on in the Environment, i.e. the Life Conditions, and how the vMemes are shaping Identity and Values & Beliefs to cope with the Life Condition changes in the Environment.

In my book, *Knowing Me, Knowing You* (2006), I used the following example of a man who had mastered change at the Nominal Level, "At work, he's a Manager; with his partner, he's a Lover." Nominal Level Adaptation appears to be successful.

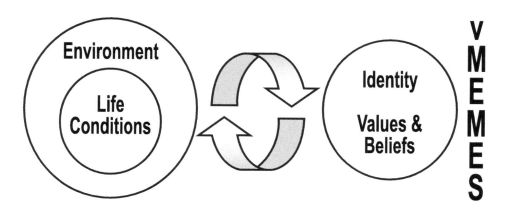

Figure 5: Deeper Level Adaptation.

However, successful Nominal Level Adaptation depends on what is happening at the Deeper Level which can be much more complex. If the man's partner is loving and caring (B/Purple Life Conditions in the Environment of their relationship), which vMeme would match? O/Purple would be the best fit and would strongly support the Identity of Lover, with Values of love, caring, belonging, etc.

However, if the partner is concerned with getting her own way and dominating him (C/Red Life Conditions in the Environment), which vMeme will be the best match? Almost certainly P/Red. The man has to know if he is more powerful than his partner and what his position is in the "power pecking order" of the relationship. He must know who is in control?

Such a Red-led scenario will be quite different than the Purple-hued scenario we first envisioned. The Values & Beliefs of the man's Red fighting with his partner over her attempts to dominate him will be quite different to the Values & Beliefs Purple would have had. This may start to compromise the Identity of Lover, depending on what his prior beliefs about a lover's role were. Behaviour, of course, is most likely to reflect the Values & Beliefs and may not be what one would normally associate with a Lover. This may further compromise that Identity. In the Red-led scenario, the neurological levels will become misaligned unless the Identity starts to mutate into something more in keeping with the Values & Beliefs ("Lover" is hardly a suitable Identity to win a war for power!).

Such shifts as those described in the book excerpt clearly involve paradigm shifts: Level 2 Learning in Bateson; 2nd Order Evolution in Beck & Cowan. In extreme circumstances, the shifts in thinking may be so violent it would be more applicable to call them Level 3 Learning or 2nd Order Revolution!

When addressing two-person relationships, such as a married couple in conflict, I find it can be illuminating, if not completely revelatory, for the client to undertake Robert Dilts' (1996) Meta-Mirror exercise whereby the client gets to see him/herself as their conflicted partner sees them and also how their conflict appears to others.

For the dynamics of group inter-relationships, I have used toy soldiers and dolls to represent the players in the scenario, including a figure for the client. The client then looks down on the players as though they are on a stage and decides in godlike fashion strategies for who should do what. All through this process, I will facilitate the client by asking what vMemes and memes are in play and what attitudes and behaviour are then predictable. I have found this method allows a client to go meta to (beyond or abstracted from) their own immediate and highly subjective thoughts and feelings with regard to the situation.

Limitations Of An SDi Approach

From the above and the case studies which follow, I trust it is clear to readers that, not only do I believe SDi is an approach which can be used in therapy, but I have used it with great success and regard it as fundamental to my work as a counsellor and therapist. However, there are certain limitations as to the use of SDi as a therapeutic map.

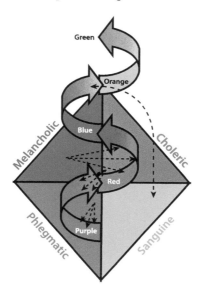

Figure 6: Associations between temperamental types and vMemes implied in the work of William Moulton Marston.

Firstly SDi outlines motivational systems and how they work. Whilst there is hardly anything more important in understanding someone than identifying what motivates their attitudes and behaviours, attitudes and behaviours are also influenced by temperament. Someone who is naturally shy, for example, is not going to become naturally gregarious through any application of SDi as such. A different understanding and different techniques are called for.

Back in 2005 I had a client whose tendency to anxiety I tried to remedy by focussing on building up her Purple and Red vMemes. What really made the difference was when I used negative reinforcement, taken directly from B F Skinner's (1938) concept of Operant Conditioning. The model that I eventually used to identify the root of this client's problems was Hans J Eysenck's construct of temperamental dimensions: Psychoticism-Extroversion-Neuroticism (Hans J Eysenck, 1967; Hans J Eysenck & Sybil B G Eysenck, 1976).

Graves (1971/2002) speculated that there was a link between temperament and motivation but had no significant evidence for it. N. N. Trauel (1961; reported in Eysenck, 1967) found a link between Extraversion and obedience/conformity. William Moulton Marston's (1928) model of Dominance, Influence, Steadiness and Compliance clearly associates temperamental descriptors with motivational descriptors in 3 of his 4 behavioural types, with a weaker association in the fourth. These associations are depicted in Figure 6 (Rice, 2006). Yet generally there seems to be little research on links between these 2 elements of personality.

Even so, SDi can be of benefit to the therapist using Behavioural techniques. As Skinner's Operant Conditioning uses reward or punishment as consequences for behaviour, so SDi enables us to identify what is rewarding and punishing for each vMeme. For example, the "naturally shy" person referred to above is likely to become more outgoing in an environment where they feel accepted for who they are (Purple) and they are made to feel good about the contributions they make, their self-esteem being boosted (Red). Similarly a loud-mouthed extravert is likely to quiet down if heavily criticised for their behaviour, a reduction of esteem which is likely to inhibit Red.

A second limitation of SDi in therapy is that it tells us nothing about the "Unconscious". While "scientific psychology" has yet to find a way to investigate the Unconscious experimentally and all kinds of unfounded assertions are made about it, there is little doubt there is some element of the mind (selfplex?) which houses repressed thoughts and memories. One study which illustrates this only too dramatically is that of Linda Meyer Williams (1994) who found 65% of a group of 117 adult women had no memory of being sexually abused when young children. (As the children had been admitted to hospital, there were medical, social work and police records which showed unequivocally that the abuse had taken place.) As Sigmund Freud (1923) thought the Id and, to a lesser extent, the Superego were located in the Unconscious and these factors in the Freudian mind can be mapped to vMemes, it will be interesting to see what crossovers will develop between Psychoanalysis and SDi in years to come.

The Case Studies

The two case studies which follow are typical of the work I do in that they deal with maladaptive schemas formed during childhood and then reinforced via experience. The work is focussed on giving back the maladaptive schema to the person who gave it to the client, thus freeing Purple and Red to develop more healthily. The case of "Shirley" also includes what is arguably a realisation from the Unconscious. These and similar case studies can be found in the Services section of my web site, *www.integratedsociopsychology.net*. Names and peripheral details have been changed in the case studies, for confidentiality purposes. Otherwise, the stories in the case studies are pretty much what happened.

Case Study #1: Susan

"Susan" first came to me because she wanted rid of a phobia she had about having men in the front passenger seat of her car. This was proving particularly problematic as she had recently struck up a new relationship, her irrational fear resulting in them always having to travel in the boyfriend's car.

When I meta-modelled her, using an NLP/cognitive questioning technique, it soon emerged that the phobia was rooted in the partly-repressed memory of a traumatic experience several years back. Then a man sitting in the front seat of her car had tried to rape her. Since the event was a clear-cut single traumatic episode, I used the NLP Trauma Cure to recode the patterns of that memory in terms of the sensory modalities in which they were encoded. This resulted in the memories being far less immediate and, thus, far less threatening to her. I future-paced Susan driving with a man sitting next to her and she now seemed quite comfortable with that thought. A few days later she rang me to report that she was indeed now driving her boyfriend about quite happily.

So all seemed well; yet I suspected there were more deep-rooted problems. The amount of guilt Susan had expressed over the attempted rape was significantly beyond what might have been expected. Yes, she and her assailant had been on a date. Yes, they had been parked in a quiet country spot. Yes, they had been doing a little kissing and "canoodling". But she made it very clear to him that she was not up for anything further; and that was a reflection of statements she had made to him earlier. It also perplexed me that, although she had a well-paid job, she drove a beat-up old car she hated. Even after the Trauma Cure, she was still contemptuous of the car. So it was no great surprise when Susan turned up three months later, miserable, frustrated and calling herself "a failure".

Enough Dissonance To Make A Change...?

Susan was still driving the car she hated. The relationship with the boyfriend, "Carl", was blossoming yet she felt she couldn't love him unreservedly. She was a talented musician and was asked frequently to play with bands or at events; yet she turned most of these invitations down. She also didn't feel she could allow herself the time to practice (too many other pressing priorities!) and she would have sounded better on a decent instrument. She had the opportunity to go self-employed, doing more personally-satisfying work than her current job, but didn't feel she was up to it.

At the Purple level of SDi Susan had a dependency on her daughter, "Julia", whom she over-indulged and which the daughter sometimes abused. When Julia spent time away with the divorced father, Susan would go partly to pieces, mingling fits of tears with bouts of drunkenness, and then spoiling the daughter on her return.

Her Red vMeme tended to be expressed only intermittently. Then it was all too often explosively, as if it been kept all pent up inside. Carl apparently also had a temper which made for some heated rows, for which Susan always took the blame.

Of Blue there was barely a sign in her life. There was just enough for her to organise her work; but her house was a mess, and there was little sense of timing, regularity or organisation in her personal life. She lived largely from crisis to indulgence.

It was clear to me that the problems were manifesting themselves at the Red level, with low self-esteem and consequently poor self-efficacy. I meta-modelled Susan to discover that the root (core) belief preventing her looking after herself was that she was not good enough to be herself. (She had even had a "nervous breakdown" when Julia was born, believing that she wasn't good enough to have such a beautiful, healthy child!) From this, I deduced that, vMemetically, there had been some failure of Red to develop healthily in the Purple-to-Red transition.

Further meta-modelling revealed that the root belief of not being good enough to be herself stemmed from early-middle childhood experiences with her late father. He should have been the magical shamanic figure Purple needs but he suppressed her self-expression. "Be quiet! Shut up! Don't do that!" etc., were the responses she got to any form of loud or noisy play she did while he was in the house. As a teenager, he discouraged Susan's interest in music, saying "You can't eat your music", and refused to support her going to Music College. Unsurprisingly, Susan's Red had not developed healthily. She allowed herself to be abused (psychologically) by one of her brothers and ended up married to a man who also abused her verbally and reinforced the I'm-not-good-enough motif.

The strategy I decided to work with for her was Penny Park's Mistaken Belief Visualisation (1994). This is a powerful visualisation exercise which involves recognising that the disabling and dysfunctional core belief is (usually) passed on to the young child from a trusted significant older person (usually a parent). The conceptual basis of Parks' notion is reflected in the work of Susan Blackmore (1999) that , as a young child, we form a selfplex, a confluence of ideas about our "self" which are either taught directly to us by parents and significant others or "meta-stated" by the application of existing schemas to make sense of our experiences. (To meta-state is Michael Hall's (1995) term for interpretation via frame of reference.) Support for Parks and Blackmore also comes from the work of Ralph Allison (1996) who posits that experiences particularly before the 6–8 age range are often critical in the formation of the mental models children will carry with them for the rest of their lives.

The exercise I intended using with Susan was designed to take out the unhelpful/unhealthy schema by finding the person who gave you the belief and, using metaphors for the belief, give it back to him/her. A new healthy, enabling belief, again couched in easy-to-use metaphors, is then installed and tested. However, when I explained to Susan that undertaking Parks Mistaken Belief Visualisation would mean acknowledging that her father was the cause of her problems, she decided not to proceed with the therapy.

Two weeks later Susan was back, more miserable than ever. However, she still felt she couldn't acknowledge the part her father had played, even though I explained he wouldn't have understood what he was doing. (From discussing her childhood memories, it was clear to both of us that he was a fairly repressed character who also didn't feel good about himself.) Finally, after another couple of months of misery, with her relationship with Carl on the line, Susan had enough dissonance to accept what her father had unwittingly done to her.

A New Enabling Belief

I resourced Susan for the therapy by getting her to do Penny Parks' Resourceful You exercise which is about visualising "you" as potent and fulfilled as you could possibly be. Effectively the genotype (your raw genetic potential at the moment of conception) is fulfilled in the phenotype (what you become). As this exercise effectively boots Red's self-esteem, the exercise in itself was an antidote of sorts to Susan's problem! We then did the Mistaken Belief Visualisation and Susan's father, dead several years in real life, was duly handed back his debilitating belief. After this, Susan created an enabling belief for herself to replace it. We future-paced the new belief to test it. Susan told me, after the exercise was complete, that one of the future scenarios she used for the test was her accepting Carl's asking her to marry him because she deserved his love and she wanted him to enjoy all the love she had to give him!

Susan was then given a number of tasks to carry out as part of reinforcing her new sense of self-worth. Among these activities was the keeping of a "happy book", a fairly standard practice in CBT. This is a daily recording of positive events and the positive feelings that went hand-in-hand with them. Although it took some effort at first, Susan quickly came to treasure her happy book! The changes she experienced over the next year or so were phenomenal.

In her early-mid 40s, Susan started behaving like a full-of-herself teenager. She got rid of her "old banger" and spent £6,000 on a car worthy of her status in life and which she thoroughly enjoyed driving. Next up was £1,200 on a new musical instrument, for which she took the time to practise. She was experiencing the blossoming of healthy Red and beginning to love herself in a whole new way. Then came the Blue. Within just a few months of the therapy, Susan was organising her house, putting in place rules and schedules (particularly important for Julia entering her teens) and starting to future-pace concerns. Susan took the plunge employment-wise and started her own self-employed one-woman business. And, Carl did ask her to marry him...and she did accept!

Case Study #2: Shirley

"Shirley" was a middle manager who came to me for therapy because she was being made redundant and her sense of self-esteem was rather low. On the one hand she could see that her organisation was in turmoil. It was run by a self-referencing Red "king" who recognised intellectually the need for the organisation to enter what Ichak Adizes (1988) calls "Adolescence" in its growth but couldn't bring himself to share control emotionally. (Adolescence is the time when the organisation has to systemise and develop a professional management structure.) The result was an aggressive, almost brutal personal management style, an organisation that lacked the structure to support its expansion, and staff either leaving or being pushed out. (Adizes typifies this state of being unable to make the transition from an entrepreneurial style to a corporate structure as "Pathological Go-Go".)

On the other hand, Shirley, who was one of those being pushed out, blamed herself for her redundancy. She told me she was under-confident with "people who matter" work-wise, e.g. bosses, and did not project herself well. She had even "crumbled" under questioning at some recent presentations. Her fear of not living up to the Red king's expectations turned into a self-fulfilling prophecy when she failed to meet certain targets. Despite the lack of management support and the turmoil the organisation was in, Shirley roundly blamed herself. "I'm not good enough!" was her summation of her experience with this organisation and she was worried that she would take this attitude forward rather self-destructively into her hunt for a new job.

Resourcing Shirley

When I asked Shirley's Unconscious Mind (she was in a light trance at the time) where the belief, "I'm not good enough", came from, she readily answered that it was her childhood stepfather, Henry. It seemed that her mother, Jocelyn, had remarried just before Shirley had hit her teens, after living alone with her two daughters since separating from her first husband years before. Henry was a cold man, briskly efficient and demanding that everyone followed the rules, his rules. Shirley found herself shouted at frequently for not meeting Henry's expectations. Shirley grew to loathe the man to the point where she would leave the room when he entered.

Shirley knew enough about SDi for me to explain that her Red vMeme had been repressed at a time in life when its role was critical in shaping her teenage identity. She hadn't been allowed to express herself freely. Being herself, rather than the rigid conformist Henry required, only brought vicious criticism. As a consequence, she didn't learn to project herself well and she developed a fear of failing to meet others' expectations.

Shirley also revealed that she didn't feel like she had been loved or belonged as a youngster. This indicated damaged Purple. That Shirley had had a string of partners without ever settling into a relationship anything like long enough to get married also told of a problem in forming secure attachments, again an indication of unhealthy Purple. (It was the famous "Love Quiz" studies by Cindy Hazan & Phil Shaver (1987, 1993) which first established that attachment experiences as a child strongly influence romantic/sexual attachment experiences in adult life.) However, Shirley was reluctant to discuss her pre-Henry existence. Since her immediate needs centered on building her self-esteem and self-efficacy so that she could find herself a suitable new job, I left off her childhood and undertook Penny Parks' Resourceful You exercise with her. This involved Shirley visualising herself with every last little bit of potential developed - her genotype fulfilled as phenotype! When she realised that she could be competent, confident, assertive, powerful and impressive, she burst into tears with relief! From then on, finding a new job seemed nothing like as daunting.

Acknowledging Deep Hurts

Shirley returned to see me a few months later. With her current relationship on the rocks, she felt unloved, unable to cope with certain activities of her lover, Simon, and unwilling to go any deeper with the commitment. After some discussion, I started Penny Parks' Mistaken Belief Visualisation on the presumption that it had been Henry who had made her feel unloved. Suddenly Shirley snapped out of her light trance and exclaimed: "Bloody hell, it was my mother as well!"

Now she was ready to talk about her pre-Henry existence when Jocelyn and her two daughters had been a tight single parent family unit. Jocelyn had doted on her children and spent lots of time on activities with them. Shirley brought out many memories of happy times with her mother, saying several times how much love there had been in the household. Then Jocelyn had fallen in love with Henry and Shirley's world began to change in ways she found bewildering. Jocelyn spent little time on activities with her daughters; now she saw Henry as much as she could. When they married and Henry moved in, Shirley's life rapidly became one of firstly conflict and then suppression. What made it so difficult for her to assert herself and the thing that hurt her so much was that Jocelyn always took Henry's side, even when he was being outrightly nasty to the girls. Shirley felt betrayed. Not only did her mother clearly love this man more than her daughters, it seemed much of the time like she had no love left for them at all. Jocelyn did little or nothing to reassure her daughters of her affection for them. No wonder the Red had failed to develop healthily. Not only was it suppressed but the Purple foundation beneath it had been devastatingly undermined.

To enable Shirley to resolve her past, I used another Penny Parks exercise, the Trauma Resolution Experience. This exercise enables people to visualise how major figures in their past, such as parents, could have been and would have acted if they had been able to achieve their maximum potential. However, such was the intensity of Shirley's emotions that I conducted a variation of the exercise in which she visualised Jocelyn's and Henry's ultimate phenotypes separately. (Ethical, since they had separated some years previous.) At the end of this rather draining exercise, Shirley made a comment that puzzled me. She said she felt "much safer" now. I later learned that she went home, told Simon she loved him deeply and then gave him an ultimatum about changing those things she found unacceptable. Four months later Shirley secured an influential position with a prestigious employer. She thoroughly enjoys the work and is making her mark on the organisation. And she and Simon are still together.

Bibliography

Adizes, Ichak (1988): *Corporate LifeCycles* (Prentice Hall, Eaglewood Cliffs, NJ)

Allison, Ralph (1995): "Critical Issues: MPD and DID should be used for Two Separate Groups of Dissociators" in CANDID (California News of Dissociation and Identity Disorder) #3/4

Bateson, Gregory (1972): *Steps to an Ecology of Mind: Collected Essays in Anthropology, Psychiatry, Evolution & Epistemology* (University Of Chicago Press, Chicago, IL)

Beck, Aaron (1972): *Depression: Causes and Treatment* (University of Pennsylvania Press, Philadelphia, PA)

Beck, Don (2002): Personal e-mail communication

Beck, Don (2008): "The Heart and Soul of the Spiral Dynamics Movement" (Spiral Dynamics Integral) *http://www.spiraldynamics.net/spiral-dynamics-integral-sdi/spiral-dynamics-integral.html* (Accessed: 28/012/13)

Beck, Don & Chris Cowan (1996): *Spiral Dynamics: Mastering Change, Values and Leadership* (Blackwell, Cambridge, MA)

Blackmore, Susan (1999): *The Meme Machine* (Oxford University Press, Oxford)

Dilts, Robert (1990): *Changing Belief Systems with NLP* (Meta Publications, Capitola,CA)

Dilts, Robert (1996): *Visionary Leadership Skills: Creating a World to Which People Want to Belong* (Meta Publications, Capitola, CA)

Eysenck, Hans J. (1967): *The Biological Basis of Personality* (Charles C. Thomas, Springfield, IL)

Eysenck, Hans J. & Sybil B. G. Eysenck (1976): *Psychoticism as a Dimension of Personality* (Charles C Thomas, Springfield, IL)

Freud, Sigmund (1900; translated by A. A. Brill, 1913): *The Interpretation of Dreams* (The Macmillan Company, New York, NY)

Freud, Sigmund (1901; translated by A. A. Brill, 1914): *The Psychopathology of Everyday Life* (T Fisher Unwin, London)

Freud, Sigmund (1920; translated by C. J. M. Hubback, 1922): *Beyond the Pleasure Principle* (The International Psycho-Analytic Press, London)

Freud, Sigmund (1923; translated by Joan Riviere, 1927), *The Ego & the Id* (Hogarth Press/Institute of Psycho-Analysis, London)

Freud, Sigmund (1924; translated by Joan Riviere): "The Passing of the Oedipus Complex" in International Journal of Psycho-Analysis 5/4

Graves, Clare W. (1971; transcribed by William R. Lee, 2002): *Levels of Human Existence* (ECLET, Santa Barbara, CA)

Hall, L. Michael (1995): *Meta States: a Domain of Logical Levels* (ET Publications, Grand Junction, CO)

Hay, Dale & Jo Ellen Vespo (1988): "Social Learning Perspectives on the Mother-Child Relationship" in Beverley Birns and Dale Hay (eds.): *The Different Faces of Motherhood* (Plenum Press, New York, NY)

Hazen, Cindy & Phil Shaver (1987): "Romantic Love conceptualised as an Attachment Process" in Journal of Personality & Social Psychology #52

Hazen, Cindy & Phil Shaver (1993): "Adult Romantic Attachment: Theory and Evidence" in D. Perlman & W. Jones: *Advances in Personal Relationships* Vol. 4 (Kingsley, London)

Marston, William Moulton (1928): *Emotions of Normal People* (Taylor & Francis, New York, NY)

Mead, George Herbert (1913): "The Social Self" in Journal of Philosophy, Psychology & Scientific Methods #10

Palmer, Stephen & Ray Wolfe (1999): *Integrative and Eclectic Counselling and Psychotherapy* (Sage Publications)

Parks, Penny (1994): *The Counsellor's Guide to Parks Inner Child Therapy* (Souvenir Press, London)

Rice, Keith E. (2006): *Knowing Me, Knowing You: an Integrated SocioPsychology Guide to Personal Fulfilment & Better Relationships* (Trafford, Victoria, BC)

Skinner, B. F. (1938): *The Behaviour of Organisms* (Appleton-Century-Crofts, New York, NY)

Sloane, Bruce, Fred Staples, Allan Cristol, Neil Yorkston & Katherine Whipple (1975): *Psychotherapy versus Behaviour Therapy* (Harvard University Press, Cambridge, MA)

Trauel, N. N. (1961): "The Effects of Perceptual Isolation on Introverts and Extraverts" (unpublished PhD thesis, Washington State University)

Williams, Linda Mayer (1994): "Recall of Childhood Trauma: a Prospective Study of Women's Memories of Child Sexual Abuse" in Journal of Consulting & Clinical Psychology #62

THE ROLLER COASTER AND THE WHITEWATER

By Beth Sanders MCP, MCIP, RPP

In 2007 I left my dream job because the system I was working in was on life support and new work was calling. After a few lurches on the roller coaster, the experience of seeing the world from new vantage points, I found myself in the thrill of plunging back into my life, compelled to seek change. I found myself seeking change in me.

One of the first things I did was get off the fixed-track roller coaster and began exploring. I started noticing things that had my attention. I started exploring and following a path that was laying itself out in front of me, step by step. I disengaged from the destinations that used to drive me, and engaged with my innate sense of direction. I did not know *exactly* where I was going, but I knew I was going somewhere. I knew I was no longer on a roller coaster with a fixed schedule, but rather in a raft heading down a river. At times the river is rough and calls great effort from me. At times the valley edges narrow and I know the moments ahead are going to need my full attention. And after running the rapids, there is always an eddy, a safe place to pull off to the side and be calm, a place to regroup, make any repairs to equipment, revel in the thrill, have a snack and prepare to move along. At times, the ride on the river can feel as fixed as the roller coaster; the difference is in those moments when I can circle up with my self and others. In my whitewater life, the eddy is a place for great learning.

At the south edge of Canada's Lake Manitoba, just as the ice was beginning to melt in the spring of 2008, I responded to an invitation to gather at a migratory bird field station with a community of practice for three days of inquiry. The invitation came from someone I trust, my former thesis advisor Ian Wight, who had a sense of my journey past, present and future. I introduced myself and told my story, and the principles I live by, i.e. look after self, look after others, look after our place. A voice across the circle rang out, "We have to talk!" It was Marilyn Hamilton. I had just uttered the words that conclude her, about to be published, book.

I found myself immersed in a new language of colours and quadrants, a world that appealed even when I could not articulate why. I jumped into the river and let it take me along to SDi trainings and a Training of Trainers experience in Canada, and on to the Dallas Confab in 2009. Since my first SDi training I've been teaching SDi formally and informally. I've been sharing it explicitly and implicitly in my work. My big learning, though, is the Spiral was always in me and around me, even if I didn't know it.

Beige and Purple are the first stages of my life, beginning at birth and on into my first years of life. While I can't remember many details, I do know my basic needs were met and I grew up in a loving family. I recall a Purple moment at age 14 as my family drove from Canada into the United States. I was petrified of tornados, and I knew from the news that tornados always occurred in the United States. As we drove over the border into Montana, I was scared to death that we would be caught in a tornado. It was my first time in the United States, and I was struck by how the forest looked the same, the roads and cars looked the same, and the people looked the same. But I was in the United States, so I was in danger. A mystical logic took hold, regardless of what I could see, "This is where tornados take place." I was not in control of my reactions. Purple was running the show and the tornado monster was hovering, even if invisible, just outside my window. In more recent years, as a mother, I notice Beige pops up when my children are in danger. Recently while walking my small children to school, a woman almost harmed them while parking her car. The "momma bear" in me reacted with anger, and a rare verbal explosion. I met healthy Beige, and although it wouldn't win me a neighbor of the year award, I saw its value clearly. While shocked by my response, I was grateful for the bear in me, and how she revealed my instinctual resources.

As a child, the Red vMeme was front and center when I realized I had competition, a younger brother. I have vivid recollections of taking larger portions of food and giving him the smaller. I recall just as vividly, and so does he, wrestling matches and my ability to overcome him physically. My awareness of others, and the transition to Blue, was sealed when he began to overpower me.

Family life and school were big parts of my life, setting the social norms that come along with the Blue vMeme. Religion was significant in my parents' upbringing. My family attended church sporadically, but the norms established in my parents' formative years were the expectations entailed in my upbringing. While I regularly poked at the systems I was a part of (home and school), I accepted those systems and the positions of authority. To a great degree I trusted authority, because it could accommodate my needs. In junior high and high school, for six years, I wanted to be in the orchestra and take physical education, but the system could not, on the surface, accommodate this. Each year, the Principal and I found ways to navigate the system and make it work. And when I went from junior high to senior high, he changed schools with me—the Blue system kept helping me. Even at age eleven I was able to get what I needed in the Blue system.

I have a distinct competitive streak in me, the Orange vMeme, to do the best that I can, and to find every opportunity possible to do the best that I can. It showed up in the creative work-arounds to navigate the Blue structures in high school. It also showed up in the way I chose to learn at university, a multidisciplinary undergraduate degree in Canadian studies that involved the integration of Canada's two official languages and courses in 14 different departments. I went on to a master's degree in city planning, a profession of synthesis and integration. Working in city systems, I was driven to seek opportunities to move up the ranks, starting as an entry level development officer, then district planner, to General Manager of planning and development for a small prairie city and two surrounding rural municipalities, a challenging position both administratively and politically. Then I took on the BIG challenge, general manager of the planning and development department in North America's fastest growing community, in the heart of the oil sands.

I can see the presence of the Green vMeme in me from late childhood and particularly in university. In hindsight, togetherness and harmony drove many decisions. In high school I participated in a student exchange that landed me in northern Quebec for 3½ months. This adventure lead to an intense affection for people I didn't know and didn't understand. To fill this void I took on studies in French at the University of Ottawa and a fascinating exploration of clashing Canadian cultures, i.e. the Quebec/Canada clash, the Quebec/Alberta clash and the Alberta/Canada clash. In all of this, an expanded sense of Red co-emerged with a more informed nationalism. The Green vMeme thrived in my desire to build bridges and honour the diversity in a common nation. These intense waves of learning began at age 16 and continued through my undergraduate education at the University of Ottawa, volunteer activities with the Forum for Young Canadians (an organization that brought together youth from across Canada to learn about how the federal government works) and advocacy work during my graduate degree. This advocacy work put me in the middle of media scrums on Parliament Hill in Ottawa and at Quebec's Legislature in Quebec City, at age 23.

While working on my master of city planning degree and my first few years working as a professional, the Green vMeme emerged in new territory. I stepped into the realm of social justice as I advocated for women and children's human rights. I ended up on the front page of the local newspaper when my first child was about to be born. Because of a pediatrician strike, moms like me were enjoying labor in an ambulance, on our way to another hospital, in another city, two hours away. The system was failing. This was not proper care, and I spoke up publicly. Advocacy was important but when it came time for me to deliver, Orange creativity stepped in: I played the Blue rules and labored at home long enough so they could not put me in an ambulance. When my water broke and I knew things were underway, I got a call from the newspaper and said, "Oh yeah, I'll talk!" The next morning I was on the front page and baby arrived. There was a pediatrician on hand, and the nurses all had thanks for saying what needed to be said.

My work as a city planner was exciting in my twenties, in the 1990s, yet I sensed simultaneously that Green work was not truly looking out for the collective. I was trying new language on for size, e.g. "sustainable development and its three pillars, the economic, social and environmental aspects of community." My professional practice meant I had to value these words and ideas and find a place for them in my work and life. The dissonance I experienced was in how Green accommodated social and environmental and social interests, but not the economic (Orange). As a city planner, my role is to support a city as it organizes itself, which means working with varied values. As I worked closely in city hall with a successful businessman, and the experience of working with developers, I learned a lot about the business view of the world, and how it fit into a community. I still have a lot to learn on this front, and I always will, but appreciation of other perspectives is essential to the health of my practice. I learned that a healthy practice, for me, meant being open to learning from any source, accepting that everyone has truth, that everyone is who he or she is, wherever they are. The flex and flow of Yellow was taking hold.

Today, I see that the seeds of Yellow were nurtured in my thesis work. I explored cultural values that emerged from my qualitative analysis of an extensive series of interviews of people involved in a controversial land development. I identified and explored how different perspectives have a distinct impact on people's expectations for public participation in public decision-making. Two poles were identified on a continuum, the proponents and the challengers, and the analysis revealed a power struggle of first-tier values. At the time, the Green vMeme perspective in me looked at power and where it resides, yet Yellow allowed me to see that one's culture and values has an impact on how the world is viewed. This idea was reinforced: each view of the world has truth in it.

Life since my mid-twenties is characterized by rich professional and family/personal experiences. On the professional front, the Yellow vMeme allowed me to lead an organization through a chaotic time. At the time, I thought I was strategic, but I now understand my work as "Spiral Wizardry," where I:

- Offered time and places for our shared sense of Purple family to gather and build relationships.
- Fed ideas to colleagues living in a Red world so they could come up with the ideas themselves.
- Lived in the Red passion of pride in my community and my team's work, and a bit of competitiveness too.
- Offered a clear sense of Blue purpose and reason to guide decisions amidst the chaos.
- Used Blue language to communicate with my boss and other Blue areas of the organization.
- Followed the Blue rules to keep certain colleagues happy and on track.
- Engaged Blue and Orange Wizards (I wish I had a Red one)
- Turned Orange on full power, in me, to make it through the time I spent there.

- Delegated work and let my team get on with their work and advocated for what they need (Orange).
- Offered strategic alternatives to an organization in distress (Orange).
- Hired people based on competency, not according to traditional human resources job descriptions and qualifications (Yellow).
- Remained open to any source of learning—internal, external, personal, collective (Yellow).
- Recognized that most of my staff was craving Green experiences and provided them with a habitat that allowed them to sense their collective community.
- Balanced that community focus with individual attention where a need for identity, territory, and pride and passion for our work was noted (Red).
- Coached staff to be self-aware, and supported them as they stretched themselves "up," on their terms (Yellow).
- Supported the work of people and organizations, even when in opposition to my employer, with the intention of supporting the larger community system (Yellow/Turquoise).
- Sought out opportunities to explore, with unusual co-learners, to find solutions to wicked problems (Yellow/Turquoise).

This version of the Spiral Wizard was fueled by a Red/Orange drive to succeed. I put my shoulder to the wheel to get the job done, I worked hard and I was rewarded with success and wonderful accomplishments. This was the roller coaster ride.

I chose to get off the roller coaster because I could see something different, beyond Yellow. The power of the collective, far beyond what Green offers, was surging. It started as tickles of Turquoise and I noted the power of connecting ideas, people, organizations and initiatives for solutions to problems that face humanity and our planetary habitat. I nurtured this emerging interest by setting up my own company, leaving me fully in charge of where I spend my energy in my work. Exploring has become my work; and my work has become my exploring.

My Turquoise world is alive and flourishing. I have initiated global and local communities of practice that nurture me, others and our places. The Spiral is a language I use explicitly and implicitly with everyone I interact with: clients, family, colleagues, self. This allows me, and us, to calmly work with out drama. While I have always been able to see the best in people and believe in them, the Spiral allows me to find their best and believe in them far longer.

My particular interest in the application of SDi is in city and community planning. Our drive for improvement is the very force that has created our city habitats. How we show up shapes our cities, and in return, our cities shape us; they give us challenges to improve again. Our relationship with cities is an essential part of our never-ending quest. My life work now takes me into the whitewater of city life, working with people who are learning how to improve self and relationships with others so that our work for our cities is better, somehow smarter. I call myself a city planner when a Blue label is required. I call my self a civic Meshworker.

As a civic Meshworker, I support my city's efforts to organize itself to serve citizens well, and I support citizens' efforts to serve their city well. As you can imagine, Spiral Wizardry is a large part of this practice. I am a great Blue moderator of election forums and community meetings. I can host a good Green circle. I can break silos and create the conditions for Orange brilliance to emerge. I can sit in Yellow and let people sort out their best course of action without giving them answers. I can create places for Purple stories to connect us to self, others and our place. I can walk into a room and generate a field of Turquoise energy that raises the field of possibilities. And I am full of Red passion for cities and all that we can do for them, so they, in return, can do their best for us.

NEWLY EMERGENT COGNITIVE CAPACITIES

Revised from the Original *www.IntegralWorld.net* Publication (2013)

By Tom Christensen

The capacities addressed below are those that co-emerge with the capacity for Second Tier cognition. Graves held that levels of cognitive complexity increase non-linearly. If that increase is only a doubling, and Beige is attributed a measure of 4, then we see the following: Purple 8, Red 16, Blue 32, Orange 64, Green 128, Yellow 256. To comprehend the significance of this progression, imagine that there are, say, only 4 synapses at Beige. Purple with 8 is not such a big change. But jump ahead to the change represented by Green to Yellow, First Tier to Second Tier, 128 to 256! That is a huge increase in brain potential. Graves addressed this phenomenon with his term, "The Momentous Leap". The point is, however one imagines the trajectory of increasing cognitive complexity, the leap from Green to Yellow, should entail significant new capacities in the Yellow brain. What might those dramatically different, significantly more complex, capacities be? Following is a report on this inquiry.

Through both ontology and phylogeny humans have often created intractable problems and then found themselves with new capacities ideally suited to solve these problems. We are currently beset by a plethora of intractable problems. Perhaps we have already emerged the capacities to solve these problems. If so, as in so much of personal development, we don't need to become anything different, we just need to become facile with the capacities we already have. What might those capacities be?

This inquiry rests on the following three assumptions:

1) **We have complex, intractable problems that must be solved in order for suffering to be reduced and human potential realized.** This applies to the whole spectrum of problems from parenting, relationships, employee and program management, military and corporate strategy, resource management, hunger and poverty reduction, wealth and wage inequality, health care availability, governance, technology distribution, and beyond. We see problems everywhere, and the really complex ones are not being resolved.

2) **The solutions will not be available at the level where the problem was created.** For example, to resolve the problem of whether light is a wave or a particle one has to step above the polarities and create a vision large enough to hold them both as true; to resolve the problem of inadequate health care delivery evidenced by its absence in poverty areas, we must move from the question of who deserves adequate health care and who do not, to a transcend and include perspective, i.e. what serves best to reduce suffering and free human potential for the whole Nation?

3) **Human cognitive development has a history of emerging new levels of cognitive complexity that do solve the intractable problems created by the junior level.** As the young person stabilizes their identity, in order to get along with other stabilized identities the capacity begins to emerge to defer gratification and to honor objective authority. As the objective rules are mastered and the constraint on individual creativity becomes oppressive, the capacity to see the grey areas, to make creative decisions

beyond the rules emerges. As individual achievement sores and is acknowledged, the isolation that accompanies this solo expression gives way as the capacity to include the creative thoughts and feelings of others emerges.

My interest has been focused for some time now on distinguishing what new cognitive capacities may have emerged at this time, that might be ideal for solving the complex problems of our times; capacities that have not been recognized widely yet. Could we have emerged the capacities necessary to solve the problems we have created? There is precedent for this occurrence, giving hope of being successful this time also in finding just those capacities. It is up to those who put these capacities to work to confirm their usefulness. But at this stage I believe I, on the shoulders of many before me, have found some of those capacities and putting them to work intentionally will emerge solutions that are simply not available until we do.

The initial discovery of these capacities occurred in an experiential, guided inquiry, 3 credit course I taught at the University of Wisconsin-Madison in the Fall of 2010, "Multiperspectival Thinking: Operating with all Windows open." Since them I have tested their veracity in two content related online publications, with no one choosing to challenge their accuracy. I have also on many occasions confirmed they can be recognized when described to highly complex thinkers. You, dear reader, are the next test. Do you recognize your own earlier undistinguished capacities in what follows?

Stabilized Objectivity.

General objectivity is technically defined as the capacity to think and feel about one's thoughts and feelings. Stabilized Objectivity extends this notion to the capacity to give up ANY perspective, to be able to move any thought or feeling to an object of inquiry. The human is not defined by or required to own, or otherwise accrue perspectives in order to be. Any thought or feeling can be detached from the sense of ownership, thus freeing one up from many biases, occluding beliefs, preconceptions, and other mental constructions that constrain the emergence of possibilities. As with all of these measures, it is not necessary that these capacities be active at all times, just that they are available at any time for intentional enactment.

Multiperspectival Thinking.

This is the ability to look at an object of inquiry from many different perspectives. For example Said Dawlabani, *MEMEnomics,* (2013), has us ask what a successful business is: Is it one that is profitable? Yes. Is it one that takes care of people? Yes. Is it one that serves the wellbeing of the planet? Yes. Here we have three perspectives. A less complex thinker will argue over which is right. The multiperspectival thinker will review the conditions and measures for each, and integrate them all in the final measure of success. A successful business is one that serves People, Profit and Planet.

The person who is trapped within their ideology, there fundamental truth, cannot bring the full scope of human cognition to solving our difficult problems. It is the mind that can entertain multiple truths, integrate them into a plan, and execute based on this wisdom that can show us solutions that the junior fundamentalist mind simply cannot access.

Transegoic Cognition.

It is very important and useful for the developing human to form a firm identity. However, with just a little introspection we become aware that who and what we are extends far beyond the boundaries of our identity, "I've never acted like that before. How did I know that? I surprised myself." Further, our nervous system is well known to register and process much more information than we are bothered with at the conscious level…we are up to a whole lot more than we even know we are up to. So that self we treasure so much is a construction that contains a sufficient number of markers to allow us to live as an identity. But that identity can be seen as just one more perspective we can enact, the first person, or "I" perspective. We can take other perspectives and do all the time.

It is the capacity to see and know unhindered by ego, or self-identity, and to do so intentionally that is Transegoic Cognition. We can think other than thru our construct of self. To think at a junior level, constrained by the consistencies demanded of identity, limits to a lethal degree what we can see and know and dream up about ourselves and our world. We can't solve the complex problems of our time with ego in the way, and we have an alternative capacity.

Transnarrative Cognition.

This capacity refers to the kind of knowing we have all at once, and which is not at the time it emerges a linear narrative of information. When we study something for some time, suddenly we "get it". In that "getting it" moment we don't see a paragraph with descriptive information. We know this something in a volumetric, spatial context. This kind of knowing is more imagery and only with the effort to communicate this insight does it get turned into a linear narrative. With highly complex cognition available, this way of comprehending a topic of interest is normal, usual, and much more comprehensive than even the reporting narrative can articulate. This new "normal" means that an object of inquiry can be considered in a much wider scope. There is now a vision available that reveals more contingencies, more ramifications, more possibilities.

Timeline Cognition.

While absorbed in Transnarrative Cognition, the past, present, and possible futures of the object of inquiry can appear. The object of inquiry can be appreciated within the scope of where it has come from, what it is now and what it might become. This can be understood as the facility to move attention along a timeline within the volumetric knowing of Transnarrative Cognition. When enacting this capacity the generative context and purpose is appreciated; the relationship of the object of inquiry to its source and its omega point are available; possible futures it has available are viewable. With this broad scope more relevant factors can be revealed, and more informed choices can be made. Just consider the paucity of information available in junior level cognition that can hold only one truth, and that truth, an abstracted, linearly understood, chunk from the timeline.

Attunement.

When Transnarrative Cognition is enacted, there is a sense or feeling that accompanies this whole, all at once, apprehension. There is information entailed in this feeling. It's possible that the information from the heart-brain, solar plexus-brain, and other nerve plexes are emerging in Attunement. People report the nature of this information in different ways.

Some report colors. Others sounds, words, or even melodies. Some report images, scenes, or energies. All convey something that the reporter considers germane to the object of inquiry. The value of these reports is measured by their contribution to advancing the inquiry.

Nonlocal Self.

The 1st person, or self perspective is a construct, and not who the person is. Upon objectifying ego, we still know we are doing, thinking, and feeling. We are still here, and we are nowhere that can be pinpointed. To pinpoint anything about ourselves is to objectify it, leaving the objectifier still absent a location. The most workable articulation of this phenomenon is to use the term "Nonlocal Self". We cannot be located, and we are here. To accept this characterization of one's being is to provide a huge measure of freedom for ideas to come forth unhindered by any concern for what it means to oneself...there is no one we can find that anything pertains to.

A Quiet Amygdala.

The 4 F amygdala responses have evolved to focus our resources on immediate threats. We all have experienced diminished capacities for creative thought when, say, an authority walks into the middle of our presentation, or we are terribly nervous when meeting someone, or a loud noise freezes us in place. In probably all cases of amygdala activation the higher cortical functions are compromised: One doesn't compose a critique of Heidegger's identity claims when the enemy is threatening to breach the wall. If highly complex thinking occurs in the absence of fear and threat, there is promise of many more possible resolutions to emerge regarding any problem of interest.

Systems Thinking.

The vision that emerges in Transnarrative Cognition is more complex than narrative speaking can convey. Experience has shown that the most complex idiom available to convey the insights of Transnarrative Cognition is that of General Systems Theory. I have looked for a more complex narrative idiom to no avail. Manuel De Landa with his notions of aggregation might qualify, but he also veers off into systems theory often in his writing. For now, there is no narrative idiom in sight that can capture the complexity of Transnarrative Cognition as well as General Systems Theory. This is not to say that all insights must be conveyed with General Systems Theory. Smaller portions of an insight can be conveyed in any narrative idiom; poetry and song included. Imagery can also be put to use here. But if a comprehensive narrative report of the nature of one's Transnarrative insight is desired, for now General Systems Theory is the best option available. (Graves formed his bio-psycho-social theory of human emergence around General Systems Theory.)

It is very likely true that you recognized these capacities as being present when those "magic" moments have occurred for you, especially in a group effort. When "in the flow" or "creative groove", "presencing", or basking in the flow of excellent, new, and perfectly furthering ideas, ego is not present, fear is absent, vision is larger than words, you feel the nature of the project as if it lives itself, and you can effortlessly move in and out of any perspective presented or desired. This is not normal. Over a period of 3 million years this is the first time any critical mass of two-leggeds has been able to do this. Why now?

I have proposed that these are nine newly stabilized cognitive capacities and that these have emerged ideally suited to resolve the otherwise intractable problems of our times. I don't have to be right about either of these claims. If these capacities are not anything special, why not? If these are not the capacities we need at this time, what are?

Note: The fact that you are still reading this says that you have highly complex cognitive capacities. This is not trivial.

Bibliography

Baggini, J. (2011). *The Ego Trick: What does it Mean to be You?* London, GB. Granta Publications.

Beck, Don and Cowan, C. (2006). *Spiral Dynamics: Mastering Values, Leadership and Change.* Hoboken, NJ: Blackwell Publishing.

Christensen, Tom. "Leading Edge Cognitive Capacities". (Nov, 2013) *http://www.integralworld.net/christensen1.html*

Christensen, Tom. "Game is Over. You are Enlightened." (Oct, 2012) *www.integralleadershipreview.com*

Christensen, Tom. "An Introduction To and Tutorial For Spiral Dynamics Integral (SDi)" (2012) *https://wisc.academia.edu/TomChristensen/Teaching-Documents*

Cowan, C. & Todorovic, N. Eds. Graves, Clare. (2005). *The Never Ending Quest.* San Barbara, CA: ECLET Publishing.

Damasio, A. (2010). *Self Comes To Mind: Constructing the Conscious Brain.* New York, NY. Random House.

Dawlabani, S. (2013). *MEMEnomics.* New York, NY. SelectBooks, Inc.

De Landa, M. (1997). *A Thousand Years of Nonlinear History.* Cambridge, MA. MIT Press.

Donald, Merlin. (2001). *A Mind So Rare.* NYC, NY: W. W. Norton and Company.

Donald, Merlin. (1991). *Origins of the Modern Mind: Three Stages in the Evolution of Culture and Cognition.* Cambridge, Ma: Harvard University Press.

Gazzaniga, M. (2011). *Who's In Charge: Freewill and the Science of the Brain?* New York, NY. HarperCollins.

Hood, B. (2012). *The Self Illusion.* Oxford, GB. Oxford University Press.

Johnson, S. (2003) *Everything Bad Is Good For You.* New York, NY. Penguin Group.

Lee, W. Ed. Graves, Clare. (2002). *Levels of Human Existence.* Santa Barbara, CA: ECLET Publishing.

Madhavananda, Swami. Trans. (1970). *Viveakchudamani of Shri Shankaracharya.* Uttarakhand, India: Advaita Ashrama.

Satchidananada, Swami (1978). *The Yoga Sutras of Patanjali.* Buckingham, VA: Integral Yoga Publications.

Sharmer, C. Otto. (2009) *Theory U: Leading from the Future as It Emerges.* Berrett-Koehler Publishers, Inc. San Francisco, CA, USA.

Tomasello, Michael. (2008). *Origins of Human Communication.* Cambridge, MA: MIT Press.

Tomasello, Michael. (2009). *Why We Cooperate.* Cambridge, MA: MIT Press.

AGELESS WISDOM AND SDi

By Rosemary Wilkie

"If SDi were provided by the Hierarchy as an update for our times to the Ageless Wisdom, why was SDi needed now? And what does its transmission do for humanity that couldn't be done now without it?" (Tom Christensen)

Down through the ages, whenever humanity has exhausted its resources and its ability to cope with its problems, we have received divine guidance. The line of great teachers: Buddha, Krishna, Confucius, Jesus, Mohammed, runs like a beam of light through all world faiths and scriptures. They were inspired by higher levels of being they believed was God. They taught love, gave us laws and codes of ethics to live by, and founded the great religions we know today, albeit encrusted now with centuries of tinkering by theologians and political pressure.

Since 1400 there has been a stream of lesser teachers, who took the form of men and women championing successfully some truth or right cause, some human right or correct demand. They weren't always recognised at the time, but changed our thinking and pioneered new areas of achievement. In the nineteenth century Helena Blavatsky, in *The Secret Doctrine,* revealed the golden thread of secret teachings underlying all religions, introduced many ideas that flowered in the New Age movement, and bridged the gap between Western and Eastern cosmology. In the twentieth century, Alice Bailey, also under the direction of Djwhal Khul (the Tibetan), produced twenty-four books, a treasure house of unadulterated ageless wisdom.

The fundamentals have always been true, but each generation has the possibility of testing the strength of the old foundations, conserving the essentials and building wisely on them a structure to meet current needs. We are now in the twenty-first century, with overwhelming new and intractable problems, some of which threaten the very existence of life on earth. Is it time for a new revelation? Could Spiral Dynamics Integral hold the key?

Professor Graves made no claim to divine revelation. In *The Never Ending Quest,* he is quoted as saying that he did not visit the Gods on Olympus, nor had he stood on the mountain top in Sinai to procure the substance of his theory. He compared his arduous, systematic work to that of Darwin a century before. In the Galapagos, Darwin had observed subtle differences and changes over time in the animal world and only after painstaking assessment of his data came to the conclusion that these were due to evolution. In the same way, it was only after Graves had studied his own data that he realised that psychology is a process and began to produce the wonderful Spiral framework in which competing schools of psychology could find their place.

In Esoteric Psychology Vol II, the Tibetan points to the major importance of psychology and the failure of the many schools of psychology to relate their many points of view to each other (p.403). That book was published in 1942 and ten years later Graves was inspired to begin his research. While working on his accumulated data, Graves asked himself the age-old questions about human life. What is it all about? What is it meant to be? We are all born with the innate desire to find out who we are and why we are here, to find meaning and purpose in life and a higher power to believe in. Graves recognised the spiritual line of development working out in the First Tier in people's tribal and clan beliefs, in their gods, ideological systems, economic or social systems, finding their reason for existence somewhere other than in the personal self. For these reasons I suggest that Professor Graves belongs in the great stream of divinely inspired teachers.

The great tradition of divine revelation is not complete without Science. The ancient Greeks, Pythagoras, Socrates, Plato and Archimedes, created the basic philosophy and mathematics on which our western culture is based. Others followed: Galileo, Leonardo da Vinci, Newton. More recently James Lovelock's Gaia theory that our planet is a living, self-regulating system, and NASA's space photograph of our beautiful blue earth, filled us with wonder and transformed the way we see our world. The proof that matter is only a form of energy is as profound in its implications as the teachings of the Christ and Buddha. The virtue of science is that it recognises the truth when proven.

Sadly, science too often limits itself by its own assumptions: that reality is material or physical; that there is no purpose or meaning to life; that consciousness can be found in the brain; that God is just an outdated idea and that the universe is made up of dead matter. Whereas the Ageless Wisdom teaches that the universal life essence flows around and through every living thing. It forms the etheric body that controls and conditions the physical form of everything from the solar system to a puppy. Our etheric bodies are subject to constant change from cosmic energies and from the general life and vitality of the vMeme where our consciousness is normally focused. The etheric is mirrored on a material level by plasma - ninety- nine percent of the universe is made up of it. David Bohm described plasma as a gas in which a high density of electrons and positive atoms stop acting individually and behave as if they are alive and part of a whole.

So What Can SDi Do That Nothing Else Can?

We are living through a period of transformation greater than the industrial and scientific revolutions, compressed into decades rather than centuries. There is a remarkable flowering of creativity, mostly ignored by the media. But the old economic order is crumbling. Money is fragile flickering figures on a screen. The social order is changing as millions of people move across the world fleeing oppression or seeking a better life. Time is passing faster. The weather is crazy and NASA has confirmed that all the planets in the solar system are experiencing disorder. It is hardly surprising that we all feel challenged, and that many are looking for someone or something to blame. Yet our only hope for humanity to survive is to cooperate, to work together, and for that we need to understand each other, to discover why we think and act as we do.

Feedback, from the simple talks, introductory articles and book I have written on SDi *(Emergence. Vol 1 – Introduction,* Rosemary Wilkie, England (2013), shows that even people in Orange and Green Life Conditions easily relate to the idea of levels of expanding consciousness, and find it very helpful in their personal lives. And business has benefited enormously from SDi thinking, as many chapters in these two volumes show. But we need to move the teachings into the mainstream and bring them to the notice of those in influential positions, politicians, for example. So far we have only reached a few. They attain high office full of good intentions, only to find themselves besieged, not only by the opposing party, but by lobbyists, focus groups, newspaper editorials, advisers, popularity polls and events, unable, as Graves originally was, to discern what is right. If politicians understood the simplest presentation of the vMemes, they could not only reach the right decisions, they could explain them in words that various levels of the electorate could understand and accept.

There is an even greater need on the international front. Knowledge of SDi shows, for example, that invading a Purple/Red country to give them democracy is delusional, as is preaching human rights to those for whom tribal good and tribal traditions are paramount. People everywhere are crying out for change, but only SDi explains in detail what is needed for real change to occur:

Are people open to change and able to deal effectively with obstacles to further development? Or trapped in their current situation by failure to overcome barriers? These barriers might be commitments to caring, making excuses to disguise their fear, or just not uncomfortable enough in current Life Conditions to make the effort. Or are they closed to change because of past trauma, or lack of neurological or brain power? SDi considers the following as necessary conditions for change.

1) People must be unable to find solutions to inner or outer problems at the current level.

2) They must be aware that current thinking does not work in their existing situation.

3) Internal and external barriers to change must be identified and dealt with, not denied or blamed on someone else.

4) Insight is needed into what went wrong and why and how different plans for the future could be made to work.

5) Support is essential to consolidate change and prevent backsliding during the adjustment period, which may be full of confusion, false starts and the misunderstanding of those who do not understand what is happening. It is

the struggle between worn-out ideas and new ones that expands consciousness.

Hundreds of official bodies and two million NGOs are working hard to help the starving, the homeless, the disadvantaged and the impoverished; too often separately and with different purposes and ideas. How much more effective they would be if they understood those conditions for change!

Even more effective efforts could be made if these groups used Meshworks, a practice of aligning available resources, vMemes, and Life Conditions. Life Conditions would include measures in all 4 quadrants which coemerge with their adaptive vMemes. Assessments should be made in at least the areas of psychology, health, politics, religion, education, and society. Where these Life Conditions are not satisfying the vMeme needs, available resources are redirected to meet those needs.

Right human relations are our only hope of establishing a peaceful and secure future in which the whole of humanity can fulfil its potential. SDi gives us a framework that allows us to see, for the first time, the stages that people have reached and what is the right next step for them. This is immensely helpful. But it does not address the fundamental question of unfairness, of why some are born into poverty and despair, and others into Life Conditions that allow them to develop their potential and climb the Spiral.

The Ageless Wisdom describes the Law of Rebirth, which holds the answer to much human questioning. The theory of reincarnation was basic to the beliefs of ancient civilisations and remains so in the East, but disappeared from the West in Roman times. So there is no anchor for the idea in our culture. Yet the alternatives are so much worse! One is that man is ephemeral and soulless, dissolving into dust when he dies, an existence without purpose or meaning. The second is the orthodox Christian theory that an inscrutable God sends souls into incarnation for one life, and what they do determines their future for eternity.

The Law of Rebirth offers an explanation for the enormous disparity of opportunity, education and wealth, and the desperate unfairness in the world. When we first hear about reincarnation we may imagine ourselves doing something worthy in a past life, the same personality in costume. But it is not the personality that is reincarnated. Different genetic, social and cultural inheritance makes that impossible anyway. It is the Soul that endures, that carries the lessons from each life and takes one body after another to manifest its purpose until it is perfected and no longer needs to incarnate on earth. It makes so much sense to consider that we come back life after life to grow in consciousness, to climb the Spiral - which no-one could possibly do in one lifetime! So reincarnation is implied in SDi.

The Ageless Wisdom also provides the involutionary arc that precedes our arrival in Beige and teaches the expansion of consciousness on the evolutionary curve beyond the Second Tier. Graves himself noted the huge number of as yet unused brain cells we are born with, like seeds with the potential to become trees. There are many bright minds conjecturing what happens at levels above Turquoise. In the past three hundred years we have developed our minds - and most of us identify with them. But think back. As infants we identified with our physical needs, and later with our emotional desires. It is not unreasonable to expect that one day we will be able to identify with levels higher than our rational minds?

It has taken aeons to develop our individuality, and we are extremely reluctant to let go of it! We experienced group life in Purple, and in Turquoise we are faced with the difficult exercise of working in groups *without* losing our individuality. This is an entirely new way of living, only possible when we are united in our purpose. Some of us have had what felt like a magical experience in a small group, joyfully recognising that we were speaking with one mind. In the outer world we can see the trend working already, in crowdfunding, car sharing, in internet groups enlisting world-wide support for victims of cruelty or oppression.

Climbing The Spiral

In Blue Life Conditions we learned self-discipline and began to master our gross physical appetites. The Ageless Wisdom says that when those appetites, gluttony, drink, drugs, licentiousness, have been mastered we have reached the First Initiation. This does not involve a ceremony. We are unlikely to be aware of our new status. It marks a point of attainment in living. The divine spark within us has been vitalised, enabling us to embark on the next stage of spiritual growth, mastering our emotions. The First Initiation also marks the completion of the involutionary journey into materiality and the significant upward turn on to the long evolutionary journey back to the Source.

The leap into Yellow can be seen as the Second Initiation. It indicates that we have largely mastered our emotions, though of course there is always room for finer feelings, such as compassion, wonder, joy and altruistic love. We seek to impose the will of the Soul, essentially Divine will, on our lower nature, which we understand so much better now that the First Tier vMemes are transparent to us. We are free to fulfil our spiritual potential, to become who we truly are. Graves describes Yellow as the threshold of being human, and the theme as: *Express self for what self desires, but never at the expense of others and in a manner that all life, not just my life, will profit.* Fear drops away, we are free from the constraints of former Life Conditions, cooperate, do more in less time, and lose interest in material possessions, status and power. We are not dependent or independent. We are interdependent. We seek better, non-violent and non-submissive ways of being. We require little, compared to our First Tier lives. With our new universal perspective on life we can see what each person, organisation or country needs to assist it to grow to the next level. Life is magnificent and it is supremely important to us that life on Earth should survive. These huge adjustments, and the bewilderment of those around us, may explain why we withdraw or disappear from the world for a while before moving into Turquoise, where we begin to think and act globally, and promote group consciousness.

The Third Initiation, mastery of the mind, lies much higher up the Spiral and a very long way ahead in time for most of us. Indeed the period between Second and Third Initiations is one of the most difficult as we struggle to master the monkey mind with which we still identify. Thoughts are more powerful than we realise, so the first step is to take responsibility for every thought allowed into our minds and refuse entry to harmful material - far from easy as we are constantly bombarded by the media, the internet and our surroundings. At the Third Initiation the entire personality is flooded with light from above and the spiritual intuition is awakened. An astronaut interviewed on television said when he saw the earth from space he knew that we are one humanity. This was spiritual intuition.

There are more initiations, beyond our current capacity to imagine, until we have triumphed over matter, struggled through every physical, emotional and mental difficulty known on Earth during countless lives, plumbed the depths of pain and sorrow and renounced all worldly interests. No longer needing to return to Earth, we become adepts and Masters, part of the Hierarchy, working to awaken the light in human beings and expand consciousness in all levels of life.

Hierarchy? This is a cosmic concept, a cosmic law. Otherwise, what would be the foundation of evolution? The Hierarchy stands as a wall between humanity and excessive evil from cosmic sources. It is directed from the higher kingdom of Shambhala. The Masters work through meditation, impressing ideas into human minds that are ready (which is why scientific discoveries can happen at the same time and far apart, leading to furious claims to be first), suggesting ways to end separateness and prejudice, to let go of hatred and forgive, or to foster goodwill and right human relations.

Masters have no interest whatsoever in our personality lives. They recognise us by the light that we radiate. We might think a little more active assistance would be welcome, but the whole point is for us to discover spiritual values for ourselves and to make the needed changes of our own freewill. That is how we grow. Otherwise we would be like children, relying on a parent to get us what we want and clear up our messes. We would never grow in consciousness.

Meanwhile the world screams for help. Right human relations are the key to solving the world's problems, and to achieve them we have to address the disparity in living conditions. Ensuring food, shelter and opportunity for everyone on Earth must be the highest priority, and SDi seems to be one of the few ways to achieve this with understanding and compassion, so that every single human being has the opportunity to grow.

The link with the Ageless Wisdom is strong. In October 1927 Alice Bailey made the distinction between Piscean (First Tier) and Aquarian (Second Tier) methods of work, "Groups in the Aquarian Age will surely be associations of free souls, self-reliant and self-centred in the spiritual sense, yet banded together for the general uplift of the race. They will not be built up around some dominating personality, but will be organisations of illuminated men and women, submerging their personalities in the general good. At present our world is the field for the play of Piscean force plus the growing Aquarian influence. Movements which have grown up along Piscean lines are completing their work, and must necessarily and rightly do so. Movements which are hall-marked as Aquarian, being groups of people, thinking independently and refusing to give unquestioning allegiance to any human being, are beginning to be noted amongst us. Many people with Aquarian inclinations, free souls, tolerant yet standing squarely on their own feet, harmonious yet siding with no group, catholic in their outlook, yet clear in their definition, are everywhere to be found.

I believe that SDi has a place in the golden thread of divine teachings, nestling in the vast embrace of the Ageless Wisdom. As we climb the Spiral towards those dizzying higher vMemes we will *know* we are all one—and think and act accordingly.

Bibliography

Graves—Divine Revelation?

Clare W. Graves. *The Never Ending Quest,* Ed. Cowan and Todorovic. Eclet, Santa Barbara (2005).

- "The Emergent cyclical theory of adult behaviour did not arise capriciously, nor is it a product of armchair theorising. I did not visit the Gods on Olympus nor have I stood on the mountaintop in Sinai to procure the substance in its words. It came to me in an arduous, systematic fashion." (p.51)

- "These data produced in me an experience similar to the one Darwin must have had when he visited the Galapagos Islands. . . He observed subtle differences in the finches and iguanas and how these differences varied from island to island. These differences, it occurred to him, were part of a slow and developing process, the process he was to call evolution." (p. 51)

- "…time was taken to think through the situation created by the accumulated information. This period of contemplation directed me to reopen an age-old question - the question about the essence of human life. Pursuant to this train of thought I asked: 'What is human life about? What is it meant to be?' If it is not, as I have questioned, a transformation of man's perversity into decency, if it is not a search for the proper way for man to live and for how to condition him to live that way, if it is not a search for one's self and for the expression of all of one's potential, than what is it? What is human life like and what is it meant to be? This is a question which needs to be answered if ever we are to understand mature human life and if ever we are to find more constructive approaches to the many of man's problems." (p. 52)

- "As I say above, I didn't stand on the mountaintop of Sinai and get the word of Jehovah to develop this theory." (p. 370)

The Law of Rebirth

Alice Bailey. *Esoteric Healing,* Lucis Trust, London (1967)

- "A particular incarnation is not an isolated event in the life of the soul, but is a part and an aspect of a sequence of experience, which are intended to lead to one, clear, definite goal - the goal of free choice, and a deliberate return out of matter to spirit, and eventual liberation." (p.259)

Alice Bailey. *Esoteric Psychology Volume 1,* Lucis Trust, London. (1967)

- "All souls incarnate and re-incarnate under the Law of Rebirth. Hence each life is not only a recapitulation of life experience, but an assuming of ancient obligations, a recovery of old relations, an opportunity for the paying of old indebtedness, a chance to make restitution and progress, an awakening of deep-seated qualities, the recognition of old friends and enemies, the solution of revolting injustices, and the explanation of that which conditions the man, and makes him what he is. Such is the law which is crying now for universal recognition." (pp. 338/9)

The Hierarchy

Alice Bailey. *Esoteric Psychology Volume 2,* Lucis Trust, London. (1960)

- "…the five kingdoms of nature on the evolutionary arc might be defined as follows: the mineral kingdom, the vegetable kingdom, the animal kingdom, the human kingdom, and the spiritual kingdom. All these kingdoms embody some type of consciousness, and it is the work of the Hierarchy to develop these types to perfection." (p.716)

- "This Hierarchy is composed of Those Who have triumphed over matter, and who have achieved the goal by the very self-same steps that individuals tread today. These spiritual personalities, these adepts and Masters, have wrestled and fought for victory and mastery upon the physical plane and struggled with the miasmas, the fogs, the dangers, the troubles, the sorrows and pains of everyday living. They have trodden every step of the path of suffering, have undergone every experience, have surmounted every difficulty, and have won out…characterised by a love which endures, and which acts ever for the good of the group." (p 716)

Harold Balyoz. *Three Remarkable Women,* (Altai Publishers 1986)

- "The Masters of Wisdom are advanced Souls who, through self-sacrificing service, intense striving, and great thought, have conquered the physical plane…Starting as ordinary human beings, they have raised themselves to such a height of achievement, of great beingness, that they have actually entered consciously the fifth, or divine, kingdom in nature…working ceaselessly for the benefit of mankind and helping all those who are struggling and sacrificing to raise themselves up also!… she taught a small part of their great knowledge about the beginnings of our world."

- "Nineteenth century science was developing its lower, strictly physical aspect so rapidly that the minds of men were in danger of swinging to the hopelessness of materialism…At this critical juncture in human thought H. P. Blavatsky appeared with her brightly lit lamp of Ancient Wisdom." (p.8)

Second Initiation And SDi Level 2

Alice Bailey. *Initiation Human and Solar,* Lucis Trust, London. (1967)

- "At the first initiation, the control of the Ego [Soul] over the physical body must have reached a high degree of attainment. The sins of the flesh, as the Christian phraseology has it, must be dominated: gluttony, drink and licentiousness must no longer hold sway." (p. 82)

- "The second initiation forms the crisis in the control of the astral body. Just as, at the first initiation, the control of the dense physical has been demonstrated, so here the control of the astral is similarly demonstrated. The sacrifice and death of desire has been the goal of endeavour…and only that is longed for which is for the good of the whole." (p. 85)

Alice Bailey. *The Rays and the Initiations,* Lucis Trust, London. (1965)

- "Freedom is the keynote of the individual who is facing the second initiation and its aftermath, preparation for the third initiation. Freedom is the keynote for the world disciple today, and it is freedom to live, freedom to think and freedom to know and plan which humanity demands at this time." (p. 684)

- "...initiation is not really the curious mixture of self-satisfied attainment, ceremonial, and hierarchical recognition as portrayed by the major occult groups. It is far more a process of excessively hard work, during which process the initiate becomes what he is. This may entail hierarchical recognition, but not in the form usually pictured. The initiate finds himself in the company of those who have preceded him, and he is not rejected but is seen and noted and then put to work..." (p. 7)

- "I would like to have you study initiation from the angle of liberation, looking upon it as a process of strenuously attained freedoms. This basic aspect of initiation, when realised by the initiate, ties his experience into a firm relation with that of the whole of humanity, whose fundamental struggle is the attainment of that freedom whereby the soul and its powers can unfold, and all men be free because of an individually attained freedom." (p. 685)

The Etheric Body

Alice Bailey. *Telepathy and the Etheric Vehicle,* Lucis Trust, London. (1963)

- "There is nothing in the manifest universe, solar, planetary, or the various kingdoms in nature, which does not possess an energy form, subtle and intangible yet substantial, which controls, governs, and conditions the outer physical body. This is the etheric body." (p. 142)

General Introduction To Ageless Wisdom

Kathy Newburn. *A Planetary Awakening,* Blue Dolphin, Grass Valley, CA. (2007)

Annie Besant. *A Study in Consciousness,* Theosophical Society, London (1904)

SDi–KEEPING ROMANCE ALIVE

By Tom Bruno-Madich & Philippa Waller

After attending training in Spiral Dynamics Integral (SDi) with Don Beck in Santa Barbara, we began to incorporate SDi into our work in the corporate arena. We developed a series of influencing, leadership and communication skills tools integrating the 4 Dimensions (Physical, Emotional, Intellectual and Intentional/Spiritual) with SDi. We also developed and created the innovative 4D Spiralgraph coaching tool. This integral orientation tool enabled us to raise a 4D psychograph to look at our clients not only from a single SDi perspective, but also to understand which of their dimensions were at what stage in the Spiral helping to define where to begin with a client and also creating a deeper and richer map of the client's progress.

Increasingly we found we were helping people develop and coaching them to manage their challenging work-based relationships, from seemingly difficult bosses, supposedly stubborn team members, to apparently unassertive assistants, always using an approach firmly grounded in SDi. We soon found an escalation in requests to help our clients manage their personal relationships. Our 4 Dimensional map coupled with the theory of SDi was already a model we had personally used in our private lives, friendships, family dynamics and of course our own relationship. Now we found we were beginning to coach couples and individuals who were looking for support in finding love, maintaining love or breaking away from broken love. We had brought the wonderfully powerful work of SDi into the dating game, marriage and romantic partnerships. Our work with SDi had expanded from the world of business to the business of keeping long-term love alive.

This new and exciting branch of our work sprang up quite naturally. We have since been asked to speak about our work in person and on radio shows and last year published our book *"Spiral Into Love" (spiralintolove. com).* This chapter is based on our work using SDi in the arena of love, romance and lasting relationships: How to use the power of SDi to "Stop falling in love with the wrong ones and stay in love with the right ones."

Spiral Into Love

As we all know, we humans love to love and we won't give up until we find it. However, there's no doubt that finding the love of our life isn't always easy. Even in an internet age of uber-connectivity, where every day we can Facebook new friends and Twitter like love birds, it is becoming increasingly hard to find our special soul-mate for life. There are many fine books, full of helpful advice telling us why lasting love is so hard to find. We read that it may simply be down to differing personality traits, cognitive differences, hormonal imbalances or which planet we're from. We can discover why men marry bitches, how to be a good husband and are even given advice on the sixty-minute marriage. While such books offer us some useful insights, they don't necessarily show us the entire picture. If the relationship challenges we face are only down to gender why do gay relationships and same-sex friendships break down? If love comes down to whether we both speak the same language how is it we can sometimes completely understand the language the other person is speaking and still never want to see them again? If love is actually about *Why Men Marry Bitches,* why are we also encouraged to pop *Why Men Divorce Bitches* into our shopping baskets? If a man needs to read a book like *How to be a Good Husband,* should he also be reading *Women Really Do Love Bastards?* And should we be advising people to read *The Sixty Minute Marriage* or *Fit to be Tied: Making Marriage Last a Lifetime?* The reality is that much advice around relationships focuses in on one, superficial or fashionable fad around the many aspects of human interactions, often the latest piece of research that offers up a single, misinterpreted but commercially lucrative sound-bite.

Today we understand more about human nature than ever before, yet many of us don't seem to be putting this knowledge into practice when it comes to love. And it's not like we're getting better at it. When it comes to love, we've been going in blindly. We need to stop listening to those old proverbs! If "love is blind" is it any wonder we stumble, trip and crash to the ground, a bleeding wreck in its pursuit? It's time to understand love a little better. It's time to place some value on love. It's also time for a new proverb: *Those who know they value love, love to know their values!*

For all the poems, songs and self-help books ever written, the research has revealed that lasting romantic happiness, relationship success and marital bliss depends on one factor more than any other: *values!* Yes, what you and your chosen partner individually value will determine the length and quality of your relationship more than any other aspect. That's why our approach to finding, building and maintaining loving relationships is based on one of the most comprehensive maps of the development of human values to date, SDi.

SDi is a model of evolving human values. It grew out of the work of the American psychologist and doctor of philosophy, Clare W. Graves (1914–1986), and suggests that human nature is not fixed. Rather, humans are able to adapt, change and evolve according to their Life Conditions. As we encounter new and potentially challenging situations, our values may shift, enabling us to better respond to the given circumstances. Dr Graves proposed that personality is a continuous process that evolves through time. Rather than having a set personality, human beings move and flow through various stages throughout their lives according to what they're doing, what they need and who they are with. This constant, fluid and ever-changing process can be imagined as a personal energy that flows up and down a Spiral of different values. In other words as we move, shift, change and grow, we can imagine our experience being shaped by the active dynamic of our values shifting up and down the Spiral.

The following descriptions of the main First Tier value sets outline the key concepts of SDi. These five value sets are the key stages of adult development and it is by understanding them that we can begin to Spiral into love. Here, we look at them in the context of romantic partnerships from all 4 dimensions of each Spiral stage, the physical behavior, the emotional expressions, the intellectual thinking style and the core intentional or spiritual value drives. We will begin at what is known as the Purple stage of values development.

The Partner At The Purple Stage—"We" Oriented

Purple values are about bonding to one's family and tribe. In humankind's distant evolutionary past, survival and security was ensured by safety in numbers. Tribal communities formed with beliefs and rituals to explain and manage their Life Conditions. A partner expressing Purple values tends to look after only those very close to them. They seek security and safety and will look to the group or family to provide it. It's important to know, partners with strong Purple values won't strike out on their own to make something happen in the world. Rather they will always follow the pack, do what the rest of their tribe does and often go into the trusted family business or a similar line of work to their relations, hence why this value set is referred to as "We" oriented.

This set of values operates heavily from emotions rather than rational thought. Purple values drive people to make decisions based on their feelings or intuitions rather than on pure reason or logic. Purple thinking is informed by inherited knowledge that has been filtered down from the immediate family, gang or tribal elders. Decision-making will revolve around accepted customs, superstitions and rituals, unquestioningly honoring laws like "Don't go out on Friday the thirteenth" or "Never buy a green car because they are unlucky". Any new concepts or ideas that don't fit in with the tribe will be rejected.

Purple behavior is imitative. People expressing this value will often copy the behaviors and phrases used by their family, close group of friends, local community, team or organization. As a result they can be over-sensitive to unfamiliar body language, environments and tone of voice. Physical characteristics and habits shared between family members are seen as a sign of belonging and are greatly valued. Dress sense is influenced by the need to display membership of group loyalty to a brand, e.g. branded T-shirts, football stripes and tribal symbols.

Purple's emotions are tied up with ritual and custom and they are quick to interpret meaning in the context of their own belief systems. Purple values usually include magical and superstitious beliefs. A reliance on omens and spells can be a big part of their biological, psychological and social habits. They may refer to powerful supernatural forces, guardian angels or the spirits of their ancestors who watch over the tribe. As dreams, magic and luck are seen as likely causes for events in life, the placebo effect can be a powerful remedy for people expressing Purple.

Bonding with the trusted, familiar group is very much where Purple emotions are focused. The same goes for Purple within a partnership. A couple expressing Purple values will be very close-knit and wary of outsiders who are different from them. These relationships are often all about the immediate family, with couples tending to stay living close to their relatives. Habits, home-making and child-rearing will often mirror the style, customs and rituals of their parents. Behavior and emotion is driven by loyalty to the family and tribe, regardless of any abuses that may take place behind closed family doors.

Because of this sense of tribal loyalty, reciprocity is a key influencer, "You scratch my back and I'll scratch yours." Although, as connection and belonging are the principal drivers, Purple will only help out those who are part of their tribe. Trust is highly important within Purple cultures and will be demonstrated through personal sacrifice and investment in people close to them. The mantra of a couple expressing strong Purple values might be "Blood is thicker than water".

The healthy expression of Purple is in a well-functioning, loving family or group full of tradition and care. However, unhealthy emotions are expressed in rampant xenophobia, racism and intolerance of the customs and religions of others. We see Purple values in strong grass-roots family communities as well as in street gangs and organized crime syndicates like the Mafia.

The Partner At The Red Stage—"Me" Oriented

Red values are all about strengthening the ego by affirming one's individuality. A person at this stage will often behave assertively. They may also display narcissistic qualities and often seek to dominate others in a quest for power and control, hence Red being referred to as 'ME' oriented.

When Red values are expressed healthily, a partner's behavior can be an energizing, creative and heroic force that makes things happen in the relationship and in the world at large. However, in terms of human evolution, this stage is essentially pre-law and order and can cause a person to show minimum regard for right and wrong.

This behavior is most often first seen when a toddler reaches the terrible twos: they can't understand logic, are unable to see things from another person's perspective and behave in an egocentric manner. However, plenty of adults still default to this stage. Some of them are highly successful CEOs!

The truth is that most of us have Red stage values alive and well and active within us. Some of us may deny or suppress these values but they are in fact essential for survival and, some believe, success in the world. Red behavior can return at any time in life and is seen in the regressive, moody and aggressive behavior of rebellious teens, tired and angry parents, offended adults and power-hungry business leaders.

When Red values surface within a couple, the relationship becomes about the absolute power and rule of the dominant partner. A person expressing Red values demands respect and always comes first, even if it's at the expense of the other person in the relationship. Red partners are great if you like someone very strong and independent who will do what they like, when they like, how they like and where they want to. But don't expect constant attention or support from a partner at peak Red as they are egocentric and narcissistic in love. Their mantra is, "Do as I say and leave me alone to do what I want!" On the other hand, however, there won't be many dull moments with a partner in Red!

A Red partner's personal power is often expressed in a dominant physicality. In healthy mode, your Red partner will dazzle you with displays of confidence, strength and energy. The healthy expression of this emotional energy manifests in heroic deeds and a strong, dominant leadership when required. The unhealthy emotional expression shows in aggression, intolerance or even random violence. When Red values are in the unhealthy mode, body language can be aggressive and posturing, deliberately taking up space in an environment and sometimes disregarding the personal space of others. Coming out of tribal Purple, the Red value set is self-serving and seeks emotional independence. This is about ego development and the evolution of a sense of self.

A quick shift from "normal" feelings and behaviors into sudden rage can be an indication that Red values are energizing your own or your partner's emotions. The motivating principle of Red is that self-expression takes precedence over everything, regardless of the consequences, as shame and loss of face is unbearable at this stage of development.

"Knowledge is power" could be the motto for Red. Thoughts and concepts are mostly self-centered. Their intellect is in service of self to gain control of persons, places and things and they will reject any thoughts of responsibility or guilt. Mental toughness and thinking that supports instant gratification through quick wins will be their focus. Knowledge is acquired only to support a "What's in it for me?" attitude. An individual living Red values will think that learning anything that does not command the respect of others, or doesn't deliver a large reward, is a waste of time.

When it comes to Red, the intellect will be entirely the slave of the emotions. Whatever Red feels is what they will express and sudden waves of emotion, be it love or rage, will totally consume them. Conflict will often play a big part in Red's relationships and when Red's emotions are in full swing, there's no point trying to reason with them. It's like trying to reason with a toddler. When the ego is inflated to that extent, no rational or intellectual argument will get through. Red sees himself or herself as the sole creator of their world and destiny, and will challenge any force or power that claims to be above them.

On the positive side, healthy Red is spiritually independent and autonomous. In early childhood we need to develop a separate ego so we can set healthy boundaries with others and move into adulthood. We could not differentiate as individuals without going through the Red value stage. It is also vital for creativity and confidence. When unhealthy Red is expressed, the world is seen to be full of threats, causing one to be aggressively defensive, stubborn and unreasonable. Red can be seen popping up in every walk of life, from the boardroom to the classroom to a night out with the girls.

The Partner at the Blue Stage—"We" Oriented

After the self-oriented, powerful, willful and emotional behaviors of the Red values stage, it is time to create some stability and order. This is when the Blue values emerge to demand obedience to the rules laid down by a higher authority. A person's values evolve into Blue after having transcended and included Red, so the highly expressed emotions of Red now become restrained and controlled by the obedient energy of the Blue values. This stage of development is essentially about creating order out of chaos.

The central principle of Blue is that one must sacrifice one's own needs now to serve a higher purpose and gain bigger, better rewards later, even if those rewards come after death. It is at this point in human history that we find the beginnings of monotheistic religions where the majority of people were expected to submit to the few who have supposedly been given authority by the higher powers. Judaism, Christianity and Islam are examples of peak Blue religions.

In terms of childhood development, the Blue value set emerges around the age of nine to twelve. It is at this time that children begin to think logically about life events, but still have difficulty understanding abstract or hypothetical concepts. They need concrete rules and regulations to help them understand the world and their place in it. A partner expressing healthy Blue values looks for order and meaning in their everyday lives. They often tend to be organized. They believe in a social and moral system in which there are laws and codes laid down that we must all abide by. Hence Blue values being referred to as "We'" oriented.

If your partner is at the Blue values stage your relationship may well have rules you must abide by and expectations you must meet. From a Blue partner's standpoint, those who obey the rules will be rewarded and those who don't should be punished. A partner with Blue values sees the world in very black and white, right and wrong and non-negotiable terms. They may seem like they always want to be in charge but in fact they are happy to submit to another's rules if they feel those rules are right. Unlike Red, who hates being told what to do, someone expressing strong Blue values will be comfortable being told what to do by a person in authority whom they respect. Your Blue partner's belief system is an incredibly important part of their lives – and not to be messed with. When someone with Blue values finds themselves in a situation where their old belief system no longer serves them or is crushed, they feel it very strongly. Suddenly the certainty they had in the world has gone, and Blue very much values certainty.

A person embodying Blue values won't bend the rules to accommodate anyone, not even their life partner. So, while offering a high degree of loyalty, predictability and stability, a relationship with a Blue partner can sometimes be inflexible and pedantic. They will want to get things right and expect you to do the same. They can have high expectations in terms of what's right and wrong about you in the relationship and their behavior towards you can be driven by a sense of reward and punishment.

Conforming to the rules and being validated by academics and institutions, Blue will be physically expressed in compliant, controlled and restrained physical behavior. Conservative dress and orderly demeanor might best describe the physical appearance of your peak Blue partner. They will most likely be very comfortable wearing a uniform of some sort. And they will love to hang their framed certificates all over the house.

When emotions are present in Blue, they are galvanized around the rules of fairness and judgment. There is an emotional shift from Red's "express yourself", to Blue's "sacrifice yourself" in order to preserve the law. Spontaneity must yield to compliance to keep emotions in check. This can manifest as a rigid and dogmatic attitude to life and work, with little emotion. Your Blue partner will probably value judgment over compassion and express limited tolerance or understanding of others who break the rules or become highly emotional. On the positive side, your Blue partner will bring order and structure to any chaotic emotional situations. However, when expressed negatively they will look to find fault rather than building on strengths.

Following the letter of the law is the prime focus of Blue thinking. Blue partners can be highly logical and rational, but they risk becoming dogmatic and immovable to the extent of insisting people follow a particular set of rules and orders regardless of personal feelings and thoughts. There is only one right way and it must be learned thoroughly and adhered to. The mind of somebody expressing Blue values is unquestioning of authority and merely focuses on preserving the accuracy of learned knowledge. Always working by the book, obediently following the straight and narrow path, Blue's intellect is disciplined and obsessed with getting things correct. A healthy Blue intellect is accurate, precise and thorough. However, pedantry, stubbornness and closed-mindedness can be the signs of unhealthy Blue thinking.

In healthy mode, your Blue partner can be a wonderful stabilizing force that seems to guide you both towards truth and feel like a source of security and comfort in times of uncertainty. In Abraham Lincoln's words, "Let's have faith that right makes might; and in that faith let us, to the end, dare to do our duty as we understand it." Or as Margaret Thatcher said, "I am in politics because of the conflict between good and evil and I believe that in the end good will triumph." In its unhealthy expression there can be a fundamentalist intolerance of alternative worldviews, with an adherence to hierarchical laws, systems or religions.

The Partner At The Orange Stage—"Me" Oriented

Transcending the superstitions of Purple, containing and including the egocentrism of Red and challenging Blue's myth-laden, dogmatic rules, the partner in Orange is innovative, rational, opportunistic and success-oriented. People at this stage are entrepreneurial and independent. Hence Orange is referred to as "Me" oriented. Someone with Orange values loves to compete and especially loves to win. Achievement means everything to Orange. Like Red, they will sacrifice others for their own selfish gain, but unlike Red they are strategic and enterprising. This stage appears in children at around twelve years old onwards when they develop the ability to understand abstract concepts. At this stage, although children begin to consider the possible consequences of their actions, they also start to develop the capacity to manipulate information, using deductive reasoning and strategic planning.

Orange values are prevalent in the western world. Capitalism thrives on them. It is thinking and behavior in service of Orange values that has created so much innovation, wealth and opportunity in the world. However, it is also these same values that allowed excess human greed to bring the world economy crashing to its knees. People expressing peak Orange values may be able to predict the consequences of their actions, but if they can get away unscathed, they won't feel guilty if others suffer as a result.

When in love, an Orange partner is often highly inventive and progressive and can sometimes behave in Machiavellian ways. They are driven to succeed at all costs. Orange can be challenging when conflict occurs within a relationship as they may only be concerned with their own feelings and merely see their partner's emotion as a weakness. On the positive side, you may well enjoy the material fruits of being in a relationship with a partner at Orange. The Orange partner wants the best of everything and will work hard to make sure they get it. Life is all about keeping up with the neighbors, exceeding expectations and striving towards constant achievement.

Being so competitive, entrepreneurial and expressive, Orange partners are often highly skilled communicators with a front foot physical attitude. Because they tend to always be looking out for the next opportunity, they often have an underlying physical restlessness. Orange expects both themselves and their partner to always be on top of their game and looking their best. They may even start looking elsewhere for a partner if they feel standards of self-presentation and physical attractiveness are slipping!

A person expressing Orange values physically would most likely have a highly developed self-awareness and the ability to mirror and match the energy levels and body language of others in order to manage communication and gain the advantage. An Orange-inspired dress code would include high fashion and exclusive styles bearing designer labels.

Emotionally, Orange partners are proactive and impulsive. They can often be emotionally independent and self-centered, making it difficult to get close to them in a relationship. They express occasional sympathy but have little genuine empathy. While seeming to need validation and often requesting feedback, they rarely act on any response that does not support their own agenda and self-perception. A person with high Orange energy thrives on a connection with others, but only if you are helping them acquire and achieve success. Ultimately, they will disconnect once you cease to be of use, even when in a long-term relationship.

Negative Orange emotion includes distrust, ruthlessness, insensitivity or even a lack of emotion. On the plus side, they exhibit self-confidence, are entrepreneurial and innovative, have high levels of personal drive and are often positively contagious. Their daily mantra might be, "What's the next bright idea?" Your Orange partner is always on the go intellectually. Thinking from an Orange perspective means looking for the next big thing. Experimenting with current knowledge and concepts, their intelligence drives them towards the discovery and creation of innovations in order to beat the competition and stand at the leading edge. Seeking to create niches, thoughts are focused on ideas that support autonomy, personal ambition and individualism. The mind in service to Orange enjoys applying itself to risk and change that leads to progress and material gain. Science, knowledge and inquiry are valued over faith, belief and religion.

Unhealthy Orange thinking may ignore vital information, offer up only partial truths and manipulate data in the pursuit of results. In other words, your Orange partner may suddenly get a brilliant idea and risk your shared savings, income and family home on the venture. An Orange partner can be highly driven to take risks and gamble with hard-earned assets.

Orange spirituality is often expressed as secular humanism and is centered on mastering the material world and the mechanical laws of nature. Positive Orange wants to make the world a healthier, better-educated and safer place for those that can afford it. If you work hard, the rewards are not in heaven but right here on earth. Unhealthy Orange will disregard or even reject dogmatic religions and mock "soft and fluffy" new-agers.

The Partner At The Green Stage—"We" Oriented

Along the Spiral from the more self-serving, materialistic Orange perspective, we move into the sharing and caring Green values stage. This value set is relativistic, communal, sharing, affiliate and consensual, i.e. very much about "we". A partner expressing Green will seek unity and authenticity in their lives and their relationships. They prefer collaborative, cooperative interactions with a focus on ethics and morality. Green thrives on harmony, empathy and love. There is an emphasis on joining together with others across nations and cultures for mutual growth as one big, global family. Everyone is welcome and everyone's opinion is right. This value set embraces diversity and seeks to help others realize their potential.

Green pluralism can lead to debilitating levels of political correctness and the inability to lead or make tough but important decisions. Also, people expressing Green values can be so overly trusting and blinkered in their belief that all people are kind and sharing that they can end up being easily exploited by others.

Green relationships are the archetypal touchy-feely, warm and cuddly, lovey-dovey experience. A Green partner will seek a close and loving relationship, with everyone. So if you are with a partner in Green you may find you have to share their attention with friends, colleagues, even strangers who might need them or who Green can help in any way. Honesty, authenticity and trust are highly valued, and you can expect some serious sharing, caring and long-term communal living. Your Green partner will have an open home policy together with a "What's mine is yours and vice versa." agenda. There are no proprietorial rights. Everything belongs to everyone in the Green house.

Most people expressing this value will be physically inclusive, open and comfortable around others, unless high Orange or Red values start to upset the group. If that happens, someone with Green values may feel nervous or physically distressed. But if all is agreeable, Greens will enjoy the physical presence of others. They are far more inclined than other value systems to get into close proximity with others and embrace people, be they friends or strangers. Your Green partner will often leave the bathroom door unlocked and probably the front door too, which only makes it easier for them to strike up long conversations with the religious and charity doorknockers that others dismiss out of hand.

Able to quickly establish rapport, people in Green will often display a relaxed, informal posture and dress sense. Their clothing is likely to be an eclectic mix of styles, perhaps favoring ethically sourced fabrics or recycled items. Even though Green has experienced all previous values, they may look at Orange and Blue and see high fashion or strict dress code as a waste of time, money and energy. They have a whole new way of thinking now. External physical appearance doesn't matter that much. It's the inner world of self that is important.

For the most part Green will put their focus on people and the environment. Their emotional drivers are all about bonding with and supporting others, selflessness, inclusiveness and sharing. They have high levels of tolerance and, when it comes to relationship disputes, being liked and accepted is more important than winning.

Negative expressions of Green include excessive permissiveness, lack of self-assertion and over-emphasizing equality. This can lead to an inability to recognize, and intervene in, situations when emotional abuse takes place. A Green partner can be in danger of being dominated, tricked or bullied within a relationship.

Green believes all knowledge is equal, none being any better than any other, simply different. In this mind-set, the primary driver is for cohesion and acceptance and, therefore, non-linear and lateral thinking is valued above logical and rational thought. Green reaches decisions through reconciliation and consensus, though a down-side might be a lack of discernment in terms of the real value of ideas and information. Everyone and everything is equal and right in Green.

A Green partner will want to accept and embrace all types of spirituality and religions as well as new-age beliefs. Anything goes as far as Green is concerned and when it comes to love, Green wants harmony, acceptance and kindness to be the dominant factor in their relationship, every day.

Moving Through The Spiral

Throughout our lives, as our values develop along the Spiral, each transcends and includes the previous value. We may find ourselves at different stages on the Spiral at different stages in our lives. Within our relationships, these shifts and changes need to be understood, acknowledged and managed otherwise the relationship can lose its sense of balance and become conflict driven. Relationships are not fixed entities. At any one time, a certain value set will be more dominant for each partner. A shift in values can be brought about through a global or personal crisis, or perhaps through a more long-term period of personal growth. For example:

- Shaun Casey was a happy family man expressing dominant Purple values, until the terrorist attacks on the Twin Towers on 9/11. Shaun suddenly shifted along the Spiral into Blue and was compelled to join the military and serve his nation in the fight against terror. His values shifted up Spiral overnight, from family and security to nation and honor.
- A London-based trader called Jeremy went into a personal crisis after the financial meltdown of 2008. Suddenly seeing only futility and selfishness in his previous job, Jeremy left the city and took up work as a teacher. In the space of a few critical weeks, his values had moved from an Orange value set of personal ambition and material gain up Spiral to a Green value set of helping and nurturing others.
- We can of course also down Spiral, as the disaster of Hurricane Katrina showed us. Hundreds of families and individuals found themselves thrust from their everyday lives into a situation of chaos and a fight for survival. The atrocities that occurred over that time only went to show how quickly our values can shift from being caring towards our neighbor (Green) to self-survival at any cost (Red).

The Second Tier Perspective

Now that we've looked at the dynamics of the various value set combinations, Purple to Green, we can look at how we can begin to understand and manage our relationships from a whole new perspective. In the SDi model, after Green comes the evolution to the Second Tier and this begins with the Yellow stage. While we may have a dominant First Tier value expression, we will often express the less dominant values at different times of our life or even different times of the day. Different people will surface different value systems within us. From the Yellow perspective, we can see and acknowledge the full range of values that both we and our partners hold and express, while not allowing ourselves to be hijacked by any single one of them. Well, not for too long at least!

This new way of looking at your relationship will enable you to identify and manage the different values and attitudes as they arise within yourself and your partner. Taking the Yellow Perspective really puts you in the driver's seat and enables you to author your own, lasting happiness. Yellow is less about living in service to a set of values, and much more about taking a new perspective that takes into account all the other value sets. In other words this is about recognizing your partner's current values and being able to adapt your thinking and behavior to meet them wherever they are.

The Partner Taking the Yellow Perspective—'ME' Oriented

By taking the Yellow perspective we can remain in First Tier as long as is appropriate and yet still see the importance of our partner's values, even if they are different from our own. As a result, we will have an objective view that enables us to Spiral along the five value sets from Purple to Green. Someone operating from Yellow understands that all the values along the Spiral are valid, but they don't feel the need to get locked into any single one of them. They acknowledge that they need to take different value perspectives depending on where they are, who they're dealing with and what they're trying to achieve.

Whatever kind of relationships we are in, it can be extremely challenging when we're faced with other people holding belief systems and worldviews that differ from our own. Even the most rational of individuals can suddenly become irrational and angry when someone confronts them with an entirely different outlook or tramples on their values. Our main challenge, of course, is that we are often only able to understand feelings and thoughts based on the perspective of our own values, beliefs and worldview. When it comes to relationships, this can often make communication between couples who have different values somewhat challenging, but *not* impossible, especially once you shift into the Yellow Perspective.

The fact is people are easier to understand if we take a moment to stop and work out what's driving them. Research has revealed that while most of us can be motivated to take action for financial gain and reward, human beings are even *more* motivated to do something if it has intrinsic value for them, if something is perceived to be in alignment with our own core values. As people are more inclined to engage with a person, place or thing if they are intrinsically motivated, it is important to understand which values are active within your partner, and indeed yourself, because that's the quickest route to the longest lasting love.

When you recognize, respect and nurture your partner's values, the love between you will grow and strengthen into something truly astounding. When a human being feels heard, understood and loved, there is no limit to the love they can return. But if you have a high understanding of your partner's values and use that information to manipulate or torment them, the relationship will quickly become toxic. As Francis Bacon said, "Knowledge is power," but if you use this knowledge for evil then your power will lead to nothing but hurt and misery. Use the knowledge you have gained to support and develop your love for one another. It's easy to use knowledge about a loved one to hurt them. It takes strength, intelligence, creativity and foresight to use that information to reach the next stage of the Spiral that will inform and support your love together. You have everything you need to create the very best and avoid creating the very worst. Ask yourself, "Are you pointing out the negative aspects of your relationship or reaffirming the positive ones?" How are you using the information you have about your partner's needs and values? After all, you do have a choice.

Many people inadvertently fall into what we call the "Phase Two Trap" without even being aware they had a choice to avoid it. The relationship Phase Two Trap comes right after the initial euphoria of Phase One. Phase One is the intoxicating oxytocin-fuelled bliss state at the start of a new relationship. It's all about having fun, falling in love and getting to know your new partner. During this phase, you love everything about them, even the annoying things. You believe you will always feel that way, but before you know it, the two of you are bickering about the small things and chipping away at your love by constantly reminding each other of your faults. As an ex-boyfriend of Phillipa's once put it, "You spend your first year with your partner finding out as much about them as possible and the rest of your life using that information against them." That is the Phase Two Trap. But happy couples don't do that. When happy couples are asked to rate which specific aspects of their relationships are most important to the success of their partnership, they generally point to the aspects of their partner and relationship that are the most positive. Individuals with this tendency are the ones who are the happiest with their relationships overall and who remain in long-term relationships.

It can be frustrating when our partner has habits that we don't like, though again it's interesting to keep reminding ourselves that these habits bothered us little in the initial stages of our relationship! As Philippa's partner said to her when she complained about shaving residue around the bathroom sink, "Just think how much you'd miss it if I was no longer here." What he meant, of course, was "Think how much you'd miss *me* if I wasn't here." A fairly Red statement, yes! But he was right. It really made her stop and think. From her perspective, she wants her partner around. She wants him to be at peace, to energize and enforce their life together. She wants him to be able to be who he is. She wants him to feel comfortable and free and to know he is enough; he doesn't lack anything. She doesn't want him to feel less than he is, because that's not when he's at his best. He's at his best in their relationship when he most fulfills her Green need for harmony and collaboration or her Orange need for innovation, ideas sharing and productivity.

There are countless things her partner does for her every day that makes her life full of fun, creativity, laughter and love. What future life would she be creating if she headed down the route of nagging him about supposed faults or irritations every day? How helpful are those niggling comments in nurturing and growing their love? How much would *she* want to be around someone who reminded her on a daily basis exactly what she was lacking and why she is such a disappointment?

If we focus on the negative aspects of our partner's values, how surprised can we really be if that relationship begins to lose its charm, if communication breaks down, or if the relationship self-destructs entirely? We're creating the relationship, every minute of every day. So what choices are we making about what we say and do in response to our partner? What aspects of their value set are we choosing to focus on? We always have a choice to focus on the positive or the negative.

Of course, those positives and negatives will vary depending on the value set combination. For example, if someone with peak Blue values were in a relationship with a more Red partner, they might need to look at the Red value set in a slightly different way from someone with more Green values would view Red. Where someone in Green might look at Red's creativity and fun and see how valuable those aspects were to the relationship, Blue might better appreciate looking at Red's power and self-determination to get things done. If Blue focuses on the negative, they might find Red's independence rather daunting, but by focusing on how Red gets results and doesn't put responsibility onto others, Blue can once again open their eyes to why they feel so much love for Red.

Abi and Jeff have been together for eighteen years. Abi expresses mainly Orange, aspirational values. Jeff expresses a rules-based Blue value set. Abi and Jeff's relationship had lost its sparkle. Abi felt they were bickering on a daily basis, and even at times avoiding each other. When asked what Jeff was like, this is what she said, "Jeff is really fussy. Everything has to be just so. There's no room for error or a change of plans. He gets frustrated with me if I suddenly land something on him like having to go to a work function or even a friend's for a barbecue at the last minute. He'll go, though he's initially quite reluctant. He doesn't like change. We've lived in the same house and he's been in the same job for fifteen years. As I've gotten older, I realize I want more from life than Jeff seems to, or certainly different things. We constantly bicker about his lack of get up and go."

Abi has understood Jeff's Blue values. She knows what is important to him and yet has almost exclusively focused on the aspects of those values that annoy her and that she sees as negative, like Jeff's need for stability and security, control and planning. The more she looks at Jeff's Blue values from a negative perspective, the more dominant that perspective will become for her. Until "fussy, staid old Jeff" is the only perspective she has on the man she supposedly loves. Abi doesn't like that perspective, but she's the one who has created it!

What if Abi started to focus more on the positive aspects of Jeff's Blue values? What if Abi looked at how Jeff's Blue values support and complement her Orange values? She did just that and from her Orange perspective that reframe sounded like this, "Jeff can be quite a perfectionist. He loves to plan and get things in order. He wants the best for me and the family. He needs things to be organized before he's comfortable enough to try something new. He creates an incredibly stable environment, which allows me more freedom in my own life. Jeff can get a little irritable when I suddenly land an impromptu social or work event on him. However, we always have a good time and end up laughing about the fact that he didn't want to go! He's very popular and likes it when people ask his advice. I feel proud of him in company. Jeff would never let me down and always supports my ideas. I realize, however, that if I want change to happen in our lives, I need to make Jeff feel safe. Rather than expecting him to lead the change, I need to assign him the more organizational aspects of a project and take the lead myself. He's a great support, whereas I'm more of a go-getter. I can see now that I've been frustrated with Jeff for not doing the things that I could have been doing all along. Jeff made some really sensible decisions to stay in this house. Although I've always wanted to move, Jeff insisted we stay put. He said this area was up and coming. It turns out he was right. We've made a lot of money on the house and I know I can now persuade him to retire somewhere really fabulous, maybe even in the sun. When I look around, I realize some friends of mine haven't got such stable, thoughtful and caring partners. Without him I could have gone wrong so many times. I'm pretty lucky."

The ability to use the Yellow perspective totally changed Abi's outlook on her partner. She was able to understand and really see how Jeff's Blue values served and nurtured her own Orange values. Rather than looking at where she felt they clashed, she could see where she and Jeff harmonized and collaborated. Abi pushed back against Jeff's Blue values because she saw them as representing rigidity and authority. This clashed with Abi's need for freedom and change, but by understanding that Jeff didn't need change in the same way, Abi could stop being so frustrated with him and start to find a way to lead the changes herself and still keep Jeff feeling secure.

Taking the Yellow perspective on your relationship means looking at your partner's values and seeing how they serve and nourish both you and your relationship. It all starts by shifting your perspective from the negative to the positive as the chart below lays out.

The Yellow Stage Perspective Chart

Value Pairing	Negative Perspective	Positive Perspective
Purple to Purple	We're so stuck in our ways.	We're safe together forever.
Purple to Red	I sometimes feel alone.	I feel so protected.
Purple to Blue	You put rules before family and love.	I always know where I am with you and where we're headed.
Purple to Orange	Sometimes I don't know if I can trust you.	You always want to bring the best to the family.
Purple to Green	You seem to love everybody; sometimes I don't feel special to you.	I always feel I belong with you; you bring out the best in me.
Red to Red	You always have to have the last word and life feels like we're always fighting.	Look at us! We're both so powerful, independent and decisive and yet together we could do anything.
Red to Purple	You're too needy.	I know you're always there.
Red to Blue	You're always bossing me around.	You've kept me out of trouble.
Red to Orange	I don't always trust you.	You totally understand me.
Red to Green	You're naïve.	You totally accept me for who and what I am.
Blue to Purple	You're too lead by your emotions and instinct.	You're very loyal.
Blue to Red	You're a total nightmare.	I can rely on you to take action and get things done.
Blue to Blue	You always think you're right.	You respect the rules.
Blue to Orange	You're selfish and manipulative.	You're a great strategist.

Blue to Green	You're flaky.	You're incredibly kind and caring.
Orange to Purple	You're so unadventurous.	I can always rely on you.
Orange to Red	You're dangerous.	You energize me.
Orange to Blue	You're uptight.	You're my rock.
Orange to Orange	I feel like we're always competing.	Together we can rule the world.
Orange to Green	You're not living in the real world.	You give me hope.
Green to Purple	You're so narrow-minded.	I feel we're so connected.
Green to Red	You're terrifying.	You make me strong.
Green to Blue	You're so inflexible.	You have such integrity.
Green to Orange	You're so wrapped up in yourself.	You're so creative.
Green to Green	We're so indecisive.	We're so supportive and forgiving.

Finally, once you've shifted your internal perspective on your partner to Yellow, it only remains to talk to them in a way they will understand and respond to positively.

Of course, when all is going well in your relationship, great. Enjoy every moment of it. Just stay awake and alert to areas of conflict. They can catch us unawares. That's not to say conflict is always a bad thing. We are in no way suggesting the Pollyanna approach to life of skipping through the metaphorical meadow pretending everything is fine when it clearly isn't. Conflict can be healthy, invigorating and energizing, a renewing and refreshing force. A bust-up doesn't have to mean a break-up. Conflict can be important in a relationship. It can temporarily bring us down from the peak feelings of love that in reality are unsustainable. When we argue, we break the untenable tension of joyful love. We need to. Sometimes we need to release energy and express our negative feelings. We can do this in a positive, awake way when we:

1) Understand our own values.
2) Understand our partner's values.

3)   Have the tools and techniques to help each other Spiral back up to the peak experience of love.

When conflict arises within your relationship, ask yourself what's motivating your partner to say the things they are saying. When you get caught up in the moment those words can feel extremely personal, but if you put that feeling aside for a second you can start to ask yourself what is underlying this emotional release of energy. For example, let's take an argument over jealousy. Along with money, communication and domestic chores, jealousy is one of the most common points of conflict in a relationship, but the root cause of jealousy will vary depending on what values underlie this damaging emotion:

- For a Purple partner, it will be the sense of family betrayal, "How could you break up our home?"
- For someone expressing Red values, it will be an outraged ego, "How dare you humiliate me?"
- For Blue, it will be that their partner broke the rules, vows or promises they had made and brought shame on the partnership, "But you promised."
- For Orange, it will be a sense of competition, "What have they got that I haven't got?"
- For Green, it will be hurt and pain but at the same time a selfless love, "Do what you need to do, I want you to be happy more than anything else."

By understanding the values at work beneath everyday conflict, we can start to resolve it as well as use it to move the relationship forward. Always remember a value clash is a two-way street. It is as annoying for your partner as it is for you!

Managing the Values

So whether you're on your first date or your forty-year anniversary, how can you tell which value is dominant in your partner? Let's take a look now at what to listen for in order to recognize which value set is present in your loved one as well as what language to use to manage those values. Here's a look at the language patterns and triggers of all five value systems in terms of:

- **What they might say**—some typical phrases to identify the value set being expressed.
- **What they don't want to hear**—words or phrases that will push their buttons, wind them up and drive them up the wall.
- **What they do want to hear**—phrases that will calm them down, build an emotional bridge towards them and make them feel understood, safe and ready to talk.
- **When they can hear you**—a good time to influence your partner or ask them to do something for you.
- **What they need**—the core essentials to keep this value set loving you deeper every day.

How To Manage Purple

What they might say:

- Everything happens for a reason.
- We need to talk about the family.
- It's our tradition.
- My family/parents think…
- My sister/brother says…
- It's a bad omen.
- We always do things this way.
- Are you part of this family or not?
- That will come back to haunt you.
- My mother was right about you.
- That's not how we do things.
- Why does anything have to change?
- But we always go there.
- I'd need to talk to my family about that.

What they don't want to hear:

- I don't care what your family thinks.
- Let's go through this step by step, totally logically.
- You need to be a bit more independent.
- You rely too much on your parents.
- We're not inviting your family.

- Your superstitions are stupid.
- You shouldn't listen to your sister so much.
- Get a mind of your own.
- Your grandmother was a loony.
- You need to cut the apron strings.
- You should be more adventurous.
- I've never felt part of your family.

What they do want to hear:

- Let's not fight. Give me a hug and let's forget it.
- We don't need to talk about it. I love you.
- Let's invite the family over.
- Is there anything I can do for your parents/sister/brother/cousin?
- How do you feel about this?
- Let's go back to your favorite restaurant/holiday destination.
- You're safe with me.
- Charity begins at home.
- Family comes first.
- If that's the way you've always done things, that's fine with me.
- Let's keep it simple.
- As long as you and the family are happy.
- Blood is thicker than water.
- I love your family.
- Let's keep things the same.
- Let's ask your mother/father/sister/brother/cousin what they think.
- Your family's important to me too.

When they can hear you:

- When you have the support of the entire family or community or your partner feels safe, secure and loved.

What they need:

- Reassurance.
- Stability.
- Sameness.

- Strength, but not dominance.
- Direction.
- Tradition.
- Secure parameters.
- Predictability.
- Sense of belonging.
- Unity.

How To Manage Red

What they might say:

- I'll do it when I'm ready.
- I'll win.
- I'd rather do it alone.
- I don't care what you or anyone else thinks.
- I'm going to do it my way.
- I'm in charge.
- I'm not doing that.
- Don't tell me what to do.
- I want this.
- I'm going with or without you.
- Leave me alone.

What they don't want to hear:

- You're pathetic.
- I don't respect you.
- You've disappointed me.
- What's so special about you?
- You're wrong.
- You're an embarrassment.
- It's your duty.
- We need to do this together.
- You can't just do what you want.
- Do what I tell you.
- You're not in charge.
- So and so does this so much better than you.

- Everyone else thinks you should do this.
- What will people think?
- Calm down and we'll talk later.
- Grow up.

What they do want to hear:

- "You" (not "we").
- You're the best.
- You're so strong.
- Do whatever you like.
- You decide.
- No pressure.
- I trust you.
- I wish I was like you.
- You can do anything.
- It's totally up to you.
- I'll never leave you.
- For me, there's no one else but you.
- Can I borrow your brilliance for a moment?
- Take me to bed.

When they can hear you:

- After sex.

What they need:

- Independence.
- Space.
- Admiration.
- Praise.
- Power.
- Status.
- Sex.

How To Manage Blue

What they might say:

- We need to do the right thing.
- I'm fixed on this. I won't change my mind.
- That's not what we agreed.
- We need to get this organized and sorted out.
- There's no other way to look at it.
- It's black and white issue.
- We made a promise.
- There's a time and a place.
- That's not in the plan.
- We mustn't do the wrong thing here.
- Can we stick to the agenda?
- I don't want to say anything I'd regret.
- Those are the rules.

What they don't want to hear

- Let's break the rules.
- You need to loosen up.
- Let's just see what happens.
- I don't care if it's not right.
- There's more than one way of looking at it.
- You're narrow-minded.
- I don't agree with your rules.
- I know it's wrong but sod it, let's do it anyway.
- I can't give you any specifics.
- Anything could change at any minute.
- Just go with the flow.
- Let's jump in feet first.
- I've reorganized your things for you.
- You got that wrong.
- You can't apply logic to this. It's just how I feel.

What they do want to hear:

- Let's stick to the guidelines.
- Can you show me how to organize this?
- I want to do what is right by you.
- Help me understand where we went wrong.
- You're absolutely right.
- Let's bring some order to this chaos.
- Let's sort out this mess we're in.
- Tell me the right way to do this.
- I value your opinion.
- Shall we take some of the emotion out of this?
- I need your expert advice.
- Let's consult an authority on this subject.

When they can hear you:

- When everything else is sorted, organized and tidy.

What they need:

- Structure.
- Order.
- Integrity.
- Honor.
- Rules.
- System.
- Regularity.
- Codes of conduct.
- Procedure.

How To Manage Orange

What they might say:

- I've got a great idea.
- I've got a better idea.
- Let's just deal with this and move along.

- Anything's possible.
- I'm in to win.
- Let's take the risk.
- I can see where you're coming from but I think you'll find I'm right.
- I've thought about this and I know what to do.
- I'm bored with this.
- Let's just go for it.
- Let's try something new.
- I have my own strategy.

What they don't want to hear:

- You need to stop dreaming.
- That's not possible.
- I don't want any more change.
- It's bound to fail.
- You're not in my league.
- You don't have what it takes.
- There are other people to consider.
- It's too risky.
- You need to calm down and play safe.
- Life isn't a game.
- Why can't you be more consistent?
- You're so manipulative.

What they do want to hear:

- You can do it!
- I'm up for anything.
- Let's do it your way.
- How can we benefit from this?
- Let's innovate.
- Can we look at this strategically?
- Let's use this to our advantage.
- I have a surprise for you.
- You're so exciting and fun.
- I love how unpredictable you are.
- So we screwed up. Let's learn from it.

- We just get better and better.
- I'm proud of you.
- You're the best.

When they can hear you:

- After they've received a gift or won a deal.

What they need:

- Flexibility.
- Spontaneity.
- Freedom.
- Energy.
- Creativity.
- Independence.
- Opportunity.
- Possibility.
- Vision.
- Admiration.
- Reward.

How To Manage Green

What they might say:

- What do you think?
- Whatever you like.
- How can I help?
- Let's do it together.
- I understand you and I want to make this better.
- Let's share this.
- Let me take care of you.
- I hear exactly what you're saying.
- We can do whatever you need.
- I really don't mind.
- Whatever's right or easy for you.

What they don't want to hear:

- I don't care.
- I'm only interested in myself.
- You need to stop being so nice to everyone and toughen up.
- You're naive.
- People are generally horrid.
- This is going to end in a fight.
- Recycling is a waste of time.
- Human rights laws have created more problems than they've solved.
- People take advantage of you.
- Humans are fundamentally selfish.
- There's no point.
- You're a mug.
- You're far too idealistic.

What they do want to hear:

- We're all in this together.
- Thank you for helping me.
- You're so understanding.
- I couldn't have done this without you.
- I'll never forget you.
- We're stronger together.
- You've been so kind and thoughtful.
- My life wouldn't be the same without you.
- We're such a great team.
- What's mine is yours.
- I'm right there with you.
- Tell me how you really feel – I want to be better.
- Let's agree on this.
- Nothing's more important than our relationship.
- We're both right.
- It would help me if you were totally honest with me.
- Let's help each other.
- You've changed people's lives.
- You have so much love to give.

When they can hear you:

- After they've helped you or helped someone else.

What they need:

- Acceptance.
- Cohesion.
- Unity.
- Social contact.
- Potential.
- Growth.
- Learning.
- Love.
- Harmony.
- Peace.
- Generosity.
- Understanding.

Time To "Spiral Into Love"

That was an introduction on how to use SDi to maximize the dynamics of your relationship. We have found it incredibly powerful in both our personal lives and our professional work. We hope you too enjoy a whole new way to Spiral into love, every day. But don't just take it from us. Dr. Don Beck has been using the SDi theory to broker peace across the world including working alongside Nelson Mandela in the 1980s. It has been acknowledged by F.W. De Klerk that Dr. Don played a fundamental role in bringing about change and a peaceful transition out of apartheid in South Africa. Dr. Don is currently applying SDi in the Middle East, working with groups of young Israelis and Palestinians. The theory and practice of SDi is working towards peace between peoples and nations all over the world. Imagine what it could do for your relationship.

PERSONAL PSYCHOLOGY AND THE JOURNEY OF EMERGENCE

By Jon Freeman

Qualifying remarks: This is a personal perspective. It is personal in the sense that it is rooted in my own experience and journey, but also because the SDi lens through which I view that journey is mine, rather than validated theory. It is in that sense merely a point of view. Nevertheless, as the outcome of quite deep consideration it is intended to provide some useful observations on how Graves' theory has affected my view of psychology.

I am not a graduate, or professionally certified in psychology or psychotherapy. Some of my university training was in aspects of developmental and social psychology. I had spent three decades in regular workshops and other self-development conversations and read a lot of books on psychology before I encountered SDi. I have been at various times a coach, mentor and counsellor to others and have also learned some alternative ways of working with emotional and psychological issues including NLP, Emotional Freedom Technique, Hellinger Constellation work and Access Consciousness. I have done a lot of work on my subjective interior and because 40 years is a long time to spend in such study, even part time, I have a breadth of experience to rival many professionals. Which is not to say that I don't know some professionals who are more experienced and skilled than I am.

To the best of my knowledge, Clare Graves described his theory as a model of adult bio-psycho-social development, but never as a basis for therapeutic intervention. If he considered it as a tool for personal change, it would perhaps be surprising. Although psychotherapy and clinical psychology had been around for 50 years, the fashion for self-exploration was born after his core research, in the late sixties and seventies. It is only fair to him and to those such as Don Beck who later developed his theory into SDi to acknowledge that there is no theoretical validation from Graves or from the added thoughts of Ken Wilber for using the theory actively as a tool for therapy or personal transformation. Regardless of these caveats, I have no hesitation in offering my analysis. Graves' theory is about world-views, and what is psychotherapy if not a journey into a person's view of the world?

It is also possible, as Dr. Keith Rice demonstrated in his book *Knowing Me, Knowing You,* to put Graves and SDi alongside many other psychological theories. This positioning shows how SDi includes, frames and fits in with, and at times even transcends these other theories. There is a great deal of potential in this respect for SDi theory to be researched and extended in this territory. But, enough of preparation; now onto my SDi informed world view.

The Deepest Wounds

Jungian theory tells us that the two deepest sources of psychological damage are abandonment and overwhelm. It is not a huge cognitive leap to suggest that these are deep survival issues. The infant human is physically vulnerable and it is inevitable that anything which threatens that survival will have psychological impact. Survival is the Beige keynote, so the earliest and thus deepest of psychological wounds are to be found in Beige.

Beige vulnerability extends into the next, Purple, level where we find out who our Tribe is. This is a time of deep bonding with the parents, the time when those parents are the source of physical safety and nourishment. During our Purple stage we encounter the most fundamental modelling of love, affection and what it means to be a human with relationships to other humans. It is no surprise that the psychological consequences of events during this Purple stage rank very closely in impact with those at Beige. Since both are typically pre-verbal and for most people pre-date their conscious memories, both are equally likely to be hard for adults to access.

But access them we must, if we are to create the freedoms that the Possible Human promises.

Personal Power and Collective Agreements

As the infant human emerges from total immersion in the parents' world she discovers her own personhood. We have all witnessed what happens as the power-words kick in, the assertion of individuality through vocabulary such as "No" and "Mine", the first skirmishes in the battle of the terrible twos. This is the individual root of the Red stage that is echoed in human societal development, the beginning of a dance of power that oscillates between empowerment, i.e. the "power to" and dominance, i.e. the "power over". Healthy human functioning at this level derives from the ability to balance these two aspects of power.

As the young person learns the play of these forces they are influenced by others. Clare Graves describes the way that adults operating from this Red vMeme must be managed through repetition of requirements. Persuasion is not possible; the individual must be guided by authority. If they don't write between the lines, their work must be torn up so that they do it again. If the person makes an error the teacher stops him and says "start it again". He just keeps going until he gets a positive response and then the rewards.[i] Graves comments strongly on how punishment is ineffective in dealing with Red, "The tissue in the head that is able to feel, to perceive punishment, is not activated"[ii]. Red can learn only by reward.

The infant at Red similarly does not have the necessary tissue activated. The neuro-endocrine chemistry that triggers that activation has not developed and the failure to support children in the development of these dynamics is the root of many later psychological challenges. These support failures typically stem from parental orientations in two other stages, the first of which is Blue.

The task of Blue is to define the rules and set the boundaries within which the dance of power takes place. The developing child makes a long and slow transition from the egocentric state towards socialisation. By the time he is entering school this is underway. He knows some of the rules, "don't snatch", "don't hit", and has some of the impulses under control. In Red the thwarting of an impulse might trigger an ungovernable tantrum of anger or tears. By the next stage the child is learning both what is right and expected behaviour and what it takes to manage her internal state in order to comply. This stage extends for many years. There are many rules to learn and many arising capacities that will call for self-governance. In this stage failure to observe the rules can be punished because the required systems have been activated. However the goal is to get beyond external punishment, to have the individual manage their own compliance. Internalisation of the rules is accompanied by the capacity to self-punish which we label guilt, and the associated desire to atone for errors.

There are a number of balances here which affect our individual psychological health and there are many implications for child-rearing. Since punishment does not work, and most parents use punishment even for children in Purple and Red, most of us will have less than ideal experiences during the stage of establishing our healthy will forces and self-worth. Boys in particular may experience dominant, "spare the rod, spoil the child", fathering that at the extremes will lead some to life-long repression and inadequacy and others to replication of the father's violence, anger and abuse of others, sometimes delayed until they are more fully grown. I have a friend who tolerated such treatment until he decked his father at the age of 15. Now approaching 70 he is a recovering alcoholic with a recent heroism award after diving into the sea to rescue a young boy in difficulties.

At the other extreme, parents who are over-indulgent or who have strong Green will want to treat their children as equals. These Green parents will also try to reason with children who don't yet have the necessary intellectual capability. This will often create insecurity by failing to create a safe, firm container for the child's impulses. The lack of effective modelling of self-control and boundary setting does not assist the child to make the transition to healthy socialisation in the Blue stage. Often it is the kindergartens and schools who are required to address this deficit.

With so many ways for this stage to be mismanaged, many of us will have experienced challenges at the Blue developmental stage. There is a polarity dance here too. On one extreme is the failure to establish the boundaries to our individual impulses; to instil a healthy conscience and consciousness of our shared life with others, resulting in a faulty moral compass. On the other extreme is the rigid imposition of rules and over-instilling of guilt such that creativity, initiative and self-confidence are stifled. A healthy balance between these polarities is necessary for the emergence of the Possible Human.

The Nature Of Psychological Healing

It is the custom when discussing SDi at all scales, from individuals to nations, for us to talk of the colours almost as if they are concrete entities. Even though we know they are not discrete, even though we can also talk about RED-Blue and Red-BLUE as steps in a gradual transition between stages on a continuum and even though we know that people are always chords not notes in the music of existence, we focus on the centres of gravity. We have no choice, since not to do so gives us no contour marks on the map of existence and there would be nothing to talk about.

The risk in this way of thinking when applied to personal development or psychological change is that we will look upon the process as involving stepwise change from one stage (or sub-stage) to the next. The reality is that we make our change one belief, one emotional block, one insight at a time.

It is a cliché to think of all psychotherapy or analysis as starting with the enquiry "Tell me about your mother." Simplistic as that may be it does contain the unavoidable truth that our relationships with parents, or those who filled that role, are fundamental in shaping who we become. Of course there are many other influences, depending on your reality framework. Rebirthers believe that some of our most fundamental thoughts are formed at the moment we exit the birth canal into this physical reality. Family Constellation therapists would show you how influences from your ancestry can inhabit your being, often in ways that would baffle a rationalist mindset. Past-life regression therapists would tell you and even facilitate you to experience your own previous existence and recognise karmic lessons or decisions that are affecting you in this one. Caroline Myss's book, *Sacred Contracts* would lead you towards your own role in choosing the particulars of this lifetime's journey.

It does not matter if any of these possibilities are part of your reality or mine, though in the spirit of transparency I will acknowledge having experienced all of the above "realities" and finding them of use. It does not even matter whether you believe in the sense of "soul" or of non-ordinary connection that some of those imply. What does matter is that each experience, each investigation, each self-learning that we may have will generally lead to a shift in thought, belief or emotional content that affects an aspect of our reality. Some shifts can be minor, e.g. seeing how we interpreted an event in one way and locked in a conclusion that we now view as flawed. Others can be more fundamental and akin to releasing the tight fist that held a whole bunch of balloons so that they can all float away. But even these more wide-reaching awakenings will only affect a portion of our being and none of them on their own are likely to trigger a step-change, e.g. from Blue to Orange. Nevertheless a consistent focus on our areas of guilt, close attention to the beliefs that we have taken on as rules even though we don't really resonate with them and systematic efforts to release our fear of external authority may gradually and cumulatively release the constraints in our psyche. Taken together they can facilitate a new balance of the energy in our system, shifting the centre of gravity from Blue toward and into Orange.

Using The Spiral Lens

Prior to encountering SDi my own focus in self-development was essentially pragmatic. My first excursion into the territory was driven by the challenges in my first marriage when what I thought I was looking for was stress management. I was never on a path to enlightenment and for 20 years or so did not have even the notion of a long-term intention. I simply went from one issue to the next, sustained on the zigzag path of change by the experience that little by little I became more functional, had more equanimity, made better choices and was more contented. Even since encountering SDi, I still have the basic approach of dealing with one challenge at a time, though I do now believe that the journey, like the Spiral, does not end and that there are now more possibilities for who I can become and what I can do than I would have been able to imagine just 10 years ago. I have much more clarity now regarding the nature of the Possible Human and at the same time less sense of any limit to that possibility.

Yet even though there is no specific goal, no anticipation of enlightenment and no end-point, I do have a context within the Spiral that affects how I view this haphazard and emergent process. I have a general goal which relates to the shift from First to Second Tier functioning. This transition, both a momentous leap in the degree of difference between the two and a gradual development in my own capacities, I now see as essential. I see it as urgent both for me personally and for all those who have an intention or desire to support and lead the planetary transition that faces us. Dr. Michael Niblack (personal conversation) described Graves' theory not as a map, but a map-making algorithm. I believe that we can use, and I do use, that algorithm to articulate aspects of my own development. Following is what shows up on my map.

In case there is anyone who still has the erroneous view that one can "be" Second Tier in isolation from First Tier, let me say with all possible emphasis that there is no such thing. To even think this fails to understand the nature of "transcend and include" and adopts the illusion that Second Tier is a state experience rather than a stage in vMeme system development. At the spiritual level it fails to observe the obvious; "After enlightenment, chop wood, carry water". However, what happens as we engage with Second Tier values is two-fold and does have an experiential aspect:

1) The first is that the change from survival to being involves a reduction in the emotional basis of our thinking. The influence of our limbic (aka reptilian) brain affects the activation of the brain structures. It evolved to do so, adapting to our Life Conditions by turning on flight-or-fight fear, the anger to meet a threat or challenge and/or influencing the shame or guilt that makes us appropriately submissive, when that supports survival. As we engage more of the higher functions we are less subject to these limbic buffetings. Our choices are made with greater cognitive bandwidth since we are not pushed chemically towards one dominant vMeme by those chemical activations; we learn to manage our emotions. With less Beta and more Alpha wave activity, possibly supported by increases in oxytocin, the communication increases across the Corpus Callosum allowing greater integration of right-brain activity with its intuitive ability to "grok" patterns. Alpha waves are inhibited by stress and emotion (esp. adrenaline) so the lessening of these limbic influences is essential to the increase in non-linear thinking that Second Tier requires.

2) The stability of our functioning in Yellow and above rests on the First Tier platform. If you have the image of the Spiral and how the diagram grows both width and depth as higher stages emerge, you can also have an image of an inverted pyramid or a stack of blocks. If the blocks

are not centred the stack will be unstable. The un-centred positioning occurs when our vMemes, thoughts and beliefs fail to balance the polarities of existence. If our response to hostile challenge is over-submissive and fearful then we cannot exercise the expertise and authority that a Yellow leader would require. If we are polarised towards rule-based responses in a particular sphere of action then we will fail to activate effective Second Tier management of Orange creative ideas. Thus in order to be effective as Yellow leaders, even in leadership of ourselves, we must rebalance, or make accommodations in the First Tier stack.

This may seem only to say that to be fully effective we must address our weaknesses, but I suggest that it goes deeper than that. To some degree it is possible to simulate Yellow by cognitive choice. Because the Yellow perspective allows us to see what the overall system needs, and what responses from others will facilitate the shift needed, we can provide that response, or at least avoid pressing the "cold" buttons that will be counterproductive with the people we wish to influence. Indeed we may have to simulate, in a spirit of "fake it until we make it", but I believe that the limits will always show up. If we have not dealt with the emotional roots and the stuck beliefs then these will continue to affect what we see by filtering our awareness of what is going on. Then they will limit our responses because we don't have the natural capacity to BE what the situation calls for. People only respond in limited degree to simulation. You can fool their brains, but not their own limbic resonances which are detecting body language and empathic triggers.

I write this in the days following the death of Nelson Mandela, acutely aware of the difference that comes when the inner work has been done. Among the truths that Mandela demonstrated are the need for authenticity, the recognition that we humans have for someone who acts from their heart with the deepest levels of human connection and compassion. A stream of stories from people who met him attests to this response. The lesson is that decades in a monastery called Robben Island facilitated a depth of inner work that most of us can only aspire to. Cindy Wigglesworth's SQ21 *(21 Skills of Spiritual Intelligence)*[iii] rests on the image she uses of love as a bird with two wings. The wings are wisdom and compassion. Nelson Mandela exemplified this truth. From a Spiral perspective we can learn the wisdom which comes from the clarity of the Spiral lens. Compassion develops through the work we do to free the heart from its blockages and wounds.

Don't Believe What You Think

I may not aspire to enlightenment but I do seek awareness, by which I mean the capacity to see things clearly as they are. As I have freed myself little by little from my own wounds my filters have become less cloudy. The journey towards Second Tier involves a shift from the narrowed perspectives that cause those centred in First Tier stages to be unable to see or comprehend any other stage and to simply see those vMemes and their expressions as wrong. They have no perspective that sits outside their own way of seeing. As humans pass into and through Green they begin to embrace a perspective of diversity and to recognise that there are other ways of being. Self-examination, to whatever extent this is practiced, develops a kind of "meta-mind", the ability to look at one's thoughts and behaviours with a degree of objectivity. My colleague Ian McDonald has a T-shirt bearing the motto "Don't Believe what you Think". The capacity to observe, to witness and to take a more objective view of our own being is the gateway to Yellow thinking as well as the awareness that allows us to treat our emotions with some suspicion. We don't have to believe what we feel either, and can better distinguish limbic reactivity from intuitive and empathic awareness.

Historically the psychotherapeutic journey begins with our own wounds, the abandonment, overwhelm, abuse (witting or unwitting) and failures of support that we perceived ourselves to have experienced as children. It continues with exploration of the conclusions that we have internalised and the belief systems that we have adopted around who we are. We discover the judgements with which we internalise low self-worth and the perceptions that limit what we are capable of. We revisit the events that have hurt us, the failed relationships, the dysfunctional family behaviours, the awful bosses and unreliable peers. We see our own mistakes and the choices that we now avoid in case they are repeated. We see the choices of others that we have reacted against and excessively avoided. In the best cases we are able to release the psychological energy that we have locked up in order to re-evaluate those choices and beliefs, whether those were framed as positive or negative and to find a freer and more open sense of what is possible for us now. We enjoy the possibilities that are rooted in our present-time awareness of what is rather than in the misperceptions of the past.

The SDi perspective helps us to see all of this history more clearly. When we understand the vMemes of those around us we can see more of how they were doing what their vMeme stage told them was the best they could do. As we look through the SDi lens at our own perceptions we can see more of the way in which our own vMemes reflect the trajectory of our experience and our responses to the others who affected our Life Conditions. We have the option and opportunity to reframe and relearn.

Reflecting The Spiral

One of my more profound awakenings took place during an SDi Level 2 training in Personal Development that was led by Jean Houston and Don Beck. During this training I found myself asking Jean the question why I found it difficult to activate my healthy Red, which I perceived as showing up in my not being assertive at times when I needed to be and in not trusting those who do display strong and assertive behaviours even when there is no abuse of power in evidence. The bottom line was that I was disempowering myself.

In the background to this question I was already aware of a number of factors. My own preference is towards the cool colours, the "We" systems. My experience as a child was of a subtle but strong required compliance and of some incidents which suppressed my expression of a Red self. I was aware of the underlying lack of Purple kinship bonding that affected my confidence and sense of my place in the world. I acknowledged the over-intellectualised culture which asked for Blue behaviour when the internal need was for continued Purple and Red exploration. I had released some of the emotions that got stuck around these events and a lot had changed. In spite of that, the question around disempowerment remained.

Jean Houston's response took my breath away and had me instantly in tears. Her response was that I needed to call upon my Red in service of my Turquoise. In saying this she firstly put a positive value and a super-ordinate goal on my exercise of Red capability. Within that she also delivered a message around bonding and around self-expression that spoke both to my cool-colour preference and to a deeper level of bonding, a kinship with the human tribe rather than my familial origins.

Jean's gift has continued to ripple through my unfolding over the time since, supported by many other explorations and awakening processes. She demonstrates the power that arises when we don't treat aspects of our wounds or imbalances as "shadow". My view of shadow is that it is something which shows up when bright light is shining on something else (including a blockage) and when we are unable to shine light (awareness) into all places. Rebalancing the polarities of the First Tier perceptual stack means that it is no longer helpful to look at beliefs as "right" or "wrong". The development of our psychological health and behavioural potency calls for the recognition of all choices as being potentially healthy when they are appropriate to the Life Conditions that we are dealing with.

Discovering The Possible Human

I borrow the title of one of Jean's books for the above heading and it also reflects my own desire and intention to understand the Science of Possibility, which is also the title of one of my books. Ultimately I am most interested in what I and We can DO in the world. My lack of interest in enlightenment rests partly in my wish to focus on "doing the change that the world needs done" (as Don Beck would put it) more than on Being the Change that I wish to see. And yet this is a paradoxical statement to make when this article rests on the premise that by changing myself, my capacity to effect change in the world grows. That paradox is emphasised by the recognition that Second Tier as identified by Graves is about BEING rather than survival.

I have not talked at all of quadrants, but it is implicit in this article that the more we are aware of our own inner world (Upper-Left) the more we are capable of perceiving clearly that in the Right Side quadrants and the better we will manage our relationships in the Lower Left collective. Similarly, the more that our action choices, made from the Upper Left, are effective in the way that they influence the other three quadrants, the greater our capacity to do the change.

My conclusion is that our doing is of the highest importance. What we do must be grounded in our being and be a reflection of who we are. Our world is on a collision course with the unsustainable effects of human misperceptions. We must do the work to take us beyond the limited, restricted bandwidth and linear thought processes that maintain that trajectory. Achieving this requires that we create the freedom to see both ourselves and the world differently and in a connected way. That is, we have to be different and as a result think differently and do different things. When we release our old conclusions and create freedom from our restricted points of view we can glimpse possibilities that were previously beyond our imagining. We can see ourselves bigger both individually and as a collective. We are the Possible Humans. What would the world be like if we could step fully into that?

Bibliography

[i] Clare W. Graves: *The Never-ending Quest,* P. 235, Eclet Publishing: ISBN 0 9724742-1-8

[ii] *The Never-ending Quest,* P. 238

[iii] Cindy Wigglesworth. *SQ21: The 21 skills of Spiritual Intelligence,* Select Books Inc: ISBN 978-1590792353

SPIRAL WIZARDS: A TRAINING EXPERIMENT

By Claudine Villemot-Kienzle

Introduction

I have been a trainer, consultant, and project leader for over 25 years. Over this time I became acutely aware that Second Tier cognition was a powerful contribution in moving projects forward. It was equally clear that there was little guidance available that could support people in making the transition from First to Second Tier. To address this deficit I envisioned a cadre of social architects, or Spiral Wizards, to fill this guidance gap. These Spiral Wizards would have to be trained. Could Spiral Wizard training be designed? The first step would be to assemble a team who would design and launch such an education program, and in our case this would entail a significant online, webinar element. Could this team be developed to its own Second Tier capacity within a confirming SDi framework? If it could then we would have the proof that Second Tier competencies could be named, developed and supported, and we would have a team configured to do just that for others.

Towards this end I assembled a collection of SDi informed colleagues. We acknowledged our competencies for successful engagement with problems within Blue, Orange, and Green contexts. Beyond this though, personally we were recognizing and articulating the nature of our own transitions from Green to Yellow. In exploring this new territory we painfully recognized the absence of methods, skills, tools, and support especially tuned to the highly complex demands of Second Tier problems. We were hitting the limits of our competencies. But then isn't that the dissonance SDi says predicts the emergence of new competencies? We seemed to be on the right track.

We were venturing into new territory, and names such as "trainer" or "consultant" spoke too much of the past. Professor Clare Graves left us with a notion of a quantum leap available for human beings. We were attempting to address the nature of this new reality and to do so well called for fresh language in order for it to be pictured and grasped as the new possibility it is. Thus we incorporated the term Spiral Wizard. For us this affirmed the vMeme model as well as created an opening for noting and affirming the new possibilities for human being that a "quantum leap" suggested.

Setting The SDi Frame As A Guide

Our team building as well as the design of the entire project was based on setting the Spiral in the center. SDi would be the force and framework that would guide our thinking and acting in every moment. We agreed to focus on consciously reflecting our process, to map, and remap our experience against the SDi standard. We further agreed to choose and affirm a Yellow level perspective.

This orientation allowed the free and easy manifestation of the First Tier vMemes all along the different project phases. This meant addressing any vMeme need that appeared, and we often looked for these needs with such questions as these:

- What do we need, now?
- What does the system need, now?
- What does the process need, now?

To further explore the memetic landscape we often returned to questions like these:

- Which methods are functional, here, now?
- Which thinking is helpful, now?
- How will we address the emotions that are here, now?
- How do we maintain a heart-to-heart connection, now?

We welcomed this project as an exciting opportunity to apply to us what we felt called to teach and transmit. As such, our work together extended beyond the context of this project. We consciously opened a parallel space of common exploring, testing, reflecting, recalibrating along the realization of the project itself. We presumed all situations are training contexts for Spiral Wizards.

Starting The Co-Creative Team Building

As initiator of the project I naturally began with presenting to the team fellows the vision that animated me, my heart's desire and my vocational arousal around the topic. The force behind the vision is derived from the Essence, the Creative Evolutionary Impulse or the Source, and reaches beyond memetics. The vMemes will bring the vision into manifestation, into the world. My vision:

- This project will inspire and create an evolutionary community of engaged Spiral Wizards. These Spiral Wizards will engage in self-transformation processes as a matter of practice. These Spiral Wizards will also initiate and conduct concrete projects in societal domains according to their passion and unique skills.

We then opened a space for team members to connect their own Essential Impulse to this vision and to relate it to their vocational arousal. Some questions we found to be helpful for furthering this end follow:

- How do I feel connected to this vision?
- What excites me about this vision?
- What is appealing to me about this vision?
- What makes me resonate with this vision?
- How can I connect my vocational arousal to this vision?
- What business are we really in?
- What do you want to give to the project?
- What is your special gift to it?
- Which of your talents, competencies, capacities will you offer?
- Which potentials can you realize through the project?
- How can we best describe what should emerge out of our engagement?

Sharing in this inquiry on the cognitive, emotional and energetic levels led us to formulate our common higher purpose as follows:

- Our higher purpose is to co-create a field of interrelatedness between us and with our collective field of wisdom. This field of interrelatedness supports the emergence of Second Tier thinking, acting and feeling in each of us individually and in our team collectively.

This common higher purpose unified our differences in thinking and acting due to our differing memetic profiles and built the bridge to cross any gaps that would emerge.

Memetic Levels

The complex dynamics and shifting boundaries showing up in such a project cannot be translated in all their dimensions and depth through words and written communication. After reflection I have chosen to describe how we operated in focusing on one vMeme after the other in order to facilitate comprehension, while being aware that this linear chronology does not match the way SDi vMemes develop.

Beige

"Can we make a living from the webinar program?" is the first question we asked. All team members were and still are engaged in different income producing professional settings. Survival needs were being satisfied for all parties.

We considered this memetic level in wondering how we could care for the viability of the project. Like a new born baby the project would need full attention of at least one person. We agreed to give it enough time to grow through all phases, without pushing or slowing down.

Looking up the Spiral we agreed that meeting the needs of all vMemes on the Spiral as described below is the prerequisite for survival of each project or team. Furthermore the contribution of all vMeme resources and qualities were determined as essential to support the growth and maturation of the project.

Purple

Our focal question for Purple was "What in the team needs attention so that trust can emerge?" Trust and belonging seemed inseparable measures and the articulation of our shared higher purpose, as noted above, was our foundation for creating a sense of belonging. Sharing this purpose helped to develop a deep solidarity. We found ourselves feeling like family members supporting each other.

We gave attention to Purple through asking, "What do we fear regarding this project?" "How do we address those fears?" Deeply listening to each other brought us knowledge of how each of us feels, thinks, and acts. This growing familiarity fostered an atmosphere of security.

Rituals helped to consolidate the sense of feeling safe and belonging. We regularly began our meetings with some attunement process, common meditation or sharing. Upon completing any phase of the project we put attention to celebration. As we were living in remote areas and were communicating online most of the time, we found internet programs that made it possible to post our successes on a common board and celebrate each step. Doing so we used Orange technology to fulfill a Purple need. We deepened the idea of "one for all, all for one" as we responded to schedule changes by taking over tasks from members under pressure, and giving support when needed, without sticking to role definitions.

The practice of Purple "putting resources in common and sharing them with the tribe" was interpreted in a modern way, as we implemented and used an online program for sharing all intellectual resources and documents we have found interesting, and for working on them collectively. Trust emerged.

Red

Giving attention to our Red vMeme consolidated our sense of belonging as it became apparent which unique contribution each could give to the group. Acknowledging and appreciating the unique talents and gifts each member brought into the whole project also reinforced confidence and trust.

Creating space for each member for personal growth and self-expression was vital for the sustainability of the project. Some of our useful questions at this point:

- Who do I want to be?
- How will I show up in this group?

- How can I develop and behold my own identity within a common purpose?
- What are the limits to my self- expression?

Respect was agreed to be a common standard. We encouraged each other to delimit one´s territory and take actions if one felt called to do so. In defining clear roles and functions (Blue) according to personal preferences and attractions, we helped frame individual action fields. Within these fields each could take initiatives without having to report to the group. This was discussed openly so that individual actions would not be interpreted as betrayal to the group (Purple) and the Purple, Red balance could be maintained. We also introduced celebration as a Purple, Red strengthener through expressions of the sort, "I see you." "I acknowledge you."

Two dissonances emerged along the process. In the first of these one team member reported, "Many interesting encounters and opportunities have arisen in the week where the team coordinator was absent". This remark and the way it was expressed argued for attention. An inquiry was facilitated:

- Did the person feel repressed?
- Was the team coordinator perceived as too dominant?
- Did the team member dare not take actions?
- If so, what could be the reasons for that?

So we opened the space for reflecting and exploring the underlying needs and the believing systems that were involved. The team coordinator asked if the team member felt not having enough room for showing up, or the attitude of the team coordinator let assume that self-expression was not welcomed. That was not the problem. So we explored another possible trigger and shared understandings on responsibility for one´s showing up and for taking one´s space for expression. We examined fears of not being loyal to the team coordinator if becoming more autonomous, and we clarified the balance between self-realization and respect for the others. The team coordinator reassured that freedom, self- expression and emancipation from the "eldest" were legitimate interests, as long as openness was cultivated. The dissonance was resolved. It is interesting to point out that the need for wanting to break out of Purple and acting Red manifested after Purple had been established and enough trust was felt to make the emergence of Red possible.

The second tension appeared some weeks later. Our practice was to design each webinar within the team and then decide who would take which role and part. Most decisions resulted from the Yellow perspective, i.e. the person with required competencies and capacities in a specific field would take responsibility for that field. In this way we built quality and authenticity for our participants. But this time, one team member proposed to provide content that had already been taught in a previous webinar by another member with higher competence in this field. The thrust of the argument was that the content should not be attached to one person and it is not about a "one-man or one-woman show". The wording and the tone suggested that there was some Red energy expressing itself in this situation. Paying attention to the situation showed that the team member feared they would not get enough visibility from the participants as a competent teacher and wanted to step more "on the scene" in this role. Yet, giving a team member the opportunity to show up in delivering content he is not deeply connected with, would not be functional and appropriate. Doing so might be a Green reaction to keep harmony and stick to the idea "we are all equal" and so we can all teach the same contents, without regard to own capacity, needs of students and the teaching context.

Recalibrating in this situation meant to first recognize the lack of fit as well as the needs underlying the member's request. Then we searched for ways to enable Red to manifest itself without putting the quality and the credibility of the teaching at stake. This resulted in giving the team member more room for specific talents and competencies while reinforcing their value in front of the team and of the participants. Creating a webinar content focusing on capacities and knowledge of the person and with added value for the participants was considered. We also considered opening a parallel "scene" that serves the project and presented the person in their singularity. The team member found ways to meet the project and participants needs and to enlarge their territory. This exercise reminded us to pay attention to this question consistently, "How do we manage connections between the individual Red needs and the big picture?"

Blue

While building trust, strengthening the sense of belonging and enjoying freedom of self-expression and individual actions, we then focused on organizing and structuring. In fact this level was already involved from the beginning, but as a minimal needed structure to enable us to start the project. Now it was about going deeper in the clarification of the structures we needed from a functional, Yellow, perspective. How often should our meetings take place and via which media? Which functions were to be fulfilled and which persons in the team were more likely to execute them with excellence as advised by their memetic profile? Which roles did we need? Functions and roles were mostly distributed according to natural aptitudes, preferences and competences. At the same time we were aware that we could switch roles, rotate and define new ones depending on context, self-evolution, new requirements etc.

This flexible morphing of structures according to changes in persons and context show how Yellow and Blue cooperate. As an example: For our online community platform we asked a team member with center of gravity in Green to take charge of the communication, facilitate sharing, and deepen interrelatedness. But regarding the technical use of the platform as a place for uploading documents and administrate contents, it became obvious that we would have to select another team member whose capacities would better fit those technical requirements. This natural memetic fitting is much more efficient and satisfying for all than trying to train the person to do something and gain competencies that are not matching their memetic profile.

Besides structure and order, an important aspect of this memetic level is the notion of meaning. Why are we doing all this? What is our mission? Collectively defining our higher purpose early on ensured that all members were willing to be in service to the whole project on a long-term perspective, beyond individual interests and short term satisfaction. This strong sense of Blue purpose was fundamental for running a project steadily through all challenges and resistances that could and did naturally emerge. Before launching the webinar and with many tasks still wanting to be completed, we however took time to reconnect with this level and gave space for each of us to remember and reassure why each had chosen to engage in this project. Towards this end, several times, one of us read the statements to the group that each had made some months ago and we let them resonate.

One tendency of the Blue meme is striving for perfection. While this can surely be a valuable quality at specific times along a project, it turned out to be an energy killer at the start. So we gave the issue of perfection attention and helped each other to relax and reconsider situations and attitudes as we felt compulsivity and pressure showing up.

Orange

Addressing the needs of the basic vMemes Beige, Purple, Red and giving Blue enough space for manifesting, provided a healthy and sustainable basis for Orange to strive. To inform this striving we undertook trainings in online marketing, consulted several experts, studied competitors in the webinar field and defined targets and success criteria. We were aware of the challenging character of the project and appreciated the challenge as a stimulating element. Within the team we developed a healthy competition in gaining new competencies and expertise relative to the online system we chose for running the webinar. The competition motivated us to give our best. We certainly were challenged by the webinar technology at the beginning. The alliance of Blue and Orange was one key to managing this issue. Blue fosters the ability to persevere, Orange triggers wanting to go beyond one´s limits. As well, our Purple was helpful, as the ones in our team who felt more comfortable with handling technology were very supportive with the others.

Our strategy was to define the first webinar series as a test version that we offered for a discounted fee. The goal was to first evaluate, improve and develop further the education program. We spent much time in defining clearly our target group. We used SDi as a very helpful and precise model for this too. We decided we would address Orange/Green and Green/Yellow and thus focus on the memetic transitions. In phases of transition most people feel uncomfortable and may be more open for new insights and changing. So we addressed what we assumed to be one of the "pain points" of our target group. A challenge was to design the website and the communication in a way that Orange/Green, Green/Yellow feel addressed and attracted by what we wanted to offer. We did end up enrolling precisely those centers of gravity in the course.

We consciously did not speak to Green as we felt that the webinar technology would not be appealing to people with this center of gravity. We observed that Green prefers meeting people in a physical space, looks for live contacts and face to face communication. Our assumption turned out to be correct as some interested persons, after having experienced a webinar sample, declined to continue because of the technology involved.

Green

We met the needs of Green by sharing our feelings and what bothered us, and also in addressing irritations and tensions as they popped up. Doing so, it was possible to sustain harmony within the team. Yet, while our standard was to start our meetings with some attunement process, we didn´t require this. We considered our time schedule and allowed ourselves to focus right away on the content if this seemed more appropriate, caring for a balance between the needs of Orange and Green.

In the celebration we organized before the launching, we designed a sequence where each spoke what they most valued in the others. We expressed gratitude for having such a supportive community. We opened this Green space intentionally during the most challenging phase of the project where a Blue/Orange drive was dominant. This prevented us from falling into an unhealthy, compulsive, pushing dynamic that could have weakened or even cancelled Green and Purple satisfiers.

We learned from SDi to be attentive to the motivation behind the manifestation. If we take "celebrating" as an example, we observed that this action can result from different memetic motivations. We looked for, and found, the real memetic motivator by asking "Why do you want to celebrate?" Orange could want celebration for the purpose of motivating and getting the best performances of people, as in sport coaching. Blue may want to celebrate because proper behavior requires this. While there is nothing wrong with these motivators they would not satisfy Green and in fact might be aversive. Thus, following a Blue/Orange celebration we attended to balancing the Spiral satisfiers by focusing on Purple, Red and Green.

When noticing the tension between individual memetic needs and our shared higher purpose we designed a win-win-win perspective, as in the following instance. One team member highly valued connecting to people in a personal way, to our students, team members, and others supporting our project. This person would look for each opportunity to be in personal contact. This member had formulated this need clearly at the beginning of the team building as one personal purpose the project should serve. We saw this as the expression of a strong need on the Green level. At the same time the Red issue of getting visibility as an individual and delimiting territory for self-expression was noticeable. Both needs were met as the team member chose to give support to people not in writing but by meeting personally. Honoring the Yellow functionality perspective we assessed whether the pursuit of fulfilling these personal needs was in accordance with the whole project. We concluded that the project clearly benefitted from solidifying personal connections, many of which would serve the project throughout its lifetime.

Second Tier

This memetic level entails the meta-perspective necessary to design the whole process as an integral one, as described above. Operating from this level means that we no longer identify ourselves with one memetic level in particular or with our memetic profile. What we personally value most and our set of priorities shaped by our personal memetic profile do not build the frame of reference for our thinking, feeling and doing. A Second Tier perspective accounts for the specific context, the present situation, and the involved people. Second Tier thinking asks "What are the next steps that would support healthy expression for the individual and serve the big picture?" We develop the capacity to step out of our personal beliefs and preferred modus operandi and to look for the needs that want to be met. Our group agreed to operate from Second Tier and was eager to "walk the talk". To train ourselves in this level of being, we experienced that some specifics are required for holding the Second Tier space:

- Steady awareness of what is occurring within oneself.
- Concurrent attention to the inner processes of all those involved.
- Deep listening.
- Emotional and energetic interconnectedness.
- Overcoming judgment.
- Active attention to tensions.
- Queries re motivation, "Why?"
- Reviewing foundations for opinions.

In our experience the pre-requisite to be able to hold this energetic space and this degree of consciousness is the health of our own vMemes. Trauma on any memetic level that is not yet healed will show up as soon as the team is challenged. Most of the time the person may go through a memetic regression and much energy flows then into dealing with the issue. In a Yellow perspective that focuses on functionality we had to find ways to express compassion for the person while protecting the purpose of the project and the group. Addressing such issues in an external therapeutic or coaching context is necessary. Without this the whole project is threatened.

The flexibility we experienced in choosing to operate from different memetic perspectives did not mean we could ignore our lst Tier vMemes and our own memetic profile. The challenge was to achieve a balance between operating from a meta-perspective and acting in lst Tier. We had to be aware of our needs in lst Tier and allow their full expression as they show up. We acknowledged these lst Tier needs and looked for ways we could best address them in a win-win-win perspective. Doing so, we behaved in an authentic way, fostered energy flowing through the entire Spiral, and stimulated the unfolding of all vMeme potentials.

Awareness, mindfulness, the willingness and capacity to design from an integral perspective were surely pre-requisites for creating conditions where Yellow could show up. Yet one question remained, "How can we maintain this level of being through all challenges in a cultural context (Germany) that is centered on Orange/Green?" While we found a way to maintain a Second Tier orientation within our project and team, we are still learning how to maintain this orientation within our larger community.

The stretch to Turquoise turned out to be inspiring for Yellow and was a profound enrichment. The Turquoise capacity to cooperate and collaborate strengthened each of us and revealed the tremendous collective potential we can rely on when we learn to become Spiral Wizards.

At the beginning of this report I mentioned the following, **"The force behind the vision is derived from the Essence, the Creative Evolutionary Impulse or the Source, and reaches beyond memetics."** We held our faith in this proposition throughout the project. We applied different methods like Vistar and Heart Coherence that support connecting to our essential self on a collective and individual level. We began most meetings focusing our attention on being aware of our essential self as the prime consciousness and then connecting essence to essence. Our intention was to explore how to design from this place, regularly bringing attention to this state with "open mind, open heart, open will" to quote Otto Scharmer. We were successful in stabilizing this connection.

We are still learners in creating Life Conditions for opening to a new paradigm in human relatedness. Beyond helpful methods and techniques, what I think we most need to maintain this connection to essence, are faith, passion and courage: faith in our essence, passion for the work, and courage to design from a future we will only see clearly when we are successful. Is it not meaningful that the word courage comes from French "coeur large" and means "big heart"?

Conclusion

As I have chosen to describe our team building in some linear order from Beige up to Green along the Spiral for facilitating understanding, I would like to recall that in fact the Spiral shows up as a dynamic. The memetic levels do have their own laws and will be triggered to arise according to our personal memetic profile, context and interactions. We will have to address needs of the different existence levels as they manifest, and then recalibrate or redesign if necessary.

In this sense we behave as choreographers in an improvisation dance where dancers (i.e. the vMemes) will move according to specific patterns, not always predictable but bringing their unique potential to the whole issue, wanting to contribute to their best if they are acknowledged and integrated. The choreographer would have the task to connect them in synergy, first within oneself and then invite dancers to do the same. That would start the co-creative memetic dance that a Second Tier perspective may initiate while holding the space for it.

Some Questions For Building A Co-Creative Team

Beige: Do we feel existential fears? How to ensure the survival of the group? Which space do we want to give to the expression of instinct and senses?

Purple: How do we create a sense of belonging and trust? What is our relationship to the other groups? What is the place we want to give rituals? How do we create a balance between loyalty to the group and self-expression?

Red: How do we design spaces for self-expression and visibility of the single team members? How can we use impulsivity as a driving force in service to the whole issue? How do we deal with "turf wars" and claim to power? How do we value respect?

Blue: Do we realize the meaning of our project? What do we define as the "higher" purpose? Whom/what do we serve with it? How do we organize ourselves? Which work processes and structures do we need? Are the different roles clear? Do we need control mechanisms for our work? How do we value morals and integrity in our team? How safe do we feel with our work and with each other?

Orange: Is our vision reformulated in clear objectives? Which strategies do we map out? Do we have evaluation and optimization systems? How do we define success for this project? Do we give enough space for intellectual explorations and experimentation? How flexible do we respond to change? Do we allow a healthy competition within and outside the group?

Green: How to become a community? Do we allow expression and sharing of feelings and banding together? Do we support self fulfilment, personal evolvement, and the exploration of the internal? If so, how do we do that? How do we create a balance between harmony and tensions? How can we deal with the principle of equality while recognizing the uniqueness of each team member? What do we need to take actions?

Second Tier: How do we achieve a balance between operating from a meta-perspective by fully integrating our being and acting in the lst Tier (and doing so ensuring authenticity)? What do we need to maintain or re-establish the connection to the essential and universal self? What is the place we give to evolutionary models and methods? How do we support autonomy and self-responsibility in our group? How do we create a functional design in a team? How much attention do we pay to synchronicities and intuition?

Acknowledgments

In deep gratitude to co-creators: Jürgen Greiner, CHE Germany- Austria-Switzerland and Ingrid Schneider, CHE Germany-Austria-Switzerland. Sincere appreciation to Marianne Froelich for her support and Michael Keller (CHE Canada) for enriching insights

SDi AND RECOVERY
INTEGRAL RECOVERY: A REVOLUTIONARY APPROACH TO THE TREATMENT OF ALCOHOLISM AND ADDICTION

New York: SUNY Press, 2013. *Chapter 5 (Edited)*

By John Dupuy

The story goes that, in the 1950s, Clare Graves was a professor at Union College in Schenectady, New York, teaching introductory psychology to his students. After Graves presented each popular school of psychology (Freudian, Jungian, behaviorist, humanistic, etc.), his students would ask, "Which one is the right one?" SDi[1] was born out of Graves' struggle to make sense of the

---

1   In Integral theory, we use many different developmental models. In Integral Recovery, however, I have chosen SDi as our developmental entry point for its beautiful applicability to the journey of recovery and its ability to help us understand not only individual development but also our development as a species, as well as the many often conflicting moral perspectives that abound in our world. There are, however, many other developmental models, such as those developed by Suzanne Cook-Greuter and Robert Kegan, that are perhaps more empirical in their research basis. But I have found that SDi is an exceptional introductory model and finds immediate resonance with my students, addicts, adolescents, and their families.

Keep in mind that SDi is measuring only one line: that of values (This is the Wilberian simplification of SDi. The Gravesian model actually puts all the lines of development in a vMeme context, influenced by the active vMemes. This is a significant difference in how the Wilberians understand Graves and SDi, which is contrary to all the other instances of Graves and SDi in these two volumes. Editor's note.) In conversation with Ken Wilber, Wilber agreed that SDi is an excellent place to start when it comes to developmental stages, but is by no means the end of the story. Wilber, in his brilliant and highly recommended work, *Integral Psychology,* places in the appendix of the book over a hundred different developmental models ranging from premodern to modern to postmodern. Here we see that there is a commonality among all of these developmental models in that the projection of growth always tends to move from simple to more complex as we move up the developmental ladder, with each senior level having the capacity to transcend but at the same time include the levels of development that preceded it.

apparently contradictory theories and answer the question. His answer was that each school of thought was correct on the level that it dealt with.

For example, Freudian psychology tends to deal with early childhood development; in fact, Freudians seem to think that most of our future is determined by what happens in our early relationships with our mothers and fathers and during toilet training. Jungian psychology, however, deals with a completely different area of psychic development, principally archetypes and spiritual "individuation." Behavioral psychology deals with exteriors, or right-hand quadrants, while virtually denying the existence of the upper left quadrant. Finally, humanistic psychology seems to work best with those who have already achieved some level of ego development and maturity. So the story goes that as Graves began to look at this data, an understanding of developmental levels emerged, which then went on to become what we call Spiral Dynamics Integral (SDi).

SDi has been tested on over fifty thousand subjects in first, second, and third world countries, and has been found to work cross-culturally in all of these diverse environments. SDi offers a hugely important and effective lens to look at human development, both individual and collective. Not only does it help us understand where we are at, but also where we have been and where we are going. SDi helps us understand ethical and moral development as an existential response to ever-changing environmental conditions (in all four quadrants).

As we examine SDi more closely, I believe it will soon become abundantly clear how this tool can add greater understanding and effectiveness to any situation involving our species and how it is an extraordinary tool in understanding and treating addiction. By adding this vertical developmental understanding to treatment, we go a very long way in addressing some of the major issues that have, in the past, stood in the way of developing effective, attractive, and responsive treatment methods.

Let's take a basic overview and see how SDi illuminates the landscape we must inhabit and traverse in our journey of Integral Recovery. Developmental stages in SDi are color coded, and unfold sequentially. They describe eight levels of world views (called "value memes" or "vMemes") that human beings can evolve through over the course of a lifetime. This is an open-ended system that allows for a lot of variation at each particular level, and no discernible upper limit to evolution and growth. Everyone is born at square one and moves on from there. The unfolding stages not only track our individual progress up the Spiral, but also our evolutionary emergence as a species. What keeps the Spiral active and evolving is that the solutions for the challenges at each emergent level can only be answered and met at the next higher stage, which in turn has its own conflicts that are only resolved at the next higher stage, and so on. Thus, the problems and issues of an addict, whom the disease of addiction has dragged down to an unhealthy, Red, toxic egocentric level, can only be resolved and addressed as a healthy, Blue, ethnocentric level comes online (or back online, as the case may be).[2]

Beige, the Instinctive Self, represents the first stage. This is where we are all born; our ancestors inhabited this domain one hundred thousand years ago plus. The ethical concerns at this level are simple sensory motor survival issues. This is the terrain in the first eighteen months of life in a normal developmental process. Our ancestors at this point were living in small bands, and their main concern was eating and not being eaten.

The next stage, Purple, the Magic Animistic Self, emerged around fifty thousand years. Purple represents the shamanistic, magical, animistic stage of human development, represented beautifully in the Lascaux cave paintings in Southern France. At this stage, the world is full of spirits that must be propitiated and communicated with through rituals and sacrifice. The end value espoused here is safety in a powerful, often frightening world of nature dominated by mysterious forces. In normal development, we pass through this wave at one to three years old. Here, a child lives in a magical world, where, if he pulls the covers over his head, he can't be seen because he cannot see you. The clouds in the sky follow him as he walks. Pretty primitive stuff this, but it was at the leading edge of evolution fifty thousand years ago. As the Purple stage emerged, our ancestors were able to organize themselves into larger tribal structures that centered on blood and kinship; human sacrifice was often the order of the day.

The next level that came about (and this is where it starts getting interesting for our purposes) was Red, the Impulsive Self. Red kicked in as a major force around ten thousand years ago. This is the egocentric power level and is represented in the Greco-Roman gods, the Nordic gods, the

---

2   It should be noted that Ken Wilber later developed a stage model using a different color system than Beck. Wilber's color system follows the spectrum of the rainbow and in some places still corresponds with Beck's model. For example, Orange is still Orange, and Green is still Green. There are some subtle differences between Wilber's and Beck's model, chief among which is Wilber's presentation of a Third Tier of development.

Meso-American gods, and so on. At this point in our development, there was no sense of an all-powerful, all-wise deity. The gods were like super heroes with generally bad attitudes. They were mean, lustful, jealous, and seemed to derive pleasure out of messing with humans. In short, they can be seen as personifications and projections of the Red selfish and impulsive ego structure.[3]

In our culture, you see this level of development negatively represented in prison gangs and street gangs. Reds are narcissistic, selfish, impulsive, and basically amoral. Reds are capable of taking only one perspective, their own. This is an important level to understand, as, in my experience, when the disease of addiction takes over and progresses, the moral level of the addict devolves or slides back down the Spiral to an unhealthy, egocentric Red - no matter what stage the addict had attained prior to the onset of the disease. This is shocking to watch from the outside, if it is happening to someone you know and love. It is the horrifying transformation of a person from their Dr. Jekyll healthy self into the psychopathic Mr. Hyde.

This is not hyperbole. It is the transformation that occurs in addiction: we become walking, craving, lying, impulsive, manipulative creatures controlled by the overpowering wants of our primitive, reptilian brains. Addiction is progressive in that the disease advances along predictable lines but regressive in that no matter what level was attained prior to the addiction's onset, the addict will end up at a pathological Red, egocentric stage or lower, with occasional flashes of the old pre-addict self shining through. Others are no longer "thou" in the sense that Martin Buber spoke of, but "it," merely objects to be manipulated, lied to, stolen from, or eliminated, if they threaten the supply of the addictive substance in any way. There is a joke that I often tell in classes with addicts or their families. It goes like this. "How do you know when an addict is lying?" Answer: "When his lips are moving." This does not produce shame in addicts as one might think but is most often met with nervous laughter and relief, as in, "Somebody understands what we've been going through." As the reptilian brain and its cravings take over a person's life, all the higher emotional and intellectual capacities are subjugated to the totalitarian dictatorship of a sick and craving brain. This cancels out about five thousand years of human moral development. If the addict survives long enough, unchecked, this regression can take them all

---

3   See the Homeric literary masterpieces *The Illiad* and *The Odyssey,* paying special attention to the characters of Achilles and Agamemnon.

the way down to Beige. Imagine the addict or alcoholic living in a cardboard box in a back alley, or under a bridge, who emerges only for brief forays to get more drugs and maybe a little food: one hundred thousand years of human development down the drain of addiction.

Traditionally, in our society, it has been organized sports and the military that have served as rites of passage to get young Red vMeme men to Blue. The training goes something like this: you are less than nothing and here's a big surprise for you - you are not the center of the universe. You are going to learn to obey the rules. You are going to learn to work together. You are going to learn discipline, and you are going to earn the right to be part of this team . . . a soldier, football player, marine, and so on. Sound familiar? I was in the army, and I was amazed to watch a bunch of shucking and jiving young men turn into tough, disciplined soldiers in short order under the artful and often brilliant care of our drill sergeants.

This is an important point because in the early phase of treatment we often deal with people at a very sick Red level of development. This means that the treatment providers, while being compassionate (which literally means "to suffer with"), need to speak to clients at the level they are currently at. In Red's case, this means being firm and direct and calling a spade a spade (which would not work with a Green vMeme person, whom you'll meet later). In early treatment things need to be very structured and directive; this is the program, we get up at such and such a time, do yoga, meditate, start class at 10:00 . . . hit the gym at 3:00, and so on. There is not a lot of wiggle room and down time, except to work on assignments and possibly catch up on sleep. Structure, discipline, honesty, and consequences are all things that Reds might not like but can respect and understand. This is why recovering addicts and alcoholics are often very good teachers, because they know all the cons and self-deceptions that addicts are prone to, and addicts in early recovery know that they know.

From Red we move to Blue, The Rule/Role Self. Blue began to emerge about five thousand years ago. This is the stage of absolutist, fundamentalist religion. It first began in the era historians call "the Axial Age," as in an axle, or age of a great turning. This is when the leaders and prophets of the great wisdom traditions were first teaching and transforming their worlds. This age basically started with the sages of ancient India and went on to include the likes of Buddha, Lao Tzu, Jesus, Zoroaster, and Plato, and probably ended with Muhammad. All founders of the great religions in this period taught some version of greater kindness, forgiveness, and the Golden Rule. This was the great "turning." Turning from what? Turning from the bloody and cruel excesses of Red dominated civilizations.

Remember, all vertical stage growth happens in response to environmental pressures and problems that the current stage does not address sufficiently or successfully. Blue brought in the healing balm of a Higher Power that was good, as opposed to jealous and capricious. The concept arose of a holy or divinely chosen community, based on purpose, ultimate peace, sacred writings and teachings, hierarchy, and humility, where ego desires become subservient to a Higher Authority. This was a huge moral leap from the cruel and often chaotic compulsions of Red, reflected again in the egocentric, amoral chaos of late-stage addiction.

In most cases, AA provides a healthy Blue structure for newly recovering addicts: go to meetings, get a sponsor, work the steps, and do what God and your sponsor tell you to. This is dead-on correct in that structure, discipline, and accountability are exactly what are needed for many early recovering addicts and alcoholics to experience Red-to-Blue growth. It only becomes a problem when recovery to Blue is actually not the end goal of the process, when one is aiming for higher-level development or trying to regain the level or altitude the addict had attained prior to the onset of the disease. Early recovery often needs to be a healthy Blue-like structure, but Integral Recovery must help and facilitate recovery to the healthiest prior-inhabited level of development, and higher, if this is feasible and desired by the recovering addict.

Again, the gifts of Blue are humility, service to a higher good, and respect for higher authority, all of which are antidotes for the problems created by Red, i.e. rebellion for rebellion's sake, self-centeredness, and impulsivity. These traits make recovery very doubtful at the Red stage, because one definition of an addict is one who can't stop the downward Spiral of using without outside help, and a Red "Screw you, don't tell me what to do!" attitude makes it very difficult. This is where law enforcement and the court system can be of great assistance in getting addicts into treatment, because our Red addicts do understand power and threats to their autonomy. The Damoclean sword of jail time dangling over one's head can be a fantastic initial motivator, but eventually the motivation toward health and recovery must come from within and from a higher altitude than Red has at its disposal. So, how do we facilitate growth from Red to Blue? By speaking to Red and framing the practice in language that Red can understand. This basic technique applies to change at any level of the Spiral.

Blue is a great moral leap forward from the bloody chaos of Red, but definitely brings its own set of problems that can then only be resolved at the next stage of development, Orange. Blue moves us from egocentric first person (me) to ethnocentric second person (we), where one cares not just about oneself but for the group (family, tribe, nation, religious community, AA group, however one draws that circle). The problem with Blue is that it only allows for one perspective or accepted Truth. Anyone outside of that circle of inclusion or care is the "other," in many cases seen as the enemy to be enslaved, converted, or eliminated. As Ken Wilber is fond of saying, "The Nazis loved their children."

The next stage to emerge in our history and on our personal journey is the Orange, Achiever Self. Some scholars say that one of the major catalysts of the emergence of Orange was the "Black Death," which swept through Europe in the late 1340's and killed from one-third to two-thirds of the entire population of Europe. At this point, it was clear to many that the priests, the relics, and the pope, the whole basic mythic structure, were useless in confronting this horrible plague. In fact, the superstitious belief that cats were the consorts of witches and needed, therefore, to be killed led to an increase of the rat population, which carried the fleas that spread the disease. The attitude that began to take root was, to quote Sgt. Friday, "Just the facts, ma'am."[4] The old answers were no longer meeting current challenges and conditions.

Orange began to show up most strongly, at least in the West, around three hundred years ago. The profound flowering of Orange came with the advent of the American Revolution, the U.S. Constitution, and the Bill of Rights. Orange was characterized by a progressive moving away from the mythic, medieval Blue vMeme into a much more rational, scientific world view. With Orange emerged the scientific method, or rationalism, individualism, modern democracy, the Industrial Revolution and capitalism. Orange brought us the technological revolution that has swept the world and is continuing to transform our lives as the power of our technology increases exponentially. On an individual level, the person at an Orange center of gravity values success, individual freedom, achievement, technology, and skillfulness. The idea is that life is a game; there are winners and losers; the winners get the rewards and the losers don't.

---

4   As Sgt. Friday from the sixties television series *Dragnet* used to say.

One of the important new capacities that emerges with Orange is objectivity, the ability to think about and have feelings about one's cognition. This capacity is limited at this point, but fully flowers at Yellow. At Orange, this new level of cognitive complexity permits one to shift among a limited number of alternative perspectives. Orange can move from a first person, ethnocentric "we" perspective, to a third person, world centric "humanity" perspective. Good examples of this are the Declaration of Independence, the United States Constitution, the outlawing of slavery, and the Universal Rights of Man (the rights of women to vote came through Orange; women's liberation would continue into Green and beyond as the shift from Orange to Green began to shake the foundations of our society with the emergence of the counterculture in the sixties).

The manifold creativity and inventiveness of Orange (or modernity) can be seen everywhere, and a list of Orange's incredible accomplishments would be too long to cite here. But along with Orange's amazing fecundity came Orange's dark and negative aspects, as with all stages on the Spiral. Orange's negative aspects can be seen in the runaway greed of unregulated capitalism, the overemphasis on individual rights to the detriment of the common good, and the push for short-term profit over the long-term health of the commons, be it the health of humans or our natural environment. For all of its problems, Orange has given us many, many gifts, and we shall need these gifts in abundance in our quest for Integral Recovery.

So how does an Orange level of development relate to addiction? When you're dealing with an Orange in recovery, you can really start talking science: brain chemistry, brainwave entrainment, brainwave states, epigenetics, and so forth. As ever more scientific data becomes available, helping us to better understand the disease of addiction, recovery takes on a whole new dimension and the number of scientifically based practices that can be included in an Integral Recovery Practice just keeps on growing.

Enter Green, the Sensitive Self. Green began emerging as a powerful force in the United States around fifty years ago.[5] Among Green's many contributions are the civil rights movement, the environmental movement, women's rights, gay rights, animal rights, and rights for just about any marginalized group that was seen as neglected and misused by the dominant Orange center of gravity. Green was a reaction against the often cutthroat,

---

5   Recently, I heard an Episcopalian priest, Cynthia Bourgeault, say that the Vatican II and the Beatles were the harbingers of the Green emergence.

laissez-faire practices of Orange and unhealthy capitalism. Green represents an extremely high level of moral development and stands squarely against the marginalization of any group or minority (except for largely rejecting Orange and Blue). Green rejects classism, racism, sexism, and discrimination of any kind. Everyone is invited to the party; everyone deserves respect and even nurturing. Much goodness has come out of Green.

Certainly, new issues and problems have also arisen with the emergence of Green. Green attempts to level all values and perspectives to equal status, for to do otherwise would be oppressive, hierarchical, and judgmental. However, all-inclusive, nonjudgmental compassion can mean that Green has trouble making judgments at all, since all truth claims are of equal value. Not that there isn't great value in many of Green's critiques of past and present injustices, as in Voltaire's rallying cry for the French Revolution, "Remember the cruelties!" However, on the downside, when no truth claim is any more valid than another, the only truth is that there is no truth that is truer than any other truth, at least no absolute truth, which is accepted absolutely! This is a performative contradiction, in which the truth claim contradicts itself, and can quickly become a moral, intellectual, and spiritual dead end. A successful Green meeting often consists of everyone getting a chance to share their feelings, since opinions, especially strong ones, are suspect and possibly oppressive. Peaceful communion is the goal. This Green moral high ground can often turn into an irresolute swamp, however, where nothing actually gets done.

The traps and pitfalls on the journey to higher consciousness are many. For those at Green, the sirens' song of nihilistic, narcissistic relativism can sink the ship and end the journey. You have your truth; I have mine; it's all the same. But ultimately, Green's compassion and desire to help heal the world provide a safe harbor so that the journey can continue.

Above the Green stage, Graves found something very remarkable indeed. Instead of the next stage or rung in the ladder, he discovered a whole new tier, Second Tier. Remember, at First Tier, all the stages think their perspective is the only right one, whether it is an ethnocentric Blue perspective or a kosmocentric Green perspective. At Second Tier, however, the realization emerges that each preceding stage is part of the great evolutionary unfolding of our species, and each one is a component part of the Spiral; each stage is needed, and each has its gifts and its part to play to fulfill the symphony of life. The Second Tier approach is to adopt a pastoral attitude toward the entire Spiral, working to help each level express itself in its healthiest manifestation. At Second Tier, we become accepting of all the stages rather than rejecting that which came before. Again, we all start at Beige. There was never a person born at Green or Orange. The task becomes to assist everyone to be the best possible versions of themselves and bring forth that which is good and appropriate at each stage, since we need the gifts that each stage brings.

First Tier

Before we continue our brief survey of the human developmental Spiral, let's look at where we have been and where we are going. Clare Graves called the first six stages we have looked at the First Tier. Before we look at the next emerging stage, let's examine the characteristics shared by all the First Tier stages. Individuals at each stage in this First Tier of our human existential development are characterized by thinking that their way of seeing and valuing is the only correct perspective; all others are skewed. For example, a Blue fundamentalist will despise an Orange rationalist or sensitive Green environmentalist and believe they are both going to hell. The Orange will consider the Blue to be a nutcase Bible thumper and the Green to be a weak-minded tree hugger. The Green will agree with the Orange about the Blue, but consider the Orange to be a Gaia-wrecking, greedy capitalist. In short, First Tier is a food fight with all of these levels seeking dominance over the others. In the United States, we call this fight for dominance "culture wars."

What also occurs at First Tier stages is often a partial or sometimes complete dissociation from the prior stage of development as one grows into a new stage. This is normal and even necessary in the beginning. But it becomes a problem when the goodness and strengths of prior levels are left behind, the babies along with the bathwater. A newly emergent Orange seldom takes the good aspects of Blue along for the journey into Orange, namely the humility and orientation towards service and community. Unhealthy Orange is, in fact, often characterized by extreme individualism, greed, and an "I got mine; too bad about you" attitude. Green will often reject the great gifts of Orange as poisoned fruits of greedy capitalism, not understanding that the technological inventiveness of Orange is what allowed Green to emerge in the first place. Think of the conversations that happen around the dinner table when families get together during the holidays.

One could unpack this problem of the First Tier food fight in a thousand different ways, but as soon as one internalizes SDi on an individual level, or on the level of how humans develop in general, many things become understandable, if not easily fixable, and begin to fall into place.

If the story ended here, we would be in deep trouble, which in fact we are. But happily, as I have said before, "Stress is the mother of evolution." Because of First Tier chaos, something new is beginning to emerge on the horizon, something that is shedding light on a seemingly hopeless situation. What begins to happen at Second Tier is a healthy developmental growth characterized by transcending and including the stage that went before. As Harvard psychologist Robert Kegan says, the subject of one developmental level becomes the object of the next.[6] In Integral Recovery terms, this is represented by the shift from "I am an addict" to "I have an addiction." The formerly in-control addict self is no longer the "I" who is calling the shots, but has now becomes a "mine", something to own and do one's best to deal with responsibly. The controlling subject, at the altitude where the addiction once found its center of gravity, now becomes the object of the next developmental stage in the recovery process.

Second Tier

Transcendence, inclusion, and healing of First Tier stages of development are the tasks of Second Tier, where we can assimilate and metabolize all the strengths and gifts offered by each and every one of the prior stages. Ultimately, this includes forgiveness and reconciliation between the different stages of development. At First Tier, the preceding stages and their failings and internal contradictions are often used as the foil, motivator, or raw material with which to build the next stage of development. And because there is often flack and attacks from the members of the stage one is leaving behind, the relationship with the prior stage is often adversarial and antagonistic. For example, if one were to stand up in a conservative Christian Church and say, "My dear friends, I love you, and the last thirty years have been great, but I now feel called to go study Buddhism," well, you can imagine the reaction!

It is, therefore, in large part up to Second Tier to heal these divisions and dissociations and to work toward allowing developmental transitions

---

6   Robert Kegan, *The Evolving Self: Problem and Process in Human Development* (Cambridge, MA: Harvard University Press, 1982).

to actually become inclusive and respectful of prior stages so that each new stage is ever healthier than the last and no longer seen as threatening by those currently at a lower stage of development. This, I feel, is one of the great promises of Integral awareness, or Second Tier, as it begins to come online more fully within the human family. The agenda or mission of Second Tier is not so much to promote Second Tier thinking, but to work toward the healthy expression of First Tier, since this is where most of humanity currently resides and will continue to dwell for the foreseeable future.

Einstein once said that a problem could not be solved on the level it was created, just as in Spiral Dynamics, the problems and challenges that are created at one stage of development are only truly resolved and effectively addressed at the next stage of evolutionary growth. The stress, crises, and chaos created at one level become the creative matrix out of which the next higher level of development emerges. In the case of addiction, the dragons, the overpowering cravings for drugs, become objects that arise in a context of expanded awareness. Only now can they be assimilated, transformed, and released and are no longer the controlling demons of one's existence. In fact, without these dragons of chaos, crisis, and stress, there would be little higher-order development or growth.[7] As we move from being the controlled prisoner of our cravings to the enlightened Witness, we progressively become freer of our chains and compulsions. This process is the "up-leveling" Einstein was speaking of on the level of the human spirit.

---

7   There is a part of us, or perhaps a force in us, which some identify as Eros, that longs for and strives for health and higher evolutionary growth. But, in most cases, and especially in the case of addicts, I believe it is divine discontent that creates the channels through which this evolutionary Eros can flow.

The United States: Predominant Memetic Levels in U.S. Culture (Where We Are At)

It's important to understand that SDi does not describe levels of people, but rather levels within people. We can all pass through, and retain access to, all of these levels as we grow and evolve through life. We know that Red is concerned with regaining autonomy and honor; Blue with forgiveness and aligning oneself with one's Higher Power, or God's will; Orange with winning and actualizing one's full potential; and Green with restoring one's healthful place in the community of life. That said, here are some general examples of these levels in the world around us.[8] In the U.S., around 20 percent of the population is said to be at Blue; while the predominant center of gravity is Orange (around 50 percent). This puts modern Green at around 20 percent. That leaves a few points for Red and below and 2 to 3 percent for emergent Second Tier. It is also estimated that about 30 percent of Green is what is called "exit Green." In other words, people who have done Green for a while and are starting to find it a cul de sac, insufficient to answer their needs (or the world's for that matter). This means that in the next few years, we could see rapid growth in the ranks of people arriving at Integral Second Tier levels of development. In SDi it is said that when 10 percent of a population arrives at the next emergent level of development, it is a "tipping point" and major shifts occur in culture and society as a whole. These next few years could get very exciting with a Second Tier unfolding, and I believe Integral Recovery will play a significant role.

At each stage of development, we must balance all four quadrants and work the four essential lines or human capacities: body, mind, heart, and soul. At Second Tier, we work to create structures and conditions that will allow the health of the entire Spiral and facilitate growth to the highest levels that individuals and cultures want and are capable of reaching. One might complain this is rather elitist, but it is an elitism to which all are invited. What we begin to understand at Second Tier is that we have to

---

8   The statistics noted in the following sections are from Dr. Don Beck's dialogue on integral-naked.org. See also Beck's website Spiral Dynamics Integral at *www.spiraldynamics.net.*

approach each level of development in terms that it can understand. This is done in the spirit of wisdom and compassion.

Here is an example of how a Second Tier perspective can overcome the problems of a first-tier approach. Ken Wilber recorded a dialogue with a father, referring to the book The War Against Boys,[9] which does a brilliant job of unpacking the problem of Green parents trying to impose their values on healthy, Red little boys by not allowing them to play their very stage-appropriate games of soldiers, cowboys and Indians, and the like. This turns out to be a very unhealthy repression of natural male aggression, as play-acting is a very positive way for this energy to be incorporated and released. If this Red stage is not allowed to be worked out as a game or fantasy, it might be acted out later in life in ways that are dangerous and harmful, such as gang violence.

In the dialogue, the father explains how he taught his five-year-old son with ADD to meditate, using the example of how Spider Man can sit still for hours on end in order to watch the bad guys. Very effectively, this man taught his son how to meditate using language that totally resonated with where the boy was at developmentally. This is a beautiful example of Integral awareness in practice.

On a larger scale, let us take the issue of environmentalism. One can present Blue with all the massive amounts of scientific data available, e.g. global warming, melting ice caps, depleted top soil, polluted and dying oceans, and they just won't hear it. Blue is pre-rational. You could argue science and data until you were blue in the face (pun intended). Blue is simply not there yet. In fact, they will be annoyed. But if you show them a few verses from the Bible (or whatever sacred text they adhere to) and talk to them in terms of desecrating Creation as tantamount to disrespecting the Creator, you will get their attention. At this point, you could say something like, "Let's pray together and ask for guidance and help to be better stewards of our Lord's creation." You will find this gets remarkable results, and you may start seeing real changes. This may be difficult to pull off if you are attempting it from an Orange or Green level because Blue might detect your insincerity or discomfort. But, at Second Tier, the move is possible because you understand and are in touch with your own Blue structure, and you can speak honestly through that part of yourself, while at the same time maintaining your Second Tier perspective.

---

9   Christina Hoff Sommers, The War against Boys (New York: Simon and Schuster, 2000).

The Players and the Values They Represent

Red is an impulsive/egocentric structure, mostly seen in street and prison gangs, such as Crips, Bloods, Aryan Brotherhood, Norteños, Sudeños, etc.

Blue is a traditionalist/absolutistic/mythic structure, seen in fundamentalism, xenophobic patriotism, "law and order" advocates, the "moral majority," and the evangelical movement. On the positive side, blue can also be humble, even saintly, deeply understanding the need for self-sacrifice and putting the higher good or Higher Power first.

Orange is a modern/rationalist structure, emphasizing individualism and personal freedom, science and technology, achievement and success (often materialistic); it's mostly seen in the scientific paradigm, corporate culture, and free market ideology.

Green is a postmodern/pluralistic structure, seen in the sixties counterculture, the environmental movement, civil rights (including feminism and gay rights, basically everyone's rights), postmodernism, diversity and multiculturalism, political correctness, human rights advocacy, and the New Age.

Second Tier, which indicates a "momentous leap" into a higher order of functioning, includes Yellow and Turquoise, and is characterized by Integral and holistic thinking, and an understanding that all previous level are necessary parts of the human evolutionary Spiral. It acts on behalf of the entire Spiral, rather than only its particular level and concerns.

Currently in the U.S., it is estimated that 20+ percent of the population is Blue, 50 percent Orange, 20 percent Green, and only 2–3 percent Second Tier. On the world stage, 70 percent of the population is at the Blue level or below.

Continuing to use the environmental issue to illustrate the advantages of a Second Tier perspective, when speaking about the environment to an Orange person or group, you might say something like, "The numbers show that 70 percent of the population believes we are in the middle of an environmental crisis. If you make a sustainable product, you will gain X amount of market share in the short term, and in the long term, the projections look like this." They will say, "Let us see those numbers!" and you have them. To Green, all you have to say is, "Trees are people too." and you have them. It is preaching to the choir. To Red, the appeal is, "Cut down that tree and you'll be doing hard time!" Another, more positive, approach with Red would be to say, "The wild lands need your protection; we need your courage and strength to be a protector, so here are your uniform and weapons." Give Red an opportunity to be honored and respected. Another cogent argument in regard to wilderness protection for Red would be, "We need the wild places because this is where to go to become men." Bring forth the positive aspects of each stage and thereby neutralize the negative aspects.[10]

As I mentioned earlier, one of the problems with First Tier development is that there seems to be an unhealthy disassociation from prior levels, and many of the strengths and gifts of preceding levels are left behind. Although negation of the prior level is often a necessary catalyst to energize the leap to the next level, this may then be experienced as a death and rebirth and can be quite painful. For example, when one is leaving a mythic, absolutist religious structure (internally) and an organization (externally), it can really be a mixed bag. On the one hand, there may be a sense of liberation and freedom, and, on the other hand, there may be a sense of dread and disorientation, because when one leaves the controlling system behind, the old certainties are left behind as well. This alone can make the leap in perspective too frightening for many.

There is a continuous process of death to the old ideas and assumptions and a rebirth into a higher, freer, larger view or perspective. This is one of the great breakthroughs of Second Tier, the realization that all of our views are relative and depend on the altitude of our present developmental stage. This is not relative in the sense that all views are equal. All views are and were adequate for the challenges they needed to face, but the higher one climbs the ladder, the larger the view becomes, which broadens the perspectives one can take. This allows each higher stage to become, in a very real sense, more adequate.

On the Integral Recovery journey it is very important to make friends with the transformational process itself. Because of the powerful synergistic effects

---

10   As Napoleon is quoted, "A solider will fight long and hard for a bit of colored ribbon." Or again, "Give me enough medals and I will win every war." (Napoleon knew his Red soldiers.)

of your IRP, and the accelerated transformational potential of meditation assisted by brainwave entrainment, transformational breakthroughs may happen quite regularly. Let us state, too, that it is the right of every human being not to transform. As one student asked me, "John, what if I want to stay Blue?" The answer is, of course, that you have every right to remain Blue.

Higher Stages: Greater Abilities and More Complex Pathologies

It should be noted that while our capacities, embrace, and complexity increase at each subsequent higher stage of development, so do the complexities of our associated pathologies. For example, I have often said somewhat jokingly, "There is nothing worse than a really smart addict," meaning that the capacity to rationalize and justify the continued use of the desired substance(s) increases as our brilliant addict spins impressive, epic, and even noble reasons to continue down the road of addiction. Again, this is simply the clever and inventive neocortex serving the primitive, overpowering cravings of the reptilian brainstem. This is an example of a high cognitive level development serving a very low memetic level of development, all of which are being perverted and controlled by the progression of the disease of addiction.

Although we are not absolutely sure what causes stage growth or the transformational leap, the inner pressure or overload that throws one into chaos and upheaval tends to be characterized by dissatisfaction with and exhaustion of the present stage (at least in the case of the suffering addict). As they say in AA, "Sick and tired of being sick and tired." At the same time, there is an attraction to the prospect of growth to the next higher available stage and beyond. All stage growth, spiritual growth, or "escaping into higher order"[11] is chaotic and can feel terrifying if one does not know what is going on. Can you imagine the terror of giving birth if you did not know what was happening? It would seem that you were being destroyed and ripped apart from the inside, instead of bringing forth new life. However, if

---

11   Ilya Prigogine and Isabelle Stengers, *Order out of Chaos: Man's New Dialogue with Nature* (New York: Bantam, 1984).

one understands the process of birth and is prepared for it, it can be one of the most spiritual experiences available to human beings. So it is essential for skillful, conscious growth and evolution that we understand that practice can, and often should, be a process whereby we let the inner pressure increase, and not release it or run from it, because chaos and upheaval are truly the mothers of transformation and evolution.

This is a point that cannot be stressed enough, because early recovery can often be chaotic, and I believe it is often the fear of chaos itself that leads the addict to use drugs in the first place. As we learn to embrace chaos as friend, teacher, and transformational principle of the universe, from chemical reactions, to the human brain, to the evolution of life and consciousness itself; as we welcome and in some sense allow the changes to occur in us, we become not only vehicles of the evolutionary process, but conscious participants in our own evolution. This is exciting new ground for humanity as a whole and recovery specifically.

The developmental dimension is what adds such an important evolutionary perspective to Integral Recovery and puts it in a class by itself as far as the recovery world is concerned. To put it simply, Integral Recovery is a Second Tier approach to treatment, in a world where the cutting edge to this point has been Green. Passing the Rubicon into Second Tier has been likened to becoming a cube in a land of squares. Once SDi has been grasped and understood, one can't just go back to seeing things in the same old First Tier way. Once we can perceive the problem from a Second Tier altitude, then the challenge becomes to bring our skill level up to our ability to perceive. In Integral Recovery this means that we must learn to meet our clients where they are at, framing and individualizing our treatment modalities to meet the client's particular developmental needs. Balancing the quadrants and the five essential lines is the key to recovery and health at any level, but how those are taught and approached must be adapted to the altitude of the client.

SDi And Alcoholics Anonymous

Alcoholics Anonymous and related 12-step groups are enormously important. They have dominated the field of recovery for the last fifty years. It is useful to apply the Integral map to our understanding of AA, and specifically the lens of SDi, to help us understand AA at a deeper level, i.e. understand its successes and failures, using our knowledge of vertical developmental structures. As it is popularly practiced and interpreted, AA is largely a Blue vMeme organization. That does not mean that Bill W.'s original inspiration was not world centric Orange, or even higher, in some aspects. "A God of your understanding" is not a Blue (traditionalist) concept. It is much broader than that. And the self-governing, egalitarian traditions of AA are not conformist in a Blue sense. But many of the AA Lower-Left quadrant cultural beliefs and practices are Blue to the core. These include the centrality of the sacred text (Big Book), which is seen by many as inspired and virtually infallible; the mythic membership culture ("us" alcoholics as opposed to the "normies"); the distrust of science and "experts"; and the fact that there is no easy or honorable way to leave the fellowship of AA. Leaving AA or the group is generally considered the equivalent of relapse or backsliding in many 12-step groups.

These Blue cultural aspects of AA are a turn off to many therapists, as well as addicts, who have a center of gravity at Orange, Green, or higher. But the good news is that many of these issues could be overcome quite gracefully if AA would become more Integrally informed and begin to support growth into Orange, Green, and higher levels of development. In other words, we could transcend and include the positive aspects of AA, the spirituality, the sense of fellowship, the ethic of service, in a more Integral approach. Healthy developmental growth means preserving the baby as we move to our next stage of development, while throwing out the bathwater that is no longer appropriate or useful. The bathwater, however, should also be honored, because it, or the inadequacies of each prior level, is what have provided the drive and the fuel to continue the journey of growth and transcendence. This is one reason why working with addicts can be so exciting and rewarding, i.e. the egocentric addict stage has just become so bloody awful, unacceptable, and deadly that the existential given becomes, "Evolve or die!" The work of healing and growing is not a lifestyle choice but a survival imperative.

Bibliography

Beck, Don, and Christopher Cowan. *Spiral Dynamics: Mastering Values, Leadership, and Change.* Malden, MA: Blackwell, 1996.

Cook-Greuter, Susanne, ed. "Postautonomous Ego Development: Its Nature and Measurement" (1999). Doctoral dissertation, Harvard University, 1999. Dissertation Abstracts International, 60 (06), 2000.

Homer. *The Iliad.* New York: Penguin, 1950, 2003.

———. *The Odyssey.* New York: Penguin, 1946, 1991.

Kegan, Robert. *The Evolving Self: Problem and Process in Human Development.* Cambridge, MA: Harvard University Press, 1982.

———, and Lisa L. Lahey. *How the Way We Talk Can Change the Way We Work: Seven Languages for Transformation.* San Francisco: Jossey-Bass, 2001.

Miller, Melvin E., and Susanne Cook-Greuter, eds. *Creativity, Spirituality, and Transcendence: Paths to Integrity and Wisdom in the Mature Self.* Stamford, CT: Ablex, 2000.

———. *Transcendence and Mature Thought in Adulthood: The Further Reaches of Adult Development.* Lanham, MD: Rowman and Littlefield, 1994.

Prigogine, Ilya, and Isabelle Stengers. *Order out of Chaos: Man's New Dialogue with Nature.* New York: Bantam, 1984.

Sommers, Christina Hoff. *The War against Boys.* New York: Simon and Schuster, 2000.

Tarnas, Richard. *The Passion of the Western Mind: Understanding the Ideas That Have Shaped Our World View.* New York: Ballantine Books, 1991.

Wilber, Ken. *Boomeritis: A Novel That Will Set You Free.* Boston: Shambhala, 2002.

———. *A Brief History of Everything.* Boston: Shambhala, 1996, 2000.

———. *The Eye of Spirit: An Integral Vision for a World Gone Slightly Mad.* Boston: Shambhala, 2001, 2000.

————. *The Integral Operating System: Version 1.0.* CDs, DVD, workbook. Boulder: Sounds True, 2005.

————. *Integral Psychology: Consciousness, Spirit, Psychology, Therapy.* Boston: Shambhala, 2000.

————. *Integral Spirituality: A Startling New Role for Religion in the Modern and Post-modern World.* Integral Books, an imprint of Shambhala Publications, 2006.

————. *The Integral Vision: A Very Short Introduction to the Revolutionary Integral Approach to Life, God, the Universe, and Everything.* Boston: Shambhala, 2007.

————. "Introduction to Integral Theory and Practice: The AQAL Map," published on the integralnaked.org website.

————. *Sex, Ecology, Spirituality: The Spirit of Evolution.* Boston: Shambhala, 1995, 2000.

JOURNEYS INTO INTEGRAL FACILITATION

By Harry Webne-Behrman

With Important Contributions from Steve Davis and Darin Harris

When Don Beck first visited us at the University of Wisconsin-Madison in October 2005, I wasn't quite sure what to expect. Here was the luminary creator of Spiral Dynamics Integral (SDi), a complex and challenging framework that helped us understand people and culture in profound ways. We had launched a study group in September 2005, a professional development opportunity catalyzed by Alberto Vargas and Darin Harris that would be punctuated by Don Beck's appearance at our "Leadership and Management Development" Conference. That six-week learning experience attracted about 25 people, from both campus and community, across disciplines and business interests, from which was birthed an ongoing learning community committed to a deeper understanding and exploration of SDi's possible applications. The Madison Integrals, as the learning community called itself, quickly proposed bringing Don Beck *back* to campus, and this dream was fulfilled the following spring, doing what was once thought impossible: We would sponsor Don for a week of SDi 1 and SDi 2 workshops! This did occur and has led to the learning and practical application of SDi in many of both the town and gown settings.

Don Beck, the gigantic spirit from Texas, arrived in the fall of 2005. What I discovered, what we all quickly learned, is that Don Beck is a generous soul who has dedicated his professional life to solving the critical problems of the planet, and that his methodology, SDi, makes Integral Theory accessible and applicable to taking on those challenges. What I also discovered is that Don is an astute observer and listener, which then informs his capacity as a wondrous storyteller and communicator of the human condition. Members of our community basked in his attentiveness and in his ability to nimbly translate our questions, wonderments, and possibilities into the SDi framework. With all of this intellectual capacity, Don also possesses a special ability to connect with people and inspire them to fulfill their aspirations. The legacy of his visits to Madison in 2005 and 2006, is at least the exploration and development of what has come to be known as Integral Facilitation.

What I find most appealing about Integral Theory and SDi are their capacities to capture a wide swath of concepts and structures in a single bound and challenge us all to see how such things can be applied to our fields of endeavor, e.g. "What vMemes are present?" "Are people open, closed, or arrested?" "What Life Conditions are impinging upon a person?" "What change state is the individual or group in?" In my case, such questions were applied to facilitation and its various flavors of group leadership, mediation of complex disputes, and teaching people skills and processes by which to help groups be more effective. I have been fortunate to partner since 2007 with Steve Davis and Darin Harris to develop and teach a course in Integral Facilitation, "Journey of Facilitation and Collaboration (JOFC)" through which over 300 participants have now passed, and to more recently develop a "Journey Beyond (JB)" course that delves even more deeply into the connections of facilitation to Integral Theory and SDi. Integral Facilitation is alive and developing.

The JOFC course is inspired by Integral Theory and SDi to examine how facilitative leaders, whether in formal roles or simply from their various perspectives within groups, can utilize theoretical insights to more effectively understand the challenges at hand. Don Beck's influence on our thinking in JOFC has been direct and profound. His visits to Madison in 2005 and 2006 directly inspired a number of us on our campus, including Darin and myself, to examine the cultural centers of our campus and to begin to "map" the various sub-cultures of the University in holonic terms: we could see where a Yellow meta view was present or missing; where Green collegiality needed affirmation or not; where Orange achievement supported this collegiality and where Blue rigor and purpose were serving the University, or not. It also gave us a language to share our insights regarding policy and curricular issues: without Blue rules and enforcement there is no foundation for Orange achievement; without Orange achievement and success the Green inclusivity agenda could not be funded; without an inclusive Green vision, there could be no broad sensitivity to critical concerns from smaller voices. We were also sensitized to a number of challenges we were facing and were able to normalize those challenges: stuckness is a normal change state; Orange financial success is required to support Green diversity efforts; ignoring cultural characteristics, is simply forgetting to include one of 4 essential perspectives.

SDi also gave us tools through which to understand meeting process, insights we were able to apply to JOFC training: problems often emerge because important vMeme satisfiers are absent; if the change state is Alpha contentment, change is not on the agenda. In addition, I routinely enter consulting discussions and team meetings with a "4 Quadrants" diagram scribbled on my paper (see diagram below) and use it to map the conversation, understand the questions that need to be asked and the gaps in our analysis of any given situation. This is an easy and portable tool, and we have developed a more thorough "Team Meeting Integral Observation Form" and an "Integral Charter" that we teach people to use in JOFC (see appendix).

The Integral Facilitation Model

We noticed that facilitators can benefit from the four quadrants of Integral Theory as points of departure: Self Awareness (UL), Task Management (UR), Group Management (LR), and Group Culture (LL) become organizing principles for thinking about the range of challenges and needs present in groups. We then articulated 20 archetypes of effective facilitation, placing them within the four quadrants as vantage points for understanding their centers of gravity. Some archetypes serve best a Blue group, others an Orange; some serve culture oriented needs, others group management needs. We next described behaviors associated with each set of competencies (archetypes) and desired outcomes that would be results of expressing such skills: group cohesion enhanced, self-awareness refined, task management made more reliable. The result is a greatly enhanced understanding of facilitation that over 90% of our participants reflect are being applied regularly in their work (based upon feedback from over 300 participants over the past seven years).

Viewing Groups Dynamics

Your Map for the Journey
Archetypes (page 14–15)

Self Awareness	Task Facilitation
Core Values & Intentions (The Inner Guide) Theoretical Knowledge (The Scholar)	Ten Commandments of Collaboration (The Path) Assessment (The Consultant) Process Design (The Architect) Presentation (The Orator) Group Memory (The Scribe Accountability (The Warrior) Roles (The Shape Shifter)
Group Awareness	Group Management
Listening (The Friend) Inquiry (The Investigator) Understanding (The Muse) Forbearance (The Empath) Set (The Shaman)	Setting (The Lover) Facilitating Participation (The Magician) Facilitating Process (The Guide) Intervention (The Interrupter) Conflict Magic (The Mediator) Consensus Building (The Advocate)

These Archetypes help us bring a richer, more complete texture to the "competencies" of facilitation, placing the use of such skills and knowledge within the contexts of meaningful (often Heroic) narratives. We show film and video clips to reinforce the practical behaviors being demonstrated within meaningful stories, as well as consider music throughout the course that helps create a state conducive to the challenges facing learners at a given time. We also have endeavored to describe group behavior and development in terms inspired by Integral (e.g. holons, emergence, systemic dynamics), rather than the usual linear descriptors associated with our field. In so doing, we gain a deeper appreciation of the cultural and vMeme centers of groups, the language associated with such perspectives, and the challenges that facilitative, Integral leaders must navigate in order to effectively support group process and progress. Steve articulated this transformation quite well in a recent Blog post for FacilitatorU.com, as follows:

What Does It Take To Invite The Full Brilliance Of Groups?

Facilitative Structures

- In the JOFC workshop we created a confluence of Blue structures that weave throughout the 5-day journey. After reviewing our approach, you may notice that the shepherding of a fully functioning group resembles the natural cycles involved in the parenting or nurturing of any living thing.
- We design structures of individual involvement that increase in complexity and responsibility over time (honoring the Spiral).
- We introduce increasingly challenging activities that require the application of multiple skills practiced over time (Orange achievement opportunities).
- We purposely introduce and nurture the formation of factional subgroups. This is a natural stage of group evolution that allows smaller groups to create Purple, Blue, Green community with one another.
- Later in the process, we offer challenges that require the resources of the entire group which encourages them to reach outside of these factions (shifting Life Conditions).

Facilitator Attitudes And Behaviors

There are certain attitudes we hold about groups in general and certain behaviors that reflect these attitudes that we believe impact the unfolding of a highly functioning group.

- We share our knowledge of a skill and how it will help the group meet its goals, followed by opportunities to practice it (Blue Structure).
- We teach participants tools to be as present in the moment as possible and encourage them to cultivate their awareness around what's happening within the group at multiple levels (Yellow complexity).
- We believe and act as if the collective intelligence of the group will guide us in helping it emerge and we listen to its promptings (Purple developed into Turquoise).
- We expect and look for synchronicities and encourage participants to do the same.
- As the group matures, we gradually decrease facilitator interventions and contributions, culminating in nearly complete withdrawal from the group.

Participants Attitudes And Behaviors

There are certain attitudes and behaviors that we observe and encourage in participants that we believe also impact the unfolding of a highly functioning group.

- Participants have a strong desire to be part of a high functioning group.
- Participants appreciate the complexity of groups and are patient enough with themselves and others to allow the groundwork to be done.
- Participants are willing to give their all to the group's task but are not attached to particular outcomes.
- Participants share and make requests to meet their personal interests, desires, and needs.
- Participants offer each other honest and respectful feedback.
- Participants understand that no one reaches true community on their own. They reach out to participants to whom they feel less of a connection and seek to bridge divides.

- The sound of the group shifts. The sound of the voices at work in subgroups takes on a hum or buzz. Voices seem to be attuned to one another. The sound of a contained but vital flow that could be likened to the sound of a happy hive of bees.
- The silences are profound. There is an energetic sense of peace, calm, ease…a supreme presence that makes the silences feel very full. One of our participants, a police officer and K-9 handler, brought his German Shepherd into the workshop during the last two days. During the time that we sensed the group had reached a state of high-function, we noticed that the dog had fallen asleep. The room was very active, but there was a peaceful, almost sacred sense in the room.
- Expressions are more clear, direct, even poetic. People are less tentative about sharing their observations, perspectives, and feelings. Communication is more authentic, concise, and respectful. There are few wasted words. Often what's shared seems to contain a quality of wisdom and eloquence that didn't exist before.
- The group becomes more important than the individual. When a group coalesces into a highly functional team, there is less concern with individual needs. The group has evolved and aligned to meet a greater need that transcends and includes individual needs.
- The line separating personal and work life begins to blur. There's something about being part of a high functioning group that shifts our view of ourselves and the world. Being part of such an organism fulfills many of the needs we're all after

The learning communities in JOFC actually undergo such transformation themselves, so they can see groups in new, perhaps deeper ways and begin to appreciate the holonic evolution of groups using deeper, complex processes of inquiry and problem-solving. We have consistently seen this growth through the 15+ JOFC cohorts. Within JOFC and JB, we see the SDi holonics mapping our way, ever Spiraling "forward and inward" towards deeper insights and practices. By always attempting to stay centered and attuned to the needs of the group, the Yellow facilitator dramatically improves his/her capacity to guide the group through its most important questions, see relationships among those questions, and explain answers in terms that can be conveyed to audiences of varying vMemes. "Simulcasting" in this way is key to any efforts at Second Tier process.

We theorized that such learners would then be prepared to learn explicitly some "Second Tier" communication spaces in JB. Our initial effort in Nov 2013 was generally successful, and we are now gleaning insights from that first group to inform a further, more deliberate design attempt in future cohorts. The promise from teaching conscious, intentional Second Tier technologies (applying techniques like Deep Inquiry, Generative Listening, Appreciative Inquiry, Open Space facilitation, etc.) to address group development and challenges, inspires us every day.

We are also exploring states and how they may be intentionally noticed and cultivated. In JB, we paid particular attention to Attunement as a Self-Awareness process from the start of the class, returning to it in various ways throughout the three days. Consistently, the emptying process and mindful meditation practice opened participants to relaxed states of being in which new energy could be summoned. This is consistent with what Scharmer et al have discovered in "presencing" practice, a central element of "Theory U" processes. (Reference: C. Otto Scharmer, Joseph Jaworski, Peter Senge, and Betty Sue Flowers, *Theory U,* 2009). This is a challenge to which we will focus in coming months, and from which we expect to draw powerful insights for our work.

We also made intentional efforts to help participants learn the disciplined distinctions that exist among simple, complicated, and complex challenges and then use design thinking to navigate and map complexity. Simple challenges, in this context, refer to issues that can be addressed with "best practices" and certainty, and where results can be reliably replicated. A cooking recipe is often such a challenge, for example. Complicated challenges refer to those with multiple elements and potential strategies for solutions, but where there will again be agreed upon metrics of successful results. Sending a spaceship to the moon requires many computations, and there may be technical tensions and social tensions present in a group relating to academic disciplines, roles, and work styles, but the outcome for success is fairly evident. There are a number of "better practices" that may be employed. Complex challenges transcend any traditional notion of analysis, as they are characterized by dynamic interactions among elements resulting in unpredictable outcomes. Furthermore, there may be high uncertainty regarding the success metrics in the matter, and if we arrive at a stable state, we frequently discover that this stability is an interlude or an illusion. Much group work is inherently complex, especially as we move into Tier 2 holons and cultural challenges. In science, weather systems are examples of complex systems. In organizations, being able to manage the diverse needs and styles of staff, customers, and emerging conditions requires that we provide facilitative leadership that is nimble, attuned, and responsive to change.

Integral Theory provides an excellent map for understanding these diverse types of challenges and their cultural centers of gravity, and our Integral Facilitation approach is highly instructive to those who wish to express leadership that is attuned to the proper challenges at the proper times. This work emerged some powerful initial prototyping of ideas, identification of high leverage points of systems intervention, and Second Tier organizational forms that are reminiscent of those taught by Don Beck in his SDi II workshops. Coupled with efforts to teach people how to do vMemetic Simulcasting, communicating across worldviews, we believe we are venturing into some powerful new, paradigm-shifting approaches to group facilitation. We have much yet to learn about the potential of the JB element to our Journey, but we are excited by the initial results.

For now, however, our efforts in Integral Facilitation are proving extremely satisfying and are yielding continued insights and practical applications. Since Darin and I also work at the University of Wisconsin-Madison, we have been able to notice the practical application of JOFC training to our campus community: we have been able to tap JOFC graduates for several important campus projects requiring such leadership, with good results. An ongoing community of practice has developed for facilitators, as well as the Madison Integrals' focus on SDi and Integral Theory. We are encouraged these will be resources for further exploration of practical applications in the future.

To close, it has been a transformative experience to know Don Beck and to be influenced by his teachings. Several of us here in Madison have been personally affected in significant ways, and we know from JOFC and JB participants that hundreds more have been positively impacted. Thank you, Don… we look forward to continuing the Journey with you.

Appendix

The following information is used in two preprinted forms in our Integral Facilitation training and execution. Contact the author for this form. The content of these forms follows.

Integral Project Charter

>Project name:
>Project leader:
>Primary stakeholder:
>Sponsor(s):

Upper Right—Task Management (Goals, Objectives, Deliverables):

>Business Case/Statement of Need (why is the project important now?):
>Project Description and Goals (overarching and intangible):
>Objectives (specific and measurable):
>Deliverables (tangible product):
>Project Constraints (elements that may restrict, limit, or place control over project, team or action):
>Customers (direct users impacted by the project):
>Customer Needs/Requirements:
>Stakeholders (those who provide input to project, are affected by project and/or who care about project):
>Major Stakeholder Roles:
>Major Stakeholder Responsibilities:
>Project Budget or Resources Needed:
>Implementation Plan/Milestones:
>Documentation Plan:

Lower Right—Group Management (Systemic Elements, Roles):

Decisional Norms (how do they align with sponsor expectations and group outcomes):

Outcomes (result or consequence of project execution, i.e. result of pursuing objectives):

Historical Accomplishments (lessons that may inform or support this project):

Project Management (team members, roles, responsibilities):

Lower Left—Group Awareness (Cultural/Relational Elements):

Aspects of Culture That Will Support or Impede Members and Goals:
Norms and Values (operating agreements, ground rules, values, that might impact project, including organizational rewards, customs, symbols, stories, etc.):
Communication/Conflict Style Plan (observations around directness of communication and types of conflict that are expected or avoided):

Upper Left—Self-Awareness (Values, Interests and Motivations):

Stakeholder Values, Interests, Personal Expectations that May Support or Impede Project:
Facilitator Motivations, Interests and Biases that May Support or Impede Project (include triggers and methods you might use to be more aware of them):
Facilitators Assessment of Situation:

Team Meeting Integral Observation Form

Task Management Observations

What are the meeting objectives?
How well is the group staying on task?
What's working at this meeting?
What isn't working at this meeting?

Group Management Observations (Process)

What processes are being used to facilitate this meeting
How effectively are they working?
What alternatives would you use?
Are there any structural, organizational or environmental issues you are picking up on?
What interventions have been done?
What interventions could have been done?

Group Awareness Observations (Culture)

What are you sensing about the culture of this group?
How would you characterize the interactions of the participants?

Self-Awareness Observations

What are you sensing or feeling about what's happening in this meeting?
What do you sense about the leader's inner state?

General (Lessons Learned)

What is your general impression of this meeting?
What observations or overall lessons do you have to report?

SDi TRAINING APPLICATION: A SPIRAL LIFE STORY

By John Dickson

My childhood was a typical middle class Canadian experience in many ways. I would call it my Blue period. Son of a second generation banker who had volunteered for the army during World War Two, service and order were major aspects of my growing up experience. Both my father and his one brother were wounded in combat and my grandfather, an immigrant from Ireland who did well in banking, was recognized for his fundraising for local hospitals. Order discipline and service to the family, community, country, humanity was both explicit and implicit in my childhood. Our Ottawa scout troop was run by Royal Canadian Mounted Police Officers who would have made Lord Baden Powel proud with just the right combination of order, discipline, empathy and kindness resulting in boys who learned and achieved in terms of skills and leadership.

The usual school experience became even Bluer in high school when I was sent to a Jesuit high school due to poor grades and an even worse attitude. Even a bad student had to acknowledge that these men were good teachers at worst and some were exceptional. Even a disinterested student had to be impressed with the fact that it took 14 years to achieve full status as a Jesuit and be able to put 'SJ" after their names. Their sense of mission and duty resulted in a combination of high technical teaching excellence combined with a true interest in each student, even ones who were not particularly interested in education.

Service to a greater cause, contributing now for some future group benefit was the background of my life with just a dash of Orange because commerce impacted the conservative and orderly bankers of the 50s and 60s. Good business men were honored in family discussions and even the slightly unethical maneuvers that resulted in success stories were honored as "what they sometimes do to succeed". The exploits both honorable and dishonorable of entrepreneurs like Paul Demarais, founder of Power Corp, were discussed around the dinner table. Demarais' invention of the amazing reverse takeover, contrasted with paying his bus drivers in bus tickets when his first bus business was almost bankrupt in his early days.

After high school I went to Europe for 18 months with money I had earned in part time jobs during high school. Europe was a collage of colors as I stepped in and out of different cultures. I was a student in Paris learning French Blue culture. It was 1968-69 and French students were demonstrating against the ever so Blue French system and advocating communism, anarchism and free love all at the same time. It was a kaleidoscope of Red, Green, Purple and Blue. Meanwhile I learned my irregular French verbs and French Culture from blue haired grande dames who confidently assured the classes of Americans and British that French was the language of international diplomacy.

In Spain General Franco was in power and everyone respected and feared the Guardia Civil, the national police who had the power to do just about anything to keep peace and order. Spain was very safe and almost crime free. Foreigners were told not to talk politics by the government. They said Spain had had enough politics during the painful and bloody civil war. Red to Blue.

In Northern Ireland the strong Blue of British rule was being challenged by the Red of the IRA. There were barricades on the streets of Belfast and rural pubs in protestant boroughs were bombed. Bernadette Devlin was elected MP and preached revolution, and protestant and catholic gangs did battle with the soldiers and each other. This was Red with a strong Purple foundation of Irish culture. Despite hundreds of years of Catholicism, magical places and magical spells still existed as did many of "the old ways".

Having gained a taste for culture and language I took my undergraduate studies in a Mexican University to learn Spanish and Latin American History. This was the 70's so the university students were very Green and constantly challenged the ever so Blue administration. Personally I also encountered the "mean Green meme" for the first time: The cliquish anti-Vietnam war vegetarians who said everyone was equal, as long as they had the same values and world view as the "Green machine". The Vietnam war vets among us were mostly lost in space. They no longer valued the Blue or the Red that took them to war but were equally lost to Orange and Green. This was perhaps my most idealistic period so I will say it was my Green period.

Mexico was another Spiral kaleidoscope presenting a thin veneer of Blue order and good governance driven by Red politicians whose values were those of a 19th century strong man or Caudillo. Every 5 years Mexicans elected a president who could not be reelected and so took care of himself, his family, friends, and their friends. Who you know is everything, the politics of personality and personal influence dominates laws and regulations from the president down to the village mayor. At the same time there was a viable business class that straddled Orange, Blue and Red: Dealing with politicians in Red, bureaucrats and regulations in Blue and dealing in the world of commerce in Orange.

Traveling beyond the end of very rough roads one encountered some of the 260 indigenous peoples such as the Yaquis and Huicholes. They still lived in a Purple world of spirits, ancestors and changing seasons. It was a magical world that cycled through seasons but did not move forward. The spirit world was traveled with the aid of ceremonies and rituals that included peyote and magic mushrooms. Bruhos, medicine men or witches, used plants and rituals to heal the sick and travel in the spirit world.

Upon graduation from the University of the Americas I returned to Alberta in 1976 to find a job and was immediately immersed in the Red and Orange of Alberta in the middle of an oil boom. What was clear was that I was not interested in becoming a small Blue/Orange cog in a large Blue/Orange machine. The world of large corporations was not for me. So I began selling real estate, a strong shift from Green to Orange. I had to pay the bills (my Blue background coming out) and I would set aside saving the world until later. As the thinking person's Realtor, I discovered just how few thinking persons there are "out there", on the street. It was an excellent post graduate education in human nature and commerce. I survived 18% mortgage interest rates, the home grown real estate crash of 1980-83 and branched into selling businesses as a loss leader. I started a successful breakfast club and completed the 80s owning my own home and a commercial revenue property.

By 1988 I found the idea of building a larger and larger real estate portfolio boring. And so with financial security and financial independence within sight I ended my Orange period and returned to Green by accepting a volunteer posting in Papua New Guinea (PNG) to establish the first rural small business development NGO in the country. PNG is advertised as "the land of the unexpected", and indeed it was. It was most difficult to work with my fellow expatriate development workers as a tinge of the mean Green vMeme was always present. I was helping locals survive with their fledgling enterprises. Others thought we should not show the innocent villagers the evils of commerce and profit.

The work took me all over the country to isolated mountain communities where people were still wearing traditional clothes. The old ones were able to tell you that they began having regular contact with the outside world in the 1960s when the air strip was built and a mission station or government post was built. The old people who had moved from the Stone Age to the Space Age in their lives understood our computers better than most. They were clear that these were magical instruments that could only give answers to initiated adepts as with all magical tools and potions. They were right of course.

It quickly became clear to my sharp Canadian MBA colleague and myself, the experienced real estate entrepreneur, that many of the Western business rules and practices that we were recommending were totally inappropriate in that place and time. So we learned and adapted and then we adapted some more. The Purple of PNG taught us that if time is circular rather than linear you have a different perspective. Tight knit communities with no hierarchy and an implicit and explicit assumption of equality wanted to have a local shop but could not keep one open because after it opened the need to achieve equal stasis resulted in unpaid bills and a shop with no food and no capital to replace the food.

The exception to the rule of equality was the Big Man or community leader who became leader by sheer strength of personality, personal charisma, and a keen sense of what the community wanted. The Big Man was a Red leader but strongly tinged with Purple. He was only the leader as long as the community agreed that he was and so combined strong "I, Me" values carefully attenuated by the need to reflect the "We" values and desires of the community, just like any good politician.

The challenge and complexity of our simple little business development NGO led me to communicate with a small business development guru at the Cranfield School of Management and after three years in PNG I embarked on a Masters in Philosophy which quickly got out of hand and became a PhD. It must be said that Cranfield is the most Orange of business schools that I have encountered. It was a meritocracy with a Blue veneer for big traditional British businesses. But there was a sharp commercial edge under the academia. Research was always focused on practical problems that could help real businesses which resulted in their work being highly valued by business; less so by their academic peers.

My research took me back to PNG to carry out an ethnographic study of how rural small businesses survived without the aid of outside assistance. Ethnography was the method because culture and values were the issues that were the greatest challenge for the rural business men. I actually lived in a rural village for five months, sleeping in a thatched hut and sharing in the community life. This is when I lived in Purple. As a result there is a PHD thesis in the British Library and on my bookshelf that identifies all the ingenious ways that village entrepreneurs managed to survive.

Having completed my academic work a colleague hired me as a consultant in his consultancy firm that catered to small and medium size growing businesses in England. I was based in Liverpool which is a cultural phenomenon all on its own. Liverpool is a multitude of small egalitarian villages that all happen to be in one place. I struggle to characterize it in terms of the Spiral probably because Liverpool of the 90s was a city in economic and cultural transition. In 1900, as a major port of the British Empire, it was one of the richest cities in the world. By 1980 most of the industries had closed and there was over 50% unemployment, economic and social decay and then riots.

After Liverpool had gone through a decade of economic regeneration I arrived to find major infrastructure projects had been completed but no economic boom going on, despite the fact that the rest of the UK was doing well. Liverpool was making the transition from the Blue and Red of empire to Orange and Green. Workers no longer followed their fathers into the same job. It was clear that history was not going to be much help as an indicator of the economic future.

During those years I had the privilege of working with numerous small and medium size business owners and managers and found the challenge of adding value to their businesses fascinating. They essentially broke into two groups. The Low-Tec iron fabricators who had been around for generations were traditional British businesses of the 1960s, steeped in tradition. In their own words they were not "pushy" which meant they waited for their customers to call with orders. This group learned that a bit of sales and marketing could actually help their customers and rebuild their profits. The other group was the High-Tech internet and computer based businesses. They were producing world class products and growing at a ferocious rate, usually around 30% per annum. The owner was usually 30 and the VPs were in their 20s. There was no need to teach these people sales and marketing. What we could provide was basic business systems and structures, working with them to develop appropriate processes that made each person or team accountable for the quality and timeliness of their work. This was another shade of Orange in my career, qualitatively different than my first Orange period in Alberta.

In 2002 I was recruited by the International Committee of the Red Cross (ICRC) out of Geneva. This is a predominantly Swiss organization with a particular Swiss culture. It is clear that the ICRC is a Blue hierarchical organization like many until one adds the egalitarian Swiss culture to the equation. In Swiss culture everyone in the village or Canton has a right to be heard and given due attention. Consequently that apparently Blue hierarchical organization does not have the deference coming from below and the "nobles oblige" coming from above. Just when the new comer has accepted that everything is decided at the top, a situation arises in the field where "the field" vociferously disagrees with the stated plan or policy. Incredibly the executive directors and the president listen and adapt the plan based on the input from the field. I do not expect to see this kind of occurrence in the UN or General Motors.

I spent the next 6 years with the ICRC. My first posting was in the former Yugoslavia, Serbia and Montenegro. This is where I learned to be Red. Consensus management was seen as weak and indecisive. Leaders of businesses, or political parties were the essence of Red. Strong personalities were valued, rules and democracy were not. Might made right and to prove it one prime minister and one cabinet minister were assassinated for attempting to bring some Blue order to Serbia. Russian oligarchs did business with the Serbian strong men and it became a major illicit trade route for women and drugs moving into Europe. In their own minds the Serbs were not defeated by NATO bombing, they just recognized we had more bombs and guns than they did so they stopped fighting. They did not welcome the arriving foreigners after the bombing was over.

As a result of the Serb army withdrawing from Kosovo, 250,000 ethnic Serbs immediately left also. They found accommodation in empty houses and apartments throughout Serbia and Montenegro. My job was to do something completely new and untried. I was to develop a program that would return a significant number of the internally displaced people to economic activity. Any informal income generation that would take them off the bread line would do. Normally small business development programs take years to run programs that have a clientele of less than 100. We managed to ramp up a kind of enterprise MASH unit that began active programs within 3 months of my arrival in Serbia and assisted over 3,000 households over a three year period. With the aid of an agronomist who developed micro agricultural projects we developed a range of micro grants and micro loans. It was big, it was bold, and it was Red. I was driven all over Serbia and Montenegro in a peppy Peugeot, cajoling, insisting and encouraging staff. The Serbs loved it.

The ICRC was mixed in its reaction to our ideas and programs. Logistics was asked to do a myriad of new activities for which they had no expertise or systems. Other departments were jealous because the program had a high profile and an even larger budget. Rumors circulated within ICRC from Belgrade to Geneva that the projects were a disaster. My department head in Geneva defended them. Other Geneva executives came to see for themselves and found an astonishing level of successful projects. And like a summer storm, the turmoil and politics blew away. The reason for the success was that we selected motivated beneficiaries and then helped them do what they wanted to do. Simple design but complex execution not often tried by development organizations, and never tried by disaster relief organizations like the ICRC. The new economic program suddenly became "our program" within the ICRC and has grown and been adapted to many countries since that time.

In 2003 I went to the Republic of Georgia to evaluate the existing program and, in parentheses, to design a replication of the successful Serbian program. Georgia was as Red as Serbia for many of the same historical reasons. Always on the border of Russia and Turkey, the Georgians have survived with courageous fighting, devious smuggling and much breaking of imperial rules to survive. During the Soviet era they flourished because of their ability to ignore, adapt and break rules to their own benefit. Georgia had always been Red within the Blue soviet framework. I designed a similar program to the Serb one for others to execute. I was immediately sent to the Palestinian Territories, the West Bank and Gaza.

I would characterize this phase as "Red to Redder". My style of operation in my small corner became Blue, bringing order, consistent values and adherence to principles. It was clear that what was not needed was one more ego or one more hot-head. My objective was to stay alive and pass on some benefits to the Palestinians for whom I worked. It would be possible to write volumes about my 18 months in Palestine so I will be brief. My first three months were in the contentious town of Hebron, tomb of Abraham, important to Jew and Muslim. There was a Jewish settlement on the edge of Hebron that was close to the old city and the tomb of Abraham. The settler strategy was a slow war of attrition against the Palestinians, backed up by the Israeli Defense Force (IDF). Settler women would physically attack Palestinian women and humiliate Palestinian children secure that any retaliation would be prevented by the IDF. And so on Shabbat, when the settlers would walk to the tomb of Abraham to pray they would regularly be shot and killed by Palestinian snipers. Then the IDF would impose another curfew, identify the house from whence the sniper bullet had come and flatten it with a bulldozer. At least one house was always bulldozed.

Hebron was run in the traditional way by the clans. Any municipal government operated on top of this traditional clan power base. So there was a façade of a Blue government system with a true Purple governance and power system that was abandoned by many young men who joined Hamas, dysfunctional Blue, to make a difference where the old systems had clearly failed. While I was in Hebron the Gaza office of ICRC identified a need for an economist to document the breeches of the 4th Geneva Convention. The French and the Swiss perceive anything related to economics, like business, as economics and so, as the in-country "economist" I was asked to go to Gaza and help out. Things were relatively calm in Gaza at that moment and so I agreed.

There are no words that can encompass the Gaza experience. It is a small patch of land 45 kilometers long and 10 to 17 kilometers wide surrounded on three sides by a fence and patrolled on all 4 sides by the IDF. Within these boundaries 1.4 million Palestinians lived, but they did not have it all to themselves. At this time there were 4 Israeli settlements inside Gaza with major Israeli military check points at key points. As we watched, the last vestiges of the traditional clan Purple order were evaporating and Red went to Reddest. The old clans that had operated still had a role but less and less in the old way and more as the ready army of a new firebrand leader. Factions were everywhere. Fatah, the PLO, still ruled but had no credibility and many factions. The people of Gaza were embarrassed that their PLO saviors turned out to be a bunch of self-serving crooks. In the words of one old man, "We thought they would build factories but instead they built themselves palaces". Arafat's cousin had a key position and abused it to become even richer. He was known as the most hated man in Gaza and was finally assassinated by Palestinians after a number of failed attempts.

My job was to document economic problems created by "the situation". The Fourth Geneva Convention states that an occupying force must allow the civilian population to have a normal life. Of course nothing in Gaza is normal so I was documenting extreme cases. In such a polarized context it took months to get past the rhetoric and exaggerations to the facts.

During my 15 months in Gaza more than a thousand homes were bulldozed, hundreds of hectares of citrus orchards were bulldozed, the spiritual leader of Hamas was killed by a targeted IDF rocket attack and the largest IDF military operation since 1967 was launched in southern Gaza. In between all of this I documented and wrote reports and assisted with emergency relief operations when needed.

When I think of Palestine I recall great acts of kindness and great pain, heroic and honorable acts with shades of Purple and Blue as well as unhealthy manifestations of Red and Blue. I took 2 months vacation after leaving Gaza and then plunged into Sri Lanka.

The Tsunami hit on December 26, 2004 and so at the end of January I was sent as part of a team to evaluate and recommend a course of action in the east and north of Sri Lanka where a long running war had taken place between the Sinhalese Government and the Tamil Tiger minority. The government of Sri Lanka is apparently Blue with a significant Orange merchant class in the south. However there have always been ethnic tensions and administrative favoritism to the benefit of the Sinhalese (Buddhist) majority with occasional outbreaks of violence on both sides. There is a strong under belly of Red within the government ranks, encouraged by the Red Bhuddist priests who own large tracts of land and act like land owners rather than spiritual leaders. This intolerance is demonstrated by Red speeches, "My way or you pay the price." non-judicial killings and disappearances, always to the Tamil minority.

On the Tamil side they have historically been ruled by law and order, Blue. As their economic situation deteriorated after independence the Blue reverted to Red as a coping mechanism to the unequal treatment. About 25 years ago the Tamil Tigers were born with a charismatic leader who survived until the end of the war in 2009 when the Sinhalese government troops finally defeated the Tigers. The Tigers are the inventors of the suicide bomber, the poor man's smart bomb. In the years before their defeat, they had developed a web of commercial interests and an efficient network of tax collection that extended to the Tamil Diaspora in Europe and Canada. While the rhetoric was Blue, one felt that it is a Red-Blue transition stage at best.

After three months of assessing and communicating the plan I continued to implement a part of the plan in Jaffna, the heart of Tamil country. The relief plan was complex in execution but culturally and politically Jaffna was relatively calm and so my approach was Blue order.

In 2007 I accepted a job in Darfur which was a step back into tribalism and Purple. In this situation the job was to assist mountain villages to support the thousands of kin who had been driven from their homes on the Savannah. This is a piece of the world that has been pushed into self-destruct mode, assisted by a national government and foreign commercial interests. The Arab militia, the Janjaweed, who are pastoralists, and the displaced Fur tribe, who are the agriculturalists, are all victims of a government that is dominated by a different group of tribes and eager for oil profits from depopulated lands.

I have come to love the warm embrace of Purple, the order of Blue and the idealism and warm embrace of Green. I have come to appreciate how Purple communities value each community member and each family member. I understand the heavy burden or impossibility of pulling the whole community forward and thus the need for Red to launch out on its own. I appreciate much more the Blue order and good governance that we experience in Canada that allows for Orange to flourish and pay for the Blue and the Green.

After 19 years of globe-trotting I decided to become a Canadian again, sharing time with my family and experiencing my first Canadian winter in 19 years. I built relationships with aboriginal businesses and did work for Parks Canada and the department of Indian and Northern Affairs, all related to community economic development in the Canadian north, north of the 60th parallel.

As the post 2008 recession settled in, more and more funding programs for Canadian economic development were cut by the Blue order, Conservative government. Every dark cloud has a silver lining however and the economic change nudged me into sharing the Spiral with medium size Alberta businesses who still have a robust oil economy. Canada is a country of immigrants so a company must manage staff from around the world with differing mental pictures of "what is normal" and "how we do things around here", all the while delivering a consistent level of service to their clients. Orange Alberta businesses are learning how to manage Purple, Red, Blue and Green. There is a role for the Spiral in business too.

I have been working with diverse cultures assisting them to "take the next step" for 19 years. All of my work since 1989 has been based on adapting my knowledge to the local situation so that the community or individual could see around the next corner and move forward in confidence. As I become more knowledgeable and skilled in my understanding of SDi I am sure that there will be opportunities to combine my past and present experience and share them to greater effect.

TURQUOISE RESEARCH PROJECT PHASE 1 REPORT
A REPORT OF FINDINGS IN THE EMERGENCE OF A HOLISTIC WORLDVIEW.

Compiled By Peter Merry with Ard Hordijk.

Center for Human Emergence Netherlands' School of Synnervation

The Impulse

This research project arose from a need, articulated by many people in the Center for Human Emergence Netherlands during the autumn of 2010, to stop and sense into what they were being called to do at this time. Following on from an intense engagement with issues surrounding sustainability and climate change, we had been asking ourselves what would really make a difference and when do we feel energised? We felt that our current approaches, although worthy and innovative, were simply not adequate to the Life Conditions that we were encountering. Countering complexity with complexity wasn't working, we needed greater simplicity, energy and clarity. That led us to a collective feeling that we should consciously and structurally take that need seriously and organise ourselves to look into what we were sensing.

This project was designed for the CHE NL as an integral, disciplined and playful research journey into the nature of that new paradigm, which we sensed was closely related to a shift from Spiral Dynamics Integral (SDi)

Green/Yellow (Harmony-Integration driven) to Yellow/Turquoise (Integral-Holistic). We felt that this new paradigm would be likely to cover noetic sciences, intuition, subtle energetics, quantum physics and many other labels all trying to name the same thing from different perspectives. Our research would be action research, meaning an iterative cycle of testing out insights gained in our daily practices, reflecting together on the results, gaining new insights and trying those again…

Assumptions And Intentions

The assumptions we had at the start of the project that brought up the impulse for this project were:

- The complexity and intensity of the challenges we are facing in the world today can only be met from a new paradigm. From one perspective this paradigm is far more complex than the dominant one in terms of the scope of reality that it can embrace, but in its expression and form it will appear almost too simple to believe.
- The world is in a non-linear transition period. The ways to cope with the current complex challenges are a quantum leap beyond current mainstream solutions. It is our work as the Center for Human Emergence to explore, name and apply potential new ways of coping.
- Industrialised society is currently founded on a paradigm characterised by rationality, objective science, reductionism and scarcity (leading to the drive for ever-increasing growth).
- The new society, while acknowledging the importance of rationality, distinction and linear growth, will reintegrate the more feminine principles of compassion, interconnectivity and natural cycles, in a new synthesis that expands on and embraces the best of the past.
- A core component of that interconnectivity will be found in work through the heart that engages the more subtle, generative dimensions of reality that give birth to our gross, material reality.
- There is a subtle energetic dimension comprised of potential, in which the laws of quantum physics operate. It is generative. It works on principles of attraction, relationship and wholeness.
- The gross world (material, relative, bounded forms) crystallises out of the subtle dimension. In the gross dimension the laws of Newtonian physics operate. It is degenerative. It works on principles of expansion, distinction and partness.

- Human evolution over roughly the last 500 years in what is now the industrialised world has focused on developing the more masculine dimensions of growth, objective rationality and domination of the natural world. In our excitement at taking this step, we forgot to build on the rich inheritance of the previous cycle of civilisation that expressed more feminine principles that honoured the Earth, relationships and perpetual cycles. Instead we oppressed and suppressed that dimension in ourselves and others.
- A significant part of giving birth to the next expression of the feminine dimension will include healing our individual and collective relationships to the Earth, our bodies and each other.
- The new ways of being are already emerging in different areas of human society: energetic healing of individuals, organisations and eco-systems; technologies based on the earth's natural gifts of gravity, magnetism and harmonic proportions; governance models that honour individuals' contributions whilst nurturing the commons nature of natural and intellectual resources

And finally, we thought it would be of service to humanity and ourselves at this time to name new-paradigm practices more explicitly, investigate the patterns that connect them, experiment further with their application and tell a story of an emerging new civilisation that is actually already here.

At the outset we identified a purpose and some guiding principles for the project.

- **Purpose: What does this initiative want to become?**
  - An action-learning community exploring and expressing how insights and practices from new paradigm disciplines can contribute to societal transition for the good of the whole.

- **What principles might guide our practice in this initiative?**
  - We take an integral approach, honouring all relevant perspectives.

  - We acknowledge that the observer impacts the reality they observe, and explore the implications of that fact.

  - We continually challenge ourselves to push the boundaries of our assumptions.

  - We allow ourselves to be guided by open heart and mind.

  - We hold seeming contradictions in the light and wonder.

The Research Question And Process

The research question that we used in our research was:
- What expressions of Turquoise showed up in people, in the interactions between people, in the behaviours of individuals and collectives and in technologies and how does this inform our understanding of the Turquoise Value System?

There were three main phases in this first part of our research.

1) Create an Integral Research Framework, to make sure we can support/accommodate research within a defined container of practice (see below), led by Ard Hordijk.

2) Apply the research framework to 3 contexts:

   a. A scoping study for ether energy technology being undertaken by an experienced Steiner-inspired team (research lead by Lisette Schuitemaker).

   b. Solutions to Climate Change at COP16 in Mexico (research lead by Anne-Marie Voorhoeve).

   c. CHE NL's own experience of applying a Turquoise perspective to our organisational development (research lead by Jasper Rienstra).

3) Harvest and integrate findings, then present our initial reflections (lead by Peter Merry, with Ard Hordijk).

The Integral Research Framework

Inspired by Ken Wilber's Integral framework and the development of that by the Integral Research Center, we decided to create the simplest guiding framework that would ensure that all four major perspectives were explored (the interior experience of the individual, the behaviour of the individual, the shared collective experience and the structural reality), through the "big three" lenses, i.e. my individual experience as a researcher, our collective insights as a research team, and objective facts we could observe.

In this project, we translated Integral theory into this guiding framework:

Content Process	I "The Beautiful"	We "The True"	It "The Good"	Output
0. Letting Come—Create meditative state/field of unity.				
1. Self reflection. What expressions of Turquoise did I experience today?	In me?	In the interactions in the team and with others?	In the behaviors in the team and others, and technologies around me?	Artistic creative expression. Journaling, drawing, painting, etc.
2. Dialogue. Share in circle exchange. What expressions of Turquoise did I experience today?	Our individual experiences.	Our interactions in the team and with others. Clarify, understand; real in-depth check in with each other.	The behaviors in the team and others, and technologies around us.	Sensing into. Coming into resonance with expressions as impression. Output in some form of "what did we experience?"
3. Analysis. What are the patterns we just heard?	Building up an individual understanding of what Turquoise is.	Comparison and integration of what Turquoise is in patterns, analysis and experience of today. Our interactions in the team and with others.	How patterns show themselves and recognizable themes. The behaviors in the team and others, and technologies around us.	Draw conclusions for today. A comparison and integration of today's experience with our latest understanding of Turquoise.
4. Invitation. After this reflection, try to match and fit what you've found onto past experiences and describe what it is you are going to look for tomorrow.				
5. Letting Go—to make sure tomorrow brings what it can free of expectations.				

© Center for Human Emergence Netherlands 2011

Applying the Research Framework

We applied the framework in three very different contexts in different ways to see how it would work and what variety of data we might be able to generate.

1) The **ether energy technology project** involved our project lead attending all meetings of the team with the framework in mind and writing a concluding report of her findings (thus using step 0 Letting Come, 1 Self reflection and 3 Analysis). In addition, Peter Merry hosted a half-day meeting with the team to elicit individual and collective perspectives on their paradigm and experience using the framework's process steps and questions.

2) Data for the **Mexico COP16 climate change project** was gathered as our international Meshworking team from the Hague Center attended the event and reflected on their own experience of Meshworking there, as well as the solutions they encountered that seemed to be coming from a more holistic paradigm. The team went through the research process steps during the Mexico COP16 period several times and on the basis of that wrote an extensive report. On their return Peter Merry and Ard Hordijk hosted a feedback session to draw out more of the individual and collective insights and experiences again using the process steps in the framework (step 0 through 3).

3) Data for the **CHE's own context** was gathered by the project lead attending a number of internal meetings and sessions, and through the analysis of different texts produced by the organisation. A written report was produced for each of the meetings using step 0, 1 and 3 of the process steps in the research framework. The texts were analysed for expressions of Turquoise after the researcher grounded himself in a meditative state (step 0).

Harvesting and Integrating the Data

Ard Hordijk and Peter Merry gathered all the raw data from the three projects and pulled out quotes that seemed to them to be a reflection of a holistic Turquoise paradigm. Then, inspired by, but not claiming to be a rigorous application of, qualitative research, we identified qualities that the quotes seemed to be pointing to, creating labels for each quote that multiple quotes often shared. From those groups of qualities we identified emerging themes, broad-brush descriptions of the nature of this holistic paradigm. Those themes were clustered based on a sense of relatedness into five memos, which make up the five chapters of findings below.

Research Findings

The sections below represent our initial findings about the nature of this emerging holistic consciousness known as Turquoise in the SDi model. It is important to note the following:

- The research does not claim to be comprehensive or academically validated. It is simply our inquiry to the best of our ability and resources into something we sensed emerging in and around us. We welcome connections to any other research that readers are aware of that could enrich our understanding and practice.
- We are conscious of the fact that the ideas, intuitions, assumptions (as also described in the section Assumptions) on the nature of Turquoise we had at the start of the research influenced our findings. On the one hand we see these ideas, intuitions and assumptions as valuable, unavoidable and useful inputs. On the other hand we hope that the research process helped us in being as open as possible to new and contradictory findings.
- We see these findings as one step and hope they may trigger some fruitful reflection and collective exploration. They are helping us make explicit something that we have been sensing more implicitly, so that we can become more conscious of it ourselves and develop these dimensions of ourselves more adequately where and when appropriate. We certainly experienced ourselves that working on the research was psycho-active itself. We hope this report may serve you in that way too. Either way, do let us know!

The five sections below are:

1) Effortlessness, simplicity and trust.

2) Inner and outer worlds.

3) Energy fields.

4) The transrational and multi-sensory.

5) Vitality.

First we include some of the quotes to give you an impression of the raw material that we worked with and with that an impression of the nature of Turquoise.

Quotes

"And all of this in lightness! No clinging to what is heavy,
no grieving about something that did not work,
no pressure to fit into a certain perspective"

"Simplicity evokes. There is no fear that in reducing complexity
one loses content. A mastering the art of being at the heart of the
matter."

"Show up, presence, and feel what needs to happen.
Letting go of past plans. "

"Turquoise provokes a being rooted in something timeless.
The pressure existing, although felt, is not hurting you as person
and becomes inexistent within. It supports some connection within.
Everything is perfect as it is. "

"Turquoise is more spacious and at the same time more full.
It supports a way of act and re-act. In this regard it reinforces the
effortlessness."

"Clean energy attracts and is visible—there is a sparkle"

"During this time it was the first time that I deeply felt the oneness of inner and the outer work. I felt clearly the impulse to expand and contract, to open up and at the same time to focus within myself, to getting into a space of non separateness and simultaneously being aware of my uniqueness and centeredness"

"An important and powerful insight was noticing how the elements of rain, sun, wind and animals were synchronously responding to the energy that the group was experiencing. When the group was in doubt or unbalanced the sun was covered by cloud and started raining, however when the group was reaching clarity the sun would come out and light just the group or the person bringing light to a certain situation."

"It was something I was dreaming of deep inside of myself for quite some time, yet before I had no idea where to find it"

"It needs to be experienced with the sensory senses of the body, the sublimated emotions of the heart that connect us with the wisdom of spirit, the rational mind can strategize the way..."

"Being aligned in group created resonance and interaction with the environment, as a mirror and information."

Memo 1 for CHE NL Turquoise Research: Effortlessness, Simplicity and Trust

Introduction

This memo explores the relationship between a number of the themes that have been distilled out of our inquiry into Turquoise:
- Effortlessness.
- Getting to the essence.
- Sense of the sacred.
- Simplicity.
- Trust in life and spirit.
- Wholeness as goal and perspective.

This is a story of how, by trusting in life and spirit to take its natural course, each action and step is experienced, and seen by others, as effortless and simple. This brings a quality of being, more than doing, which gets to the essence.

Being

When we are in the moment, things naturally arise (or not). Experience often carries a quality of surprise and unexpectedness. Resting in being also draws the attention to the essence of things. People report a natural tendency to slow down and pay attention to the fundamental nature of reality they are experiencing. Turquoise brings forth a way of being that is rooted in something timeless.

This quality of being also creates ease with everything that arises. Experiencing that everything is perfect as it is. This also enables Turquoise consciousness to work with everything that is. For example, while you might feel inner pressures and tensions, they no longer hurt you as a person.

Turquoise is simultaneously more spacious and more "full". It supports a way of acting and responding that flows from effortlessness.

Letting go

People also describe a process and state of letting go, of expectations, of plans of how it should be, of fear that they will not end up where they wanted to be. There is no clinging to what is heavy or grieving about what did not work. Also there is no fear that in reducing complexity one loses content.

Effortlessness

The sense of effortlessness is described as open, light and imbued with curiosity. It creates space and quickens creativity, allowing subtle energies to flow and serendipity and synchronicity to happen. People also report joy and celebration of life.

Simplicity

People describe this quality of simplicity as being at once at ease and without distraction. Expressions of Turquoise are clear and complete, simple and yet pregnant with implications.

Trust

It seems that effortlessness and Turquoise consciousness start with trust, i.e. trust in spirit, in the whole of creation and in one's own experiences and impressions. If that trust is there, connection to the subtle energies can be made and effortlessness arises. People also mention trust in the unknown, or that trust enables them to step into the unknown. Being open and trusting that what can't be seen yet exists, together with the wholeness of body, mind, spirit and soul.

Memo 2 for CHE NL Turquoise Research: Inner and Outer Worlds

Introduction

This memo explores the relationship between a number of the themes that have been distilled out of our inquiry into Turquoise:

- Experience of unity between inner and outer worlds.
- Alchemy of interior states.
- Deep communion enhancing individual agency.
- Holding I-We boundaries.
- Cosmo-centric morality.
- Life-resonant forms.

This is a story of the interplay between inner and outer worlds, between what we experience inside ourselves and what manifests in the world around us and our relationships to it.

In its essence, what seems to emerge as Turquoise consciousness is a conscious awareness of how my inner state co-creates the reality around me and how forms outside of me energetically impact me. This consciousness is also conducive to practices that enhance inner states and outer forms for greater resonance and vitality.

Flow And Synchronicity

In the research data, we discover this phenomenon in experiences of flow and synchronicity, when people feel aligned and open inside and when there is an intentionally created collective field. When those individual and collective inner qualities are present, things seem to fall into their natural place. People show up at just the right time to do what needs to be done. A need has hardly been expressed before it is met in some unexpected way.

Nature Interaction

One element that was mentioned often, especially in the Mexico context, was the way in which the natural world seemed to respond to the energy of a group. When the group was coherent and vibrant, animals would often come close and observe. When things were tense, the sky would cloud over. When breakthroughs occurred, a shaft of sunlight would appear. Likewise, if people had a question or a need and they paid attention to the natural world around them, then they would often find inspiration in some resonant form of nature.

Inside-Out

This awareness of the interplay between the inner and outer worlds also is taken beyond a passive witnessing. People and groups seem to have an individual and collective self-awareness that enables them to be aware of tensions in themselves or their group, name them and transform them without judgement. This "inner alchemy" is not done just to make themselves feel better, but because there is a deep recognition that by shifting tensions in themselves, they are shifting tensions in the world around them.

Many people refer to the experience of seeing patterns in themselves or their team reflected in the groups that they are hosting. The responsibility for having a coherent field yourself is thus extended beyond your own interest to that of the people you are trying to support. Being coherent ourselves generates coherence around us, as tension in ourselves reflects tension in the field we are working with.

Morality also appears on the scene in this context. The moral orientation of an individual or group seems to impact on their access to information, synchronicity and progress. Morality certainly transcends the sole interest of the individual or group involved, and seems to orient most often to the good of life as a whole.

A particularly striking dimension of this characteristic is how inner realities seem to impact on technology. A recurring theme is that the intention of an individual or team seems to impact on the efficient functioning of technologies that work with more subtle dimensions. Should the intention be more selfish, then the technologies seem to get blocked in their development and working. A certain resonance of consciousness seems to turn them on and off.

Outside-In

Working from outside-in is also part of this consciousness. People are very aware that the physical forms that they create will impact on the energy of a field. So a lot of care goes into creating uplifting, grounded and coherent working spaces for collaboration. Principles of sacred geometry are consciously applied to the design of objects. In the distributed energy work, for example, the physical constitution of the space that is created for that energy to be accessed is carefully constructed with specific materials and proportions to be as resonant and attractive as possible.

There is also a greater awareness of the importance of the state of our physical bodies in terms of how that creates the conditions for our energetic work. Seeing our bodies and physical spaces as "temples" becomes a lived truth, rather than an espoused concept.

Another dimension to outside-in is an awareness of the energetic cycles of time. This often involves a conscious practice of attuning to the different energies that certain phases in time cycles activate, knowing that different energies are more or less supportive of certain kinds of action. It also involves noticing synchronicities between the energy of a certain time and our experience at that time.

Me, You And We

The interaction between inner and outer worlds is often most palpable in the relationship between an individual and an other or group. It would seem that as individuals express greater agency in a grounded, light and open-hearted way, then the other or collective field is also uplifted. In fact, it is reported as a 2-way experience. When an open and coherent collective field is established, individuals feel invited to really step into their own power and identity, contributing what they can uniquely contribute to the needs of the whole. Individuals in this context never have to compromise themselves for the collective; in fact, the opposite is true. We are uplifted in the expression of our individual potential in a way we could not have been when isolated, and likewise the collective is strengthened through that individual power making itself available to the whole. Connection through an open heart is mentioned many times in this context.

Memo 3 For CHE NL Turquoise Research: Energy Fields

Introduction

This memo explores the relationship between a number of the themes that have been distilled out of our inquiry into Turquoise:

- Working with subtle energy.
- Field dynamics.
- Nonlinear time.

This is a story of interconnectedness, of experiencing ourselves and the world around us as fields of energy that interweave and interact. There comes a realisation that the physical boundaries we see with our eyes are only one dimension of reality, and that at the energetic level there is a system of flow and movement within and between seemingly separate entities. We sense how our thoughts, emotions and intentions impact on the energetic dimension of reality, shifting the probabilities of one or other material reality manifesting. At the same time we notice how the frequencies of other entities resonate with us.

A Field Beyond Time And Space

A common theme was the experience of a collective field that seemed to exist as a result of the interactions of individuals in that collective, yet at the same time independent of the individuals themselves. It could be experienced beyond the moments where the team was actually physically together, yet needed regular attention to maintain its quality. Any time a group did reconvene, they could sense a reconnection to their field. When not together, people could draw support from a sense of its presence.

Within this field, time also seemed to show up differently, with past and future converging into the present. Time became more cyclical, with echoes from the past repeatedly showing up until addressed and a sense of many potential futures being present at once. It was seen as important to be aware of the history of a field that you may be stepping into or connecting to, feeling gratitude for what has been and what has brought us to where we are now, and releasing any antagonism towards that history.

People's subjective experience of time also changed, with a sense of spaciousness, e.g. having the time needed and things happening "at just the right time". Synchronicities were common (see Memo 2 for more on this topic).

Energy in Space and Time

One of the most frequently recurring themes was the importance of giving attention to the energetic quality in a physical space at a certain time. So when a group created a space to do work in, they felt how important it was to set a tone in the space through some ritual work or collective intention.

This was experienced as particularly important when creating a space for others to come into. Participants would comment on the feeling of the space. The kind of interactions that went on between people in a specific space were seen to be influenced by the quality of energy that was present and nurtured in the space.

Elements of this work included connecting to the geographical place where you are, greeting it, asking permission to do the work that you want to do, asking for the help of any energetic entities that may be present in that space, visualising clear and vital energy, connecting to more archetypal energies such as the four or seven directions (i.e. North, East, South, West, plus up, down and centre). Also important was the recognition of energy in inanimate objects. Bringing particular objects that hold meaning or symbolism was also seen to impact the energy of the space.

Processes with the group of people in the space were also seen as important in setting the tone. This function is performed by a "check-in" and "check-out" round, to bring people's voices and intentions into the space at the beginning, and then close people's energetic connections with it at the end. Reading special texts such as prayers or poems can also play a key role. Instruments like chimes and conches are also often used for this purpose.

The Importance Of Intention

The intention of an individual or collective was often experienced as critical to the energetic dynamic of a place or relationship. Greater coherence around intentions was achieved by making people's goals explicit, naming visions or dreams that may be in the room, noticing and pointing out alignment and dissonance.

In a collaboration context, having people's intention focused on supporting the collective made a big difference in the quality of the results that could to be achieved together. Developing a discipline in oneself and creating the conditions in the collective to transcend individual fears impacted very positively on the energetic field in a group and how it could support people getting things done.

It was also commonly experienced that we attract the energy that we ourselves are radiating. So if we are in a positive, creative mood, we tend to meet things that support us in that. However, if we are feeling sorry for ourselves, then we are more likely to be reinforced in that belief. We are seen to be sending out a message about ourselves based on the beliefs we are holding at a certain moment which resonate with and activate similar energies in the world around us.

Thinking And Feeling Energetically

An underlying theme in all of the sub-themes is the way we think about reality. In Turquoise consciousness, people tend to think more naturally in terms of energetic resonance, frequency and vibration. So there is more awareness about colours one may wear or work with, particular sounds one might use, the form of and proportions in objects, the use of the voice for words or music.

Once this awareness of an energetic dimension to reality is present, people tend to be more comfortable talking about different beings or entities that may exist in this dimension, and ways to interact with them. It is felt to be more acceptable for people to share information they have received from sources that others cannot see or feel.

Memo 4 for CHE NL Turquoise Research: Transrational And Multi-Sensory

This memo explores the relationship between a number of the themes that have been distilled out of our inquiry into Turquoise:

- Grounded in the body.
- Heart over mind.

- Importance of transcending the rational in full human experience.
- Working with non-rational sources of information as an aid to development.
- Acknowledging the validity of our subtle inner worlds.
- Ability to hold different states at the same time.
- All perspectives hold information.
- Holding the whole and the parts.

This is a story about the ability and need to simultaneously sense through and as body, heart, mind and soul, the rational and verbal as well as the non-rational and non-verbal.

People stressed the importance of being grounded in the body, as a means of getting a deeper sense of what was happening in and around them. Bodily sensations were seen as providing vital information. People recognised resonance between their bodily sensations and the energy of what was happening around them.

People also pointed to the importance of listening with an open heart. This leads to a deepening of presence, vulnerability and openness and enhances the quality of attention. Access to Turquoise is seen to be possible only when the attention shifts from the sometimes rigid rational mind to the openness, stillness and true vulnerability of the heart.

The intuitive and transrational, subtle senses were often mentioned and expressed. For many, this felt like reconnecting with something that had been living in them for a long time, to finally take it seriously and accept it as valid. Others described it as the process of taking less interest in the gross forms, turning inside and coming to a state of co-creation which is free of forms.

These different senses are not experienced distinctly and sequentially, but simultaneously. All senses are seen to be important. There was no particular preference for concrete facts, occasions, or bodily sensations over subtle intuitions and systemic insights or vice-versa.

In addition to this multisensory experience, comes the ability to hold paradoxical perspectives in consciousness: focused/open, gross/subtle, systemic/detailed, parts/whole. This capacity was seen as contributing to the healthy development of the system and/or individual.

Memo 5 for CHE NL Turquoise Research: Vitality

This is a short memo that covers two themes that we felt did not fit any of the other memos:

- Showing up fully.
- Vitality.

In its essence, this is about how, when we are connected to Turquoise, a strong sense of life force seems to flow through us, liberating, playful and carefree. In the first of the two themes above, the experiences were about being able to be fully present and transparent, with nothing to hide, no fear of inadequacy, and an energy of openness and radiance. In the second, people reported a sense of playfulness, creativity, being fully alive and energised. Our sense is that this more yang-like quality may be a taste of Coral emerging, as Yellow starts to shift under influence of Turquoise.

Appendix 1—Turquoise: A Starter

Peter Merry wrote this piece inspired primarily by the Spiral Dynamics book (Beck and Cowan, 1996), Barrett Brown's ideas and his own experience.

Qualities Of Turquoise From The I, We And It Perspectives

These notes are a starter to trigger the exploration in our research project at CHE NL. They are based on my latest understanding of the Turquoise (H-U) consciousness as I think I am starting to experience it, and as we start to get a sense of it in the CHE NL. These tasters attempt to describe how Turquoise might be experienced from the three perspectives.

I (as experienced in myself)

- I experience a relationship of unconditional wholeness with the world around me, as it flows and shifts in different constellations of energy.
- My heart is open and free of constriction as I fully embrace anything I encounter.
- I hold a strong awareness of who I am and how I am living in the moment.
- I see the deep-lying energetic patterns of life unfolding around me

and as me, choosing my action through my intuition and embodied knowing.

- I act in the knowing that I cannot predict the outcome of my actions.
- I hold ambiguity lightly as an invitation to discovery.
- I act in relationship with other energetic entities.
- My primary loyalty is to the flourishing of life as a whole which is largely determined by subtle energetic conditions.
- I experience Life as having elegance, grace and simplicity at its essence.
- I live in the knowing that I am both totally free and always in relationship with everything.
- We (as experienced in the space between us)
- We are fundamentally one and rejoice in the diverse expressions of that unity.
- "We" is something that emerges in the space between us.
- Relationship is full of curiosity, discovery and synergy.
- "We" is born out of an impulse that transcends and uplifts the participants.
- We constellate, dissolve and re-constellate as life in-forms us.

It (as witnessed around me)

- The patterns and qualities of the Earth hold solutions to most of our design challenges.
- Energy is always present – it is just a question of channelling it.
- Life is naturally generative and wastes nothing.
- Everything is interconnected and impacts everything else within and beyond time/space boundaries.
- Our interior state co-emerges with and as the manifestation of reality around us.
- Flow, stress and blockages have everything to do with subtle energetic conditions.
- Our reality is comprised of many different life forms in the energetic realms who we can collaborate with.
- Organisations flow organically as the dynamic balance of life.

A slide from Dr Don Beck on Turquoise:

Whole View	
Life Conditions	A delicately balanced system of interlocking forces in jeopardy at humanity's hands
Goals	Global community/life force; survival of Earth; consciousness
Coping Systems	Experientially to join with other like thinkers; holistic, transpersonal
Cultural Manifestations and personal displays	Collective individualism; cosmic spirituality; Earth changes
Location	Global Village
Drive	Synergize and macro manage
Organization	Holistic Organism

Acknowledgements

Thank you to the people who have given their time to participate in this research from the Ether Energy Group, the Mexico Meshwork Team and the Center for Human Emergence Netherlands; Helen Titchen-Beeth for reviewing and editing this report.

APPLICATION FOR SDi TRAINING

By Michael Keller

To: Marilyn Hamilton and the SDi Group Training Board
Fm: Michael Keller
Re: Application for SDi Training, Canada, December 2008
Date: 20 August 2008

How did you become aware of SDi? With whom, and when have you trained?

- Marilyn Hamilton offered the first SDi Level 1 with Don Beck in Vancouver, BC (2002) in partnership with financial scholarships offered from Royal Roads University where I was teaching, so I attended.
- 2003—Level 2, "Natural Designs," Don Beck with Marilyn Hamilton, Vancouver, BC, Canada
- 2005—Back-up support team for Level 1 and Level 2, "Designing for the Eco-Region", Don Beck with Marilyn Hamilton, Vancouver, BC, Canada
- 2006—Co-delivered Level 1 with Marilyn Hamilton, Courtney, BC, Canada, incorporating a co-designed and experiential curriculum for introducing each of the vMeme content pieces.

How have you been applying SDi?

- Recognizing patterns and the clashing, competing and reinforcing inter-play of vMeme systems; what really matters to me in any given context; how I can better align my purpose to get the results I seek; identifying others' vMeme values and meeting them where they are at to assist them in getting further towards where they want to go. This has been a translation exercise to develop both my Yellow and First Tier capabilities and overall capacity to engage in successful transformation work with self and clients.
- Co-consultant with Marilyn Hamilton and Barry Stevenson, Rogers Communications, Burnaby, BC, Canada, presenting interpersonal communication strategies and practices for engaging across Spiral vMemes; assisted Marilyn in highlighting memetic representations embedded in the Enneagram work of participants (May 2007).
- In multiple Ginger Group Collaborative annual Inquiries in order to both continue my learning and to assist/support Marilyn Hamilton by coaching Ginger Group members and other community attendees in real-time application of Spiral learning (2003 to present).
- Introducing SDi to the Westwood College, Vancouver, CIDA-funded, IYIP/YEN Internship programme participants for the purpose of enhancing their understanding and appreciation of their cross-cultural experiences while living abroad in host cultures. The 8 participants were located across a ten-hour time zone. Format was a combination of pre-readings, online group introduction to Spiral and vMemes, individual SDi Values Test debriefing and a second group follow-up support session (2007-2008).
- As a co-consultant with Marilyn Hamilton, presentation to BC Pension Corporation, Victoria, BC, Canada (March 2008).

What do you consider is possible in the further application of SDi in Canada?

- Working closely with Marilyn to publish articles related to successful applications of SDi in organizations, Integral Cities, or elsewhere. This could also include co-design and presenting at conferences and other public venues.

- Developing on-line pre-work modules for use, in particular, with cross-cultural training and support programming.
- With Marilyn, co-designing on-line, pre-work modules for SDi Level 1 & 2 trainings, on-going support modules for in-between enrichment and a marketing strategy.
- With Marilyn and other newly certified Canadian members, co-designing on-going learning support offerings to keep certified practitioners engaged and "sharpening their saw", learning from each other and building capacity together.

In what geographic area(s) would you prefer to practice?

- Western Canada and the Pacific Northwest USA, but not limited to these geographic area since my work can occur anywhere in the world. I am also interested in collaborating with other SDi certified persons anywhere to develop on-going SDi learning support programs and to co-design/deliver both SDi trainings and client contracts.

Describe your life so far in terms of the Spiral, your key experiences in the stages and your transitions from one stage to another to where you are today. What insights has the application of SDi brought to you?

Re-Storying My Self Through The Lens Of The Spiral.

Formative Years

My life began as an only child with my basic, Beige, needs provided by my mother and father, as an intact Purple family unit, until the age of seven when my parents were divorced. At that point, I continued living with my mother and seeing my father on occasional weekends until I was around 10 or 11 years old when my father began taking more interest in spending time with me. With the divorce and my father's absence, my grandparents took on a more direct role in my upbringing, supporting my mother as a single mom in a world when divorce was still an unpopular option. This was my formative Purple tribe. My grandparents took on sharing the parenting role and responsibilities. I recall some very challenging psychological discomfort around my future and, at times, my survival as my mother was not well prepared to take anything more than low-paying secretarial positions, a fluctuating Beige element for sure. Nor was she very grounded in her self and as a mom, often playing the victim and avoiding responsibilities.

My grandparents lived nearby, too, and could be readily tapped for baby-sitting/supervising me when my mother had outside activities or went on dates. In short, I grew up fast and became even more independent Red/Blue than the typical only child, taking on more and more responsibilities for myself and the household. I developed lots of Blue self and other-imposed structure and right ways to do things: getting a TV Guide delivery route when I was 10, buying all of my school clothes from 6th grade onward, making breakfast for my mother and me every day, doing laundry and household chores, along with lawn care tasks. At 15, I took my first official job as a stock boy and began to actually save Orange money for college. Throughout my childhood, I was made to attend Blue church every Sunday with my grandparents, which was not a fit for me. I Red rejected the Blue church-ism in my early teenage years. Instead, as I reflect, I recognize that I created/substituted my own versions of Red/Blue dynamics to create my own structured world, much of which was in reaction/rejection of my family's highly dysfunctional ways of living and relating.

Public School Years

My versions of Red/Blue showed up markedly in my school experiences, i.e. not much passion or positive energy for engaging in studies so I did just enough to slide by, a C-grade average student for the most part. In school at that time, all students were rank ordered in separate rooms according to ability: A-level, B-level, C-level, D-level. A very apparent socialization mechanism accompanied this stratification as well in that C-level rarely, if ever, would interact with A-level kids. Then, much to my surprise, in fifth grade a major shift occurred for me in school. I had a very progressive, male, 5th grade homeroom/math teacher who saw some potential in me enough to recommend I be moved up to the A-level room in 6th grade. This was a major change in the normal Blue rules and processes and presented me with a significant Orange performance challenge. Ironically, if there is such a thing as irony, I started getting "A" grades, a practice I continued until graduating high school.

This 5th to 6th grade time was another major transition and shift for me: it opened up in me Orange ways to be more bold, daring and enterprising in how I engaged in learning. It became fun to explore and discover, to understand things in ways that also got me right answer rewards on tests and brought a whole new group of friends into my life and previously tiny world. My Purple tribe was in expanding metamorphosis! This turned my world upside down overnight. I moved into a whole new class of school society. I had a sense of both place and purpose and mutually reliant community members. I belonged and liked it there, my first glimpses of Green! New possibilities were emerging for me and I was a member of the popular/cool, smart kids. This also had an impact on my home and family life: I began learning things that my mother and grandparents new nothing about and could not appreciate nor converse with me about. So, a greater distance grew and grew, stretching the family Purple cohesion and comfort. I spent less and less time at home, often arriving only in time to grab a cold plate of dinner and head off to my room to sleep.

As I entered puberty, I began to realize that I may not be like the other boys who were starting to become interested in girls and having girlfriends. I wrestled with being attracted to the boys much more than the girls and knew that wasn't "normal" behavior. Given all of the messages I was raised with, all the Blue-isms of fundamentalist Christians, there was clearly right-wrong, good-bad ways of behaving, and being attracted to boys was definitely on the "bad things" list. Being gay was unacceptable and torturous for me to reconcile publicly. So, I hid, passing as a straight guy by dating women in an effort not to lose my Purple tribe, my Orange status, and my emerging Green social network. In short, the risks of rejection were too high for me and I repressed my Red rebel in an effort to accommodate to the Blue ways of fitting in, my internalized homophobia tug-o-war. I no longer knew who my people were and did not know how to figure this all out alone. But "alone" was the only way I knew how to proceed. So, I threw myself into excelling at Orange school activities, playing by the rules, getting good grades, joining clubs, playing in the band, and basically being a goody-goody kid that never made trouble and that everyone liked, an effective Purple/Green mask.

School offered so many Orange ways to stimulate my thinking, stretch my imagination, uncover mysteries of science and the physical world. I loved learning! I was completely Red self-motivated, self-directed, highly Blue self-disciplined and self-actualized, Orangely independent yet interdependent within the systems that I moved through, adaptive and response-able.

However, I still trusted no one, especially in my family. Around age 14, my father began taking a renewed (disguised Red) Purple interest in our spending time together. I was with him almost every weekend. He took me places, bought me things, and tantalized me with the glitz and glamour of his world, all the things my mother could never have provided. At 16, my mother re-married (her second) and I did not get along with her Purple new husband, so I decided to move in with my Purple father and his third wife until I finished high school. In short, from day one, all that glimmered was not gold. He had won the unstated Red battle with my mother, gained the victory of the final slap in her face by wooing me away from her. That was all that mattered to him, winning the game of retribution, no matter what the price might be for me; a rude awakening that affected me quite profoundly.

Once again, I accommodated to the situation, sublimating my Red anger, disappointment, and humiliation by directing my energies even more into Blue/Orange school success. I saw this as my only pathway, via Orange success, to freedom in the future; my only option for getting out and getting away by getting exceptional grades that would allow me to go to college wherever I chose. My Purple family tribe was now fragmented beyond reconciliation, the fabric of my peer social network was my only reliable container and yet my sexuality was becoming an ever increasing pressure to contend with, my un-integrated Red. While University offered an escape and an arena for exploring who I was becoming, I remained too fearful to take any risks, acquiescing into a quiet guy who sat in the back row in most classes and rarely said anything. My Red was very repressed and sublimated. I asserted little on my own behalf and rarely challenged anything. I had become a shadow of my former and real self. I had lost my honor and my heart. I rejected academia as I was suffocating and I dropped out of school. I had a high draft lottery number and, so, had no fear of being drafted into the Vietnam war.

College and Twenties

In my late teens and early twenties, with my new living-on-my-own circumstances, I took a delivery-boy job in a local floral shop and within 6 months was apprenticing as a floral designer. This unimaginable arena released my creativity in ways that I had never before imagined. I became inspired and innovative, tapping into new ways of knowing that only designing can elicit. I actually began liking myself again. This new Blue design world gave me the foundations for Orange financial success and independence. During this time I also discovered my body which had become tight and inflexible, diminished in posture and endurance. I don't recall what prompted me but I chose to join a classical ballet class. In ballet, I discovered an avenue for both connecting with my body and using it to express my humanness in a whole new dimension. I was beginning to appreciate the body-mind interaction through the highly Blue structured format of choreography. I attended classes several times a week, subjected myself to great rigor and practice sessions, and became an exceptional dancer, able to compete for professional roles at the civic ballet level within 1.5 years. My heart and soul became alive, again. However, being just a good dancer was not actually the essence of this process for me.

It was the awakening of the body-mind connection, the recognition of interdependence, a unifying integration that had been missing in my lop-sided accommodating to the external world. I realize now that this was the healthy recalibration of my Red passion and vitality, my gusto for living! In addition, most classical male dancers were considered to be gay, so I knew that I was taking a risk and that, somehow, I was ready for this shift. My independence became much more grounded and resilient. I was able to hold my head up with pride. While I did not choose to dance professionally as a career, this was readiness work that I needed to do to get a healthy balance of my Red, Blue underpinnings in order to platform me for Orange success and Green health.

At 21, I chose to stop smoking cigarettes, eating meat, and drinking alcohol, a major healthy Blue lifestyle shift. This period also was a time for me to take Orange responsibility for me and my health, e.g. I learned to garden organically, make my own clothes, cook vegetarian meals; getting back to basics. This was my intentional Blue focus on grounding structure for wholeness and confidence in Green living lightly on the planet. I am also aware that this was another healthy re-calibration of my Red independence. Rather than being a rebel without a clue, I was instead taking full responsibility and accountability for my presence and impact on the planet. This was also a psychological re-calibration of my emotional Beige stability, an empowering of my confidence and capability to support myself in the basics of life. I have continued to eat a vegetarian diet and to plant an organic garden wherever I have lived for the past 35 consecutive years, a Green commitment to leave every place more beautiful and healthier than I found it!

Ballet was only the door-opener for my continued interest and exploration of body-mind integration. At 22, I undertook the study of T'ai Chi Ch'uan (traditional, 108 movement, long form), eventually becoming an instructor and teaching public classes, for 20 years until 1994. T'ai Chi is the quintessential meditation-in-movement discipline, integrating Yellow groundedness with energy flow. At 23, I encountered Baba Hari Das, Santa Cruz, California, and became an instant student of very Blue Ashtanga Yoga practices under his guidance. Eventually, I moved to Santa Cruz to live in the Purple/Blue Ashram and study Green/Yellow Ayurvedic healing and massage practices. It was here that I had my first glimpse of (Green/Yellow/Turquoise?) "spirit" in practice, a way of being beyond just the interplay of body-mind. As a result, I became a regular Blue practitioner of hatha yoga, continue this practice to this day and have taught Orange public classes for over 20 years. This was all designed for me to tap into more Green/Yellow human potential.

At 25, continuing my commitment to body-mind-spirit health, I returned to Ohio to live with an elderly couple on a small organic orchard, a recalibration of my withered Purple, while I undertook formal Blue training and licensure in Therapeutic Massage, graduating first in my class (1978). At that time, the State of Ohio was one of the few states in the US with Blue rigorous training and licensing standards (2000 hours) and granted licenses by exam only through the State Medical Board. For me, this Blue legitimacy was important at a time when massage was generally a parlor sport of the red light district. Once licensed, I moved back to Oregon where I opened my private practice, becoming a very financially Orange successful businessman which I continued for 17 years. This practice was my giving towards a healthier, better world by helping people in physical pain and discomfort, a whole-person Green approach embodying a rich and meaning-full life. With my massage & bodywork practice, enhanced with teaching yoga and T'ai Chi, I was living my purpose fully, in service to others and a better world, a solidly supported Orange value system manifest! I was the healthiest and most integrated that I had ever been in my life!

Still, though, throughout my twenties, I continued to wrestle with my sexuality, searching for models of healthy gay relationships and ways to connect with other gay people. There was no gay Blue structure available for me to step into and no apparent way that I could create a Purple connection or safe affiliations. This gap and my internalized fears (homophobia) continued for many years until I finally came out when I was 30 years old, getting real with myself and the world. How liberating this new self-acceptance was for me, too! I was re-writing my Blue rules and bringing my Red authenticity forward. I was finally re-connected with my Self, with a fundamental aspect of who I am that seemed to free up the repressed energy of my aberrant Blue-isms history and allowed me to regain Red self-respect and honor, taking risks towards Orange re-inventing myself. I had stepped towards a better me and a better life.

At 31 (1983), with my consistent years of financial and business success, providing money, position, status, place in a community, a sense of belonging, I realized that I was no more happy from having the markings of such success than when I had nothing. Clearly, there was something wrong with this picture. I had achieved the Orange American Dream for success. What happened? I was unable to reconcile this for myself on my own and clearly it was important to understand and resolve. So, I decided that the best way for me to get a better understanding of what was going on was to step outside of my familiar and comfortable culture, since all it could do was reinforce what was already happening. Being outside of my home culture for an extended period of time would help me get clearer about what really mattered to me, what was really important in my life. So, I decided to take a year off and travel the world. However, I got no further than Nepal and stayed there for 10 years, with one year living in Tibet.

As you might imagine, there were countless challenges and transitions that occurred for me living in such a dramatically different culture and part of the world. It would take pages and pages for me to recount the many and various insights and awakenings I experienced. I see little point in doing such an elaboration here. However, following are some of the synthesized highlights in relation to the Spiral:

- Beige—Survival challenges of altitude sickness, Typhoid fever, Amoebic Dysentery; civil unrest and martial law (pro-democracy movement/retaliation, 1989); overall unhealthy/unsanitary living conditions and food scarcities; unreliable availability of household water, electricity, and cooking fuel; no refrigerator, TV, appliances; transportation only by foot, bicycle, or public taxis/buses.

- Purple—Accepted into Nepalese and Tibetan society as an important and contributing member; invited to participate in Nepalese ritualistic ceremonies and celebratory gatherings; being considered as "belonging" to the international community.

- Red—Chose to live in a traditional, "risky" Nepali neighborhood, the only westerner, for eight of my 10 years; maintained my heart-felt convictions in the face of ridicule for being an American choosing to live within the local society; to persevere in the face of political graft and corruption without losing face; wrestled with my own sense of privilege as a westerner and the reverse discrimination that accompanied it.

- Blue—Director of Himalayan Yogic Institute, Kathmandu, an in-town center representing the Tibetan Buddhist (Kopan) Monastery; Completed my Masters in Intercultural Communication (Antioch University, 1990) with an emphasis upon Cross-Cultural Adjustment and Support Programming for Expatriates; Tibetan Meditation training and monastic retreats; Daily meditation practice; learning of Nepali and Tibetan languages (fluent in Tibetan); challenged by the many isms present in the mixed society of Nepal.

- Orange—My private massage and bodywork practice where I received referrals from the only western medicine clinic in Nepal (Kathmandu); taught yoga, body-awareness, and T'ai Chi classes, along with cross-cultural adjustment programs for US Peace Corps; led tour groups to Tibet; lived and worked as a Tour Development Director, Holiday Inn, Lhasa, Tibet, as one of only 11 westerners permitted to live in Lhasa at that time and the only one who spoke Tibetan; Tibetan Studies Program Director for the University of Wisconsin's "College Year in Nepal Program"; Manager USAID Commissary store; All-English editor for daily radio, print, and TV, Nepal News Services.

- Green—Networked with foreign aid agencies, NGOs, diplomatic missions to rectify inequities, establish respectful business and social relationships/interactions across cultures; tapped into my own potential through spiritual practices and discipline, especially

Tibetan Buddhist; completed the first ever survey/study, sponsored by UNESCO, of the Tibetan Refugee Settlement Camps conducted entirely in the Tibetan language; facilitated weekly Buddhist Dharma teachings for westerners interested in expanding their understanding of Tibetan practices and those seeking deeper inner meaning in life.

- Yellow—Doubtful if I was even aware of or able to operate in a Yellow values system directly. An exception may be where cross-cultural adjustment and bodywork were involved and I was able to recognize all aspects of vMemes 1-6, engaging a whole-systems operational view. But I didn't know that at the time; I just knew that an integrated approach worked better.

In my bodywork practice in Kathmandu, my clientele were all foreigners mostly from North America and Europe. I noticed that most clients were suffering common physical maladies, tight or hyper-contracted muscles, neck and back pain with impaired range of motion, headaches and insomnia, and general anxiety and disappointment. These problems were not because of rigorous living conditions but, rather, because of stress from not adapting successfully to the local culture/values and ways of doing things. I, too, had experienced many similar challenges in my first 2 years in Nepal. However, I had chosen intentionally to adapt and fit in to local society (Purple/Blue), learning the language, shopping in the local market, living in a Nepali neighborhood and embracing the inherent ambiguity. In contrast, the vast majority of foreigners were affiliated with Orange organizations that provided housing, car & driver, security guards, cooks & maids, modern furniture and appliances, along with privileges to shop at the Orange US Commissary.

Most causes of stress were related directly to the unreconciled disparity in living-styles/conditions and values systems combined with the lack of professional support for cross-cultural adjustment. Most foreigners gained their limited knowledge and coping skills from other seasoned foreigners and, thereby, fell victim to the transmission of all the same dysfunctional thinking and behavioral response patterns already held, prejudice and ethnocentric Blue judgmental-isms. Since all of this stress was occurring in-country and there was no apparent support mechanisms available, I chose to focus on this as the thesis topic for my graduate degree (1987-90), giving it deep Red personal Blue meaning and Orange/Green/Yellow relevance.

As you might imagine, it can be quite demanding to complete a graduate degree while living in a developing foreign country where I was also working a full-time job required to obtain a visa to remain in Nepal, managing a full-time bodywork practice and negotiating the many challenges of daily life. In addition and at that time, I found no Blue/Orange professional support for my thesis premise that the only legitimate point for positive intervention in support of more successful cross-cultural adjustment was when provided after individuals arrived in their host country and during their stay. At that time, the only sanctioned support utilized by NGOs and foreign missions was provided prior to departure and post-return. Still, I had experienced my own successful adjustment and had witnessed my bodywork clients' on-going struggles to adjust. I knew what was involved and what was required and would not let the lack of support stand in my way (Red/Orange/Yellow tension?) of addressing the core issues. This graduate work clearly inspired me towards life-long learning and consciousness development.

In 1991, when I was leading a tour group, I was offered an Orange job as the Tour Development Director for the Holiday Inn, Lhasa, Tibet. As a Tibetan speaker, this was a golden opportunity for me to live in and explore the homeland of so many Tibetan refugees that I knew from living in Nepal. Also, the Red/Blue occupation by the Han Chinese was a double-edged sword that I wanted to see close up and personal. In short, what I discovered was the overwhelming Red/Blue control imposed by the Chinese. To name just a few such impositions:

- Shadowing me every time I went out.
- Opening and reading my mail and leaving the translated Chinese characters written on the pages.
- Marching every 30 minutes through the central marketplace.
- Placing spies amongst the monks in every monastery.

I had never before lived in a repressive and oppressive place dominated by an outside cultural group that was basically enacting Red/Blue cultural genocide upon the now minority Tibetan people and their unique Buddhist culture. The city of Lhasa, once home to the Dalai Lama, had become a Red/Blue/Orange Chinese city with Tibetan monuments and where Tibetans were treated as low-class members. While I enjoyed my one year living in Lhasa as a privilege that few people will likely experience, I chose not to continue living there because of the Red/Blue intolerance and ethnocentrism perpetrated by the Chinese forceful occupation. This was a clear rub against my preferred Green ways of equitable and harmonious, interdependent relations.

Upon my return to living in Kathmandu in 1992 I was offered an Orange position as General Manager for an innovative eco-village style resort being created by a very successful German businessman and his wife. The resort was named "Kano Dada" and was designed by an American architect as an authentic Nepalese village utilizing traditional style and construction techniques (modified slightly to accommodate western sensibilities, such as attached toilets) for the various sized bungalows. In general, the Green concept was very popular amongst both the Nepalese, who had never experienced westerners honoring their local architecture or customs, and the westerners who appreciated that all food would be organically grown, power supplied via solar panels, and water stored underground with the grey water used for irrigating the hillside orchards. However, over the 2+ years of my involvement, the Orange owners continually changed Blue designs and rules, made major additions that required monumental renovations to existing built structures, hired and fired Red/Blue local staff without consultation, which had a huge Purple/Blue socio-cultural ripple-effect in the surrounding area where most of the staff was coming from. Once again, my Orange/Green mindset was my stumbling block because I was unable to translate effectively to reconcile the many transgressions and negative impacts. Finally, I chose to resign, an act of Purple/Red self-preservation of face/belonging. Unfortunately, the resort never opened.

Not long after my resignation, I decided it was time to leave Nepal primarily because of the on-going breakdown of basic needs and services combined with increasing air pollution; I needed to wear a carbon-filter face mask when riding my bicycle in the streets of Kathmandu. When I arrived in Nepal in1983, I could see the spectacular Himalayas from Kathmandu every day in the wintertime. When I left 10 years later, I had only glimpsed them 3 times the entire winter due to the valley pollution. The erosion of the Green environment in such a short period of time was mind-boggling and very distressing for me. As a foreigner, I had no idea of how I might remain and have a positive influence in turning the air quality situation around. I also was motivated to share what I had learned from living abroad with others in my home culture, another emerging Green contribution to a better world.

Forties and Purpose-Full Work

In early 1994, I returned to the USA to live in Bend, Oregon, and to work in the local Environmental Center as the Manager of the Orange/Green Household EcoTeam Program designed to assist householders in changing behaviors to become more environmentally friendly. I quickly became aware of the exclusivity of Green environmentalists, a clear "us vs them" mentality. Also, there was a very unhealthy absence of Blue structures (being able to balance the books) and underpinnings (procedures and practices) and a rampant martyrdom/self-sacrifice syndrome regarding how much better it was to work for nothing and the rejection of Orange making money as a bad thing to be avoided at all cost. I was also challenged by the stuckness of mindsets, of Blue righteous-ism. I was unable to influence any consideration of other points of view, of the value and viability of alternate approaches, of reconciling the blatant contradiction between voicing the importance for including all voices and the evident avoidance of differing opinions. As a result, I chose to return to academia and into teaching at the local Central Oregon Community College in the Blue/Orange/Green Service Learning Program, another significant transition point for me.

In 1996 (thru 2000), I began teaching Service Leadership courses as part of the educational requirement for Service Learning program participants who were placed in local non-profit Green service organizations in exchange for educational Blue/Orange scholarship funds. This was a very Orange/Green model of social responsibility and community development. For me, it was of paramount importance that the curriculum be practical and the pedagogy be experiential, applied adult learning, which was not the norm in typical undergraduate education. Again, I was reminded of how easy it can be for me to also become stuck in mean Green mental models. I noticed my one-up, one-down comparisons; my co-dependent assessments of who I must help; my tendencies to blame others and circumstances for the maladies of the world that someone else should fix; and my inability to accept responsibility for creating the disappointments I experienced.

For me, this new arena was a significant stretch in very real and healthy ways! I was teaching in ways that Red challenged the Blue status quo. Still, in short order, I became recognized for the great success our placements were having in local non-profit agencies, 95% of our program service learner placements were hired by their respective agencies, an unheard of statistic in any other co-op or service program in Oregon and not one of the intended outcomes for our program. Still my method was a clear demonstration of integrated learning by the students in my leadership courses! From such Blue/Orange success came the request from many of our Green placement agencies for me to conduct collateral training programs for their personnel who were seeing the many benefits exhibited by working with our service learner placements. In addition, I was invited to present at a variety of Service Learning Regional and National Conferences. Our Blue-Orange materials were distributed as a model for use by newly forming service programs across the country. Unfortunately, in 2000, this award-winning program was discontinued due to myopic, self-serving, competing internal Red/Blue/Orange politics.

Fifties and Intentional Living

In 2000, I was hired by Royal Roads University (RRU), Victoria, BC, to teach in the Masters in Leadership and Training (MALT) program. This program incorporated Blue/Orange/Green adult learning principles, experiential/participatory Blue/Orange pedagogy, and community/cohort Orange-Green learning and research environments, called Residencies. I thought I'd finally found where I belonged and could bring forth my best contributions. The Residency classroom was intended to be holistic and, thereby, demanded a faculty to operate both as a team and as individual models of leadership, i.e., living our learning, the RRU motto. While very attractive to me, I also had my own apprehensions since I had few good experiences working with others or in a team-based situation. I didn't like sharing (Purple/Red tension) either my toys or the sandbox. So, I knew there would be some new learning opportunities, especially around what genuine Orange/Green collaboration could mean and whether I could even make it work. Well, I not only learned how to make it work well, I received glowing evaluations for 5 consecutive years of teaching 7 residency cohorts, two of which were first-time launch residencies (BA and MA levels) in a very different from MALT RRU program.

During this time, I also began to get more and more consulting work in Canada. From amongst my many faculty team members, I forged some new Orange/Green collegial working relationships that led to new contract client work. I also became Blue/Orange stretched by keeping two consulting practices, one in Bend, Oregon and the other emerging in Victoria, BC, alive and well tended. In short, I decided that the better prospects lay in my options in Canada and, in 2003, I moved to Victoria to live and work collaboratively, choosing to not consult solo anymore nor take on anything less than whole-systems change contract work. I was raising the learning bar on myself once again, entertaining the Yellow notions of integrated, holistic and systems-thinking approaches to learning and transformative/culture-shifting change work.

For the past 5 years, I have been primarily engaged and focused on two work areas: co-designing self-improvement/personal growth seminars, and, as one of a three-consultant team, in on-going Province-wide culture-shifting contract work within the BC Ministry of Environment. This work has demanded that I develop and incorporate First Tier and Yellow thinking to address the complex issues being faced by a large, multi-stakeholder organization, as well as translate and apply integrated design for achieving the expected changes at different levels of Life Conditions and workplace environments in nine respective Regional Offices, spanning Red to Green memetic contexts, that also are expected to interact across multiple Regions collaboratively…whew…!

Upon reflection, I had put a lot of my Orange/Green hopes and dreams into RRU and in how it seemed they were taking a stand to truly "live their learning" as the motto espoused. Actually, over my five years of teaching (2001-2005), I have witnessed an erosion of their stated Blue/Orange principles and leadership/management practices, becoming more and more like every other Blue/Orange academic institution. In my judgment, the leadership capabilities that the highly interdependent world ecology is calling for and needs desperately cannot be provided by traditional Blue/Orange structured academic institutions or pedagogy. Hence, a more engaging whole-person humanistic approach is required, one that bridges Orange/Green realities without compromising the necessary Orange resources for Green social responsibility.

The current environmental climate changes are a clear Green example of the need for more collective and collaborative engagement in order to respond effectively to such a highly complex and emergent challenge that could well threaten human survival. These emerging challenges call for designing effective forums for bringing historically separate community groups together for the sole purpose of first exploring an issue in ways that support collective learning from each other, hearing what the issue means to each respective area within the overall system so that the best and most appropriate action can be taken with collective support, endorsement and committed, integrative activities. This, I pose, is the Blue/Orange/Green social responsibility hurdle of the 21st Century and the work that I am committed to addressing in order to do "the work".

Self-Identified Learning Edges

My Green healthy and unhealthy bias & blindness has been a predominant meme lens and, thereby, seems to still be the learning edge for me. I realize that, from my early twenties, I have attempted to leap into Green ways of being & living without having invested an appropriate degree in my Purple/Red/Blue/Orange infrastructures. These underpinnings are necessary for a successful living of my Green values authentically in order to contribute to a better me and a better world. Also, I don't fully understand the spectrum of ways that the "mean green meme" can show up.

My Purple remains under-developed even though my family-of-origin connections and interactions have improved significantly. For me, my sense of tribe and family seems to be comprised more of my close and long-time friendships. I would appreciate exploring this more through the lens of the Spiral.

Personally, my purpose of tapping into human potential, to develop others to develop themselves and, thereby, to enhance the evolution of human consciousness and human ecologies, represents my affinity with Yellow values. However, when I woke up to recognizing that my motivation was to do this for others and not with them, I clearly realized the important distinction between knowing about a vMeme and acknowledging that as insufficient to operationalizing those values, living them behaviorally. Enhancing my ability to translate and work with First Tier is a primary developmental edge for me.

LIVES ON THE SPIRAL: PERSONAL REFLECTIONS ON THE INFLUENCE OF SDi

By Keith E. Rice

I've had an interest in Psychology since my first year at university but being exposed to Spiral Dynamics Integral (SDi) in March-April 1998 was of a totally-different order than anything I'd encountered before. Inevitably I had come across powerful, paradigm-shaping models before, most notably William Moulton Marston's DISC (1928). With its mapping of Dominance, Influence, Steadfastness and Compliance in attitudes and behaviour, it forms the basis of the business world's second-most popular psychometric after Myers-Briggs. I had come to understand DISC well enough to be able to write and deliver training courses in it. But DISC was essentially descriptive. Just one of the things that sets SDi apart from most other models is that it can be applied causally. In other words, it answers the "why?" question.

Back in March 1998 I was a mess. Some 15 months earlier I was hospitalised for a week following a "stress reaction" in which I had rung my doctor to threaten suicide and subsequently been arrested by the police for my own protection. This episode had been triggered by a combination of my business failing and relationship problems. As I had 2 previous suicide "attempts" on my record, the doctor had reason to take my threats seriously!

I have a mildly psychoticist temperament (from Hans Eysenck's Psychoticism-Extraversion-Neuroticism model of temperament (Eysenck,

1967; Eysenck & Eysenck, 1976)) and am thus prone to impulsive and compulsive behaviour. Accordingly, I have a reckless resilience which soon saw me out of hospital and talking my way into a job in Business Link Wakefield, a branch of a government-funded agency for supporting small businesses. While my efforts were highly successful, beneath the surface I was still extremely fragile. With the funding for the job running out and no possibility of it being extended, I began to experience serious stress and anxiety symptoms including at times heart palpitations. It was in this kind of state that I was first introduced to SDi.

The story of the Business Link's involvement with Don Beck, Chris Cowan and SDi is a complex and multi-layered one. Ian Lavan, the Link's Export Development Counsellor, was an NLP Master Practitioner and far more interested in fringe psychology than exports. On his Master Practitioner training, he had been introduced to the basics of SDi by Master Trainer Wyatt Woodsmall and was encouraged to train with Beck & Cowan at their Texas headquarters. Ian used his NLP skills to persuade the Business Link to fund such a trip. He was so impressed with what he learned in Texas that he then persuaded Business Link to fund Beck & Cowan carrying out a training programme in Wakefield and putting all the advisers through that training. That, fortunately, included me.

My first impressions of SDi were that it was a ridiculous bit of woo-woo mumbo-jumbo, more akin to colour healing or chakra schematics than serious psychological science. Since I was, at the time, also highly sceptical about NLP, I was initially resistant to the teaching of Beck & Cowan, denigrating it as just more of Ian Lavan's weird stuff. By the end of the third day, though, I was an unequivocal devotee. All of a sudden life and all its manifold contradictions made sense. I could see that all the internal contradictions and the conflicts with external others came from different motivations, or, to be more accurate, motivating systems or vMemes, as SDi calls them.

For example, I now understood why I enjoyed pornography, satisfying a Beige/Red vMeme harmonic, but felt terribly guilty about it because of the Christian Blue-oriented memes (culturally-transmitted concepts) I had absorbed about male/female relationships and the control of sex in society. That was an internal conflict which had tormented me since the days when I had been a fundamentalist Christian. Now I could understand that Red wanted one thing while Blue wanted another. SDi carried a bit of Sigmund Freud's (1923) analysis of Id vs Superego conflicts, "do what pleases" vs "do what's right", but without value judgements beyond "does it work for me and not impact negatively upon others?"

I still remember turning such conundrums over and over in my head as I walked back to the Business Link one lunchtime, about a week after Beck & Cowan had jetted off back to Texas. With each step nearer the Link, it seemed my understanding grew, and a corresponding sense of euphoria seemed to spread from the pit of my stomach throughout my torso and into my extremities. In exultation I leapt repeatedly off the ground, punching the air with my fist and shouting "Yes! Yes! YES!" I've certainly experienced some ups and downs in the journey of life since those heady days of early spring 1998, but I've never looked back. And I've never been in that kind of mess again. I've often said that Don Beck & Chris Cowan saved my sanity. It's just possible they saved my life.

It really was like, "…and with one bound he was free!"

Blue Is The Color Of My Father's House

My father was nearing the end of his 2nd month in the intensive care unit in the bowels of Preston Royal Infirmary, Lancashire, in late 2002. He was suffering a prolonged acute bout of Myasthenia Gravis, a debilitating and potentially fatal condition in which the neurotransmitter acetylcholine is no longer transmitted through the synapses at the muscle platelets. Amongst the muscle networks which were no longer working were those which contracted and expanded his lungs – so a ventilator was plugged into my father's trachea to do his breathing for him. Most of the time he was able to communicate with me through a mixture of writing, gesturing and grunting. A combination of Purple affiliation and Blue duty had me spending weekends at his house nearby and travelling across the Pennines from Hull on the East Coast at least twice more in the week. With Mum dead a couple of years, I was his main visitor. He really seemed to appreciate the visits, often grasping my hand as I sat or stood by his bedside. It was a mode of Purple communication for both of us. We knew we belonged to each other.

This particular night I had travelled 3 hours from a day's consultancy on Teesside to be with Dad. I didn't get to the hospital till 9:30p and was exhausted. Dad had had a particularly bad day, at times it had come close to touch-and-go and, though he was no longer at severe risk, he was in a lot of discomfort. He barely acknowledged my presence. No hand-holding that night. His eyes followed the nurses all the time. He smiled and tried to laugh if they made a flippant comment while attending to him and he simply oozed gratitude for everything they did for him. They seemed more interested in him than I had seen them previously.

I left, emotionally crushed and feeling even more exhausted. But, as I thought it through, SDi made sense of the experience for me. Dad and I might have fed our Purple sense of belonging to each other but that day he had slipped below nodal Purple on the Spiral. That day it had been all about survival. Something I couldn't help him with. But the nurses could. To survive, he needed them and he needed them to care about him so that he survived. What I had seen was my Dad's Beige and Purple vMemes forming a vMeme harmonic, the survival motivation developing a new sense of belonging with the people who were most likely to ensure his survival. At that level, I was redundant – useless! But the nurses had the skills and access to the machinery that could save my Dad, if only he could motivate them to be that much more attentive. His was an unconscious motivation, to be sure. He seemed embarrassed and fudged commenting on that night when I raised it a couple of years later. It was a potent reminder that the lower you go on the Spiral, the more dominating the motivations can be.

My father, Ted Rice, would have been embarrassed by my raising that night in the hospital because he was essentially centred in Blue and ignoring your son to ingratiate yourself with people who, as professionals, should have done their job to the best of their ability, regardless, was hardly the right thing to do. My father's Blue largely dominated my upbringing. He was really good at saying what should and shouldn't be. So people should stop listening to pop music and listen to classical, especially the early-mid-period composers (Bach to Beethoven) whose music was very ordered, structured, mathematical and precise. Everyone should vote Conservative because people should: a) Know their place in the class hierarchy and b) Labour were dangerous with their ideas of co-education (boys and girls taught together in the same school!) and minimising the wage gaps between workers and managers. Everyone should read a broadsheet, not that tabloid trash, and watch the TV news every night because everyone should know what's going on so they could make "informed" choices (by which he really meant support the Tories!). With a bit of Purple differentiation underpinning, he was an unashamed racist because whites were superior. Blacks were unintelligent, primitive and lazy. Asians were crafty, sneaky and lazy. And once the science was unequivocal about the risks of lung cancer, everyone should stop smoking! If my father looked externally from himself, as Blue does, to find "what is right" "out there", his internalisation and interpretation of those memes into his internal schemas made him a zealot (Red/Blue) to be reckoned with. He knew how things should be and he paid little regard to the feelings of others in seeking to impose his orthodoxy on them.

In 1967, the year of flower power, when the ears of most of the teenage boys in the UK were disappearing under longer and longer hair, he insisted I should still have a "short back & sides" haircut. After a blazing row, I packed a bag to leave home in protest. He was unmoved; and only my mother's near-hysterical intervention got me to stay. It would be another year before she managed to convince him to let me have my hair just that little bit longer. When we moved to a new house in 1972 and I stood on the raised front lawn with hair down to my shoulders, held off my forehead with a hippie headband, he was so ashamed he shouted me in and forbade me to stand in such an obvious position in front of the neighbours ever again. A couple of years later, when I told him I'd smoked dope for the first time, I actually thought he was going to have a heart attack on the spot. Admittedly my fun-loving Red was now having some fun with his uptight Blue!

If I annoyed him—sometimes deliberately!—my mother frustrated the hell out of him. Centered in Purple, with frequent flashes of Red, she had no interest in doing the right thing by being informed about the current state of the economy or which was the latest African state to succumb to civil war. Mum got her news from gossiping in the village. She had no idea as to whether the pound was up or down on the currency markets but she knew the progress of Mrs Walton's illness, what the primary school teacher had decided about little Harry Benton being bullied and what the likelihood was that Phil Smith really was cheating on his wife with Susie, the flirtatious barmaid at the Fox & Grapes.

Dad called Mum "mentally lazy" because she wouldn't pay attention to the TV news broadcasts. He was so locked into his Blue worldview that he couldn't conceive that there was a values gap between them and that, to Mum, different things were important.

Mind you, Dad's Red did get the better of him on occasion—as when he had a short-lived affair. How his Red, just like Freud's Id, didn't understand consequences was amply illustrated by the fact his collaborator in the affair was our next-door neighbour. As though they would find it easy to keep that one a secret! My mother left my father when the affair was revealed. I, at the age of 7 already starting to disrespect my mother under the weight of my father's criticisms, stayed with him.

Two days later I remember my grandfather's face appearing at our rain-drenched window and summoning Dad to his house in Liverpool. Though he would soon come to disrespect his own father for his "idiotic" Socialism, there was enough Purple working in my father's head at the time for him to defer to Granddad's wishes. Both sets of grandparents were there. My parents were pushed alone together into my grandfather's front room and told to sort it out. Both my parents came from Liverpool working class families. Divorce then was uncommon; male infidelity and females coming to terms with it on the presupposition that it was "just sex" and wouldn't happen again was not that uncommon. This was Purple at work, in terms of tradition and ascription of gender roles. The pressure put on my parents to make it work "for the sake of the boy" was enormous. They emerged from the front room with faces like thunder and could barely manage a civil word to each other for weeks. But Mum did go back and, as far as I know, my Dad didn't stray again. I was never officially told about the affair, though my mother told my second wife. After Mum had died, Dad hinted at something having gone on but justified himself by saying Mum hadn't given him enough sex, effectively Red shrugging off the shame of the affair by deflecting blame onto someone else, Mum.

Mum agreeing to go back may also be read as having a Beige component. In the days before good income careers were available for most women, she needed my Dad's money for her standard of living and to raise her child. Evolutionary psychologists such as David Buss (1989) and David Waynforth & Robin Dunbar (1995) have provided convincing evidence of the importance of male resources to female reproduction strategies. In a Beige/Purple harmonic my Mum needed my Dad and his far-from-measly ability to earn a reasonable income to support her and her child. Interestingly, although it's a rather painful memory, amongst the last things my mother told me on her deathbed was that I was a failure because I hadn't given her grandchildren, a rather bitter illustration of the Beige, evolutionary drive to pass on your genes. As her only child, my mother's genetic lineage dies out with me.

It should be noted that my parents became great friends in the last decade or so before my Mum died, really seeming to find what Ellen Berscheid &

Elaine Walster (1978) termed "companionate love". They finally seemed to be comfortable in their relationship and really seemed to enjoy each other's company. That their Purple bond was strong was clear in the affectionate terms with which they referred to each other and sometimes even held each other. Who knows, if my father's testosterone levels dropped, typical of older men, and my mother's were elevated, typical of post-menopausal women, maybe they even found bed was no longer a problem?

Does Insecure Attachment Lead To Insecure Lover?

John Bowlby is one of my psychology heroes. Although methodological flaws have since been found in a number of his studies and the validity of several of his conclusions have been challenged, he led a developmental movement in the 1940s, 1950s and 1960s which changed British society's approach to caring for children. The fact that parents these days have virtually unrestricted visiting to sick children in hospital and can even stay with them overnight is almost single-handedly due to Bowlby. (Prior to Bowlby's influence, a Nursing Times survey, published in 1952, found that only 300 out of 1,300 hospitals allowed daily visiting and 150 allowed no visiting whatsoever.)

Thanks to the World Health Organisation taking up Bowlby's work in the early 1950s, his first WHO book was published in 1951, his influence spread throughout much of Western society.

Just one of the factors Bowlby and his student, Mary Ainsworth, investigated was secure and insecure attachments, with Ainsworth (Ainsworth & Bell, 1970) eventually designating 3 attachment types:

- Securely attached.
- Insecure resistant—can't trust the caregiver and tries to control by being clingy.
- Insecure avoidant—has given up on the caregiver and lives as independently as possible from them.

Although there's no indication Bowlby was aware of the contemporaneous Clare W Graves, on whose work SDi is built, effectively Bowlby and Ainsworth were working with the Purple vMeme and its need to find safety in belonging. Both the insecure categories indicate some unhealthy working of Red to compensate for Purple's attachment needs being frustrated. Bowlby was a psychoanalyst by training and was mentored by Anna Freud for quite a time. In the development of his ideas, Bowlby was much influenced by Sigmund Freud's (1940) notion that the relationship between the child and its mother is "the prototype of all later love-relations." Cindy Hazan & Phil Shaver (1987, 1993) were the first of a raft of researchers to find degrees of correlation between infant attachment type and adult romantic love style, thus lending support to the Bowlby-Freud concept.

So did my earliest childhood relationships affect my ability to conduct adult ones? Well, of course, I can't remember much below the age of 5. But some of my earliest memories are of my parents rowing. I even saw my father slap my mother across the face once with his motorcycle gauntlet. I remember feeling frightened on what seemed like numerous occasions that they were going to split up. In my early teens my mother told me that women didn't enjoy sex. These childhood incidents did indeed create mental models that greatly influenced my approach to adult relationships, but so did the TV series "Hart & Hart". The lovey-dovey relationship with just a hint of passionate naughtiness that Robert Wagner and Stephanie Powers portrayed so well was what I aspired to. The living hell of my parents' marriage, as the childhood me saw it, was to be avoided at all costs.

Thus, I've been a little double-minded in my relationships. I was at times insecure-avoidant, not trusting and unwilling to risk being emotionally intimate with someone. At other times I could be insecure-resistant with women I fell desperately in love with. At these times I would be jealous, clingy and controlling to the point of obsession and then devastated when the woman finally ended it, fed up with the jealous accusations and the demand to be loved constantly with the same intensity I loved her. Should a woman become demanding with me that I wasn't smitten by, a combination of my mild psychoticism and Red would cut her off ruthlessly, rather than submit to expectations. The destabilising of my Purple need to find safety in belonging at what seems to have been a fairly early age does indeed seem to have had an adverse effect on my ability to form lasting romantic/sexual relationships. My journey is littered with the shattered corpses of short-term relationships.

As my understanding of SDi has grown and with it my reframing of Psychology in general, so I have become more reflective and more able to control my tendency to paranoia. I see the need to do that if I am ever to meet my Purple safety-in-belonging needs. With my third wife, Caroline, on our way to our tenth wedding anniversary, I seem to have found someone who is a natural loving Purple healer. A primary school teacher, she has an intuitive understanding of young children and can speak to their Purple, making them feel secure while also stimulating their Red to make education activities fun. Perhaps, in a way, that's what she's doing with me, feeding me just the right combination of security and fun to repair those vMeme systems and expectations damaged so long ago. Even so, my mother's words ring readily in my internal ears that women don't enjoy sex. At times, despite the very obvious evidence to the contrary wrapped around me, I still struggle sometimes to believe that Caroline likes the physical side of our relationship. Obviously, there's more to it than either Freud or Bowlby thought in their respective times. But, in my experience, they were certainly right in their concept that childhood experiences can influence right throughout adult life.

A Second Tier Thinker...?

Graves (1970), like Abraham Maslow, whom he much admired and whose Hierarchy of Needs (1943) he initially tried to map his research findings to, drew a distinction between the being levels of Second Tier thinking and the subsistence or deficiency levels of First Tier thinking. Many who advocate SDi state that to really understand SDi you have to be able to perceive the world through a Second Tier lens. In which case, since I have a reasonable appreciation of Graves/SDi, when did I first start thinking in Second Tier? Undoubtedly I experienced a major release of Yellow thinking, self-actualisation in Maslow's model, as a result of the Beck & Cowan workshops in March-April 1998. At first I reasoned I had experienced a "Quantum Leap" as Beck & Cowan termed it when someone experienced the emergence of 2 or 3 levels more or less simultaneously. (While Beck has always held this can be simultaneously, Cowan later told me he thought it was more a case of sequential emergence in rapid succession.) However, as I've reflected on my own life over the years, I've come increasingly to the conclusion that I had already accessed Yellow thinking much earlier in my life, albeit briefly, and then largely succumbed to the demands of my First Tier vMemes under the pressures of daily living. What the Beck & Cowan workshops did for me was to enable me to understand this way of thinking and thus legitimise it for me.

To refer to zeitgeist, the spirit of the times, my teenage years coincided with that great outpouring of artistic, musical and life expression from the mid-1960s to the mid-1970s, the hippie era. In SDi terms, it was very much Green at a cultural level releasing Red by undermining Blue. In the name of fulfilling self, the rules and restrictions of society were ignored, effectively allowing huge amounts of self-indulgence. The expectation that sex took place within the confines of a loving and committed, married and heterosexual relationship was rejected. The new standard that you should be able to fulfil yourself with whomever and in whatever way led, more or less directly, to the so-called era of "free love".

Undoubtedly the late 60s was a remarkable time of experimentation in, eventually, just about every area of human life in the Western world. Much of the music, film and art of the time remain unsurpassed for its adventurous eclecticism. However, there were consequences. Fifty years later, well over a third of marriages in the Western world end in divorce, we have large numbers of single parent families with an explosion of attachment disorders amongst children and teenagers, not to mention drug epidemics, HIV and other sexually-transmitted diseases and very high rates of unwanted teenage pregnancies.

Our house was a microcosm of the cultural conflicts of the time: My Red/Green harmonic kicking against the Blue rules and regulations of my father. I was very attracted to the hippie culture, drawn in initially by the music of the American West Coast, from The Mamas & The Papas to Quicksilver Messenger Service and especially Jefferson Airplane who were one of the more literate and articulate exponents of hippie ideals. Peace and anti-war, anti-establishment, sex without marriage, don't trust anyone over 30 - I took it all in. How I loved singing the Airplane's infamous "Up against the wall, motherfuckers!" chant while strolling past the head teacher's open door!

But however much I embraced the Green memes put out by the Airplane and their peers, many of the underpinning expectations in life were still oriented from Blue, internalised undoubtedly from my father's quest for and insistence upon order. Thus, it was a profound shock at university when one of my tutors, whom I only remember as "Ken", laughed at me when I responded to a criticism of my work by saying, "But it says in the book...."

The realisation over the next few months that, just because it was in print, didn't necessarily mean it was valid was truly disturbing and eventually led me to doubt many of the trusted givens on which I based my life. Though it would take Beck & Cowan to legitimise and stabilise Yellow thinking for me, I think Ken's undermining of my First Tier certainties nudged me into tolerating and then accepting ambiguity and uncertainty.

Today, thanks to SDi, it makes perfect sense that people have different views, that the same person may have different views on the same issue according to the context and the stimulus they are presented with. That one news channel will present a different take on what is supposedly "hard fact news" than another and one newspaper will present a completely logical justification for voting one way while another paper will present an equally-coherent case for voting the other way, seems terribly realistic to me now. There may, after all, be only one reality, despite what the mystics say and the science fiction enthusiasts dream of. But, if there is, then there are a multitude of perspectives on that reality. How someone perceives an issue will depend on which vMeme or vMeme harmonic is dominating in what Susan Blackmore (1999) calls the selfplex, one's sense of self, and what schemas one has internalised from the memes they have been exposed to. Further, that internalisation process itself is influenced strongly by the vMemes dominating in the selfplex.

I often hear talk amongst SDi aficionados about how wonderful, revealing, meaningful and exhilarating it is living life through a Second Tier lens. It is almost as though they have reached some form of enlightenment in which they now locate themselves, especially if they believe they have accessed Turquoise thinking. When I first encountered SDi, I thought Yellow thinking sounded really interesting, But Turquoise somehow revolted me. It sounded like it was the way tree-huggers and all those precious environmentalists and do-gooders thought. Interestingly Chris Cowan later told me that he certainly didn't understand Turquoise at the time of the "Spiral Dynamics" book (1996), and that he and Beck modelled what they thought Turquoise might be as a hypothesised Second Tier combination of Purple and Green without really understanding what they were doing. Personally I'm not at all sure I understand Turquoise. It doesn't revolt me at all these days. It just seems beyond my comprehension other than as a set of words I vaguely aspire to because my Blue tells me that's the direction I should be going in.

I have no doubt I self-actualise into Yellow thinking at times. But I spend most of my time slumming it in the mud of Red and Blue. I'm terribly self-indulgent. I like sex, drinking and shoot-em-up movies and I hate the shame of admitting I'm wrong. I have strong Blue expectations of how things should be and easily become disturbed and/or offended if my expectations are disappointed.

As discussed earlier, with my wife's help, I'm working on repairing my Purple. My Orange is seriously deficient. I bumble through life without strategies or even focussed objectives beyond a desire to have my work in "Integrated SocioPsychology" becoming influential in the development of the behavioural sciences. My Green likewise is deficient. I really have to work at caring what happens to the planet, it certainly doesn't come naturally, and I am quite accepting of social inequalities. From what I would argue is a Yellow perspective, I see the growing divide between the very small numbers of the very rich and the growing and very large numbers of the very poor as becoming unsustainable systemically. But that's not a Green perspective. Strangely, though, as a teacher I abhor the message that implies that lower ability students are lacking. So my Green must be functioning to some extent.

Work And SDi

Prior to the Beck & Cowan workshops, career-wise I was very much driven by Blue. Unsurprisingly, perhaps, given the household I grew up in, once I had gotten over the peak of my hippie rebellion, unconsciously perhaps my Yellow taking in the consequences of all that Green liberated Red indulgence, I settled easily into Blue ways of thinking and ended up working as a consultant on quality standards like ISO 9000 and Investors in People. Unfortunately I very much approached this work, not from the angle of business improvement but from the perspective that what was required was rigid conformity to idealised models of business performance.

My precision and attention to detail made me effective in getting organisations to meet their desired standard but I did little or nothing to improve business performance. One printing house in London threw out the project because I was tying them up in paperwork. That was typical of Blue's emphasis on form over function. That motivation was taken to the extremes of punishing the sinner when, during a procedural audit in a care home, I castigated a nurse for not signing the care plan in the right place. The nurse was in tears but the care plan itself was fine and the actual care delivered even better. But all my myopic Blue could see was that the nurse had invalidated the plan because she hadn't signed in the right place. No wonder the care home owner threatened to physically eject me from the building! Paradoxically perhaps, my father, who was also providing ISO 9000 consultancy at the same time, was more effective at improving business performance than I was. In retrospect, there was clearly some Orange pragmatism tempering his interpretation and application of the quality standard. Once I had that astounding release of Yellow thinking following the Beck & Cowan workshops in March-April 1998, I began to focus on what the system needed, rather than what I personally thought should be done.

The problems with Business Link were resolved quickly. They didn't have the funding to carry on my work as an employee so I reinvented myself as a self-employed adviser. With Ian Lavan and another adviser, Steven Beevers, who had also been infected with the memes of SDi, we created a business network, the 21st Century Group, which was so effective in getting local small business leaders to think strategically it was commended by the government's Department of Trade & Industry (Rice, 2007a). We also supported the HemsMESH project which involved Don Beck in using an SDi Meshwork approach to look at regeneration in the South-East Wakefield former coalfields (Rice, 2007b).

Though I personally wasn't interested in money much beyond what I needed to live my fairly simple life, I made more money in the 18 months after the Beck & Cowan workshops than I ever have, before or since, both from public funds and private companies. It didn't last, of course. The new Government initiated a drastic restructure of the Business Links and I eventually returned to teaching.

As a part-time teacher, I've found the multiple perspectives facilitated by SDi invaluable in understanding how and why educational institutions do and don't work. In the early nineties I lived in Hull where the political elite were convulsed with the unpalatable fact that the city came bottom of the GCSE qualification league tables year after year. High rates of truancy were identified as a key factor, i.e. how can the students learn if they are not in school? As I pointed out to several local politicians and council/education officials I was in contact with, children and teenagers are voracious learning machines. Those truanting students just weren't learning what the system wanted them to learn. Instead they were learning how to have sex, take drugs, fight, steal cars, evade police, etc., etc., things that were relevant to their values.

This was really brought home to me around the same time when I took on a short-term supply contract in nearby Grimsby. Like Hull it was a depressed town, in good part due to the severe decline in the fishing industry. The school I was assigned to was located in a part of town where many of the former fisher folk lived. It was now wracked with unemployment, poverty, prostitution, drugs and gangs. For History lessons I had to teach 14-year-old bottom-set Year 8s about the political manoeuvring and religious schisms which had brought about the English Reformation. No matter how much I tried to make it a soap-opera narrative about Henry VIII and his wives, they lost interest as soon as I went into the political and religious contexts, resulting in bad behaviour and high-stress conflicts. When I asked, only 2 of the class had been in a church and only one had ever opened a Bible. The History topic had no relevance to them and only a few had much idea what a king was.

I suggested to the school that, since a prime objective was to teach the students how to do History, we set them a coursework project on Grimsby in the time of the fishing fleets, for which they could get information from their parents, uncles and aunts and grandparents, thus exploiting the familial and oral traditions healthy Purple is so rooted in. Unfortunately the Blue of the school insisted on sticking to the National Curriculum and not deviating at all into unapproved projects, for no matter how short a period of time.

More Than 15 Years Of SDi

Some 6 months after he had been on one of my courses, Lewis Lynch, a former novice monk turned Religious Studies teacher, told me he could find no weakness in the SDi theory. He had tested and looked for flaws. He had put up scenarios where he thought it may not have been able to give him insight. In every instance, Lewis reported that the theory held true. More than 15 years after the Beck & Cowan workshops Don's former PA Petra Pieterse has referred to me as "one of the old-timers". What Lewis reported is how I feel today about SDi.

I live my life as though 7 broad-based systemic motivations live inside my head with the potential for an 8th to emerge. I understand they conflict sometimes. I also understand that they collaborate. What they each do is not always in my global best interest in a particular circumstance. So, while I usually seek to nourish them in the way that Maslow saw them as "needs", I also understand that sometimes they also have to be restrained, all according to the current circumstances, or "Life Conditions" as Graves termed them.

I also meta-state (to use Michael Hall's (1995) term for interpretation via frame of reference) my interactions with others via the Spiral. What memes are going back and forth between us? Facilitated by what vMemes? And are those vMemes in competition or harmony?

Over time I've also come to realise what SDi is not. It patently is not "the theory that explains everything" as claimed by Nicholas Steed in Canada's Maclean's Magazine (1967), an unfortunate strapline which both Beck and Cowan have used at times in the past and which probably has done the theory no favours amongst academic sociological and psychological researchers. SDi per se has little or nothing to say about such key areas of psychological concern as:

- The unconscious, either in the psychodynamic sense of a repository for hidden drivers and unacceptable memories or the cognitive notion of unconscious processing.
- Perceptual processes, either top down or bottom up.
- Temperament.
- Memory.
- Psychopathology.

Yet, if the precepts and understandings of SDi were applied throughout the behavioural sciences, what applications to these and other areas might be uncovered? For example, Graves (1971/2002) speculated that there was most likely a connection between temperament and vMeme motivational systems, but had no credible evidence for this. Clearly, he was not aware of the unpublished work of NN Trauel (1961; reported by Hans J Eysenck, 1967) which found a link between extraversion (temperament) and disobedience (motivation). As the four types of attitude and behaviour described by Marston seem to contain describing words and phrases for both temperament and motivation, would this again imply strongly that there is some kind of link between these two dimensions of the human psyche? If Freud's Id is equated to the warm colored side of the Spiral and Red in particular, while the Ego-Superego tendency to conformity and obedience is matched to the cool colored side of the Spiral, would this imply a better understanding of the unconscious could be developed by applying SDi motivations rather than Freudian/psychoanalytic ones?

Questions such as these have led me over the past 10 years to work on formulating an approach I call "Integrated SocioPsychology". Put simply, this involves assuming that SDi is the most accurate representation of human motivations and then seeing how other psychological and sociological concepts fit with it. What I'm finding is that having SDi underpinning everything makes sense of the behavioural sciences. Disparate and sometimes contradictory assumptions increasingly seem to fit into a greater whole, in which they seem to explain different aspects of that whole without being contradictory. By finding them a place within the greater whole, these many concepts add both depth and breadth to the knowledge and understanding SDi provides. It's a huge and highly ambitious task, of course, aligning and integrating the behavioural sciences around the conceptual structure of SDi, a task I'm increasingly aware is beyond my sole capacities. Nonetheless, increasingly I'm coming to see this as my mission in life: To develop an approach for integrating and aligning the behavioural sciences based primarily on SDi.

Thus, in effect, I can say that not only did Beck & Cowan save my sanity (and possibly my life too) back in March-April 1998, but they also set me on course for discovering my mission in life. That mission also has to have a pragmatic and highly-practical face to it. Whatever Integrated SocioPsychology becomes as it develops from its core of SDi, for me it has to be something that can transform people's lives for their real benefit. Many of my early workshop programmes lost money, due to the difficulty of getting people interested in a new and relatively unknown concept. I was frequently asked why I continued to run them, often with only a small handful of attendees. The answer I used to give still applies: In SDi I've been given a wonderful gift that is effectively the key to understanding human life. It's enabled me to transform my life. When I've been given such a wonderful gift, how could I not want to share it with others?

Bibliography

Ainsworth, Mary & Sandra Bell (1970): "Attachment, Exploration and Separation: illustrated by the Behaviour of One-year-olds in a Strange Situation" in Child Development #41

Beck, Don & Chris Cowan (1996). *Spiral Dynamics: Mastering Change, Values and Leadership.* (Blackwell, Cambridge MA)

Berscheid, Ellen & Elaine Walster (1978). *Interpersonal Attraction.* (2nd edition, Addison-Wesley, Reading MA)

Blackmore, Susan (1999). *The Meme Machine.* (Oxford University Press)

Bowlby, John (1951). *Maternal Care and Mental Health.* (World Health Organisation, Geneva Switzerland)

Buss, David (1989). "Sex Differences in Human Mate Preferences; Evolutionary Hypotheses tested in 37 Cultures" in Behavioural & Brain Sciences #12

Eysenck, Hans J (1967). *The Biological Basis of Personality.* (Charles C Thomas, Springfield IL)

Eysenck, Hans J & Sybil B G Eysenck (1976). *Psychoticism as a Dimension of Personality.* (Charles C Thomas, Springfield IL)

Freud, Sigmund (1924; translated by Joan Riviere). "The Passing of the Oedipus Complex" in International Journal of Psycho-Analysis 5/4

Freud, Sigmund (1940; translated by James Strachey, 1949). *An Outline of Psycho-Analysis.* (Hogarth Press/Institute of Psycho-Analysis, London)

Graves, Clare W (1970): "Levels of Existence: an Open System Theory of Values" in Journal of Humanistic Psychology 10/2

Graves, Clare W (1971; transcribed by William R Lee, 2002). *Levels of Human Existence.* (ECLET, Santa Barbara CA)

Hall, L Michael (1995). *Meta States: a Domain of Logical Levels.* (ET Publications, Grand Junction CO)

Hazen, Cindy & Phil Shaver (1987): "Romantic Love conceptualised as an Attachment Process" in Journal of Personality & Social Psychology #52

Hazen, Cindy & Phil Shaver (1993): "Adult Romantic Attachment: Theory and Evidence" in D Perlman & W Jones: "Advances in Personal Relationships Vol 4" (Kingsley, London)

Marston, William Moulton (1928). *Emotions of Normal People.* (Taylor & Francis, New York NY)

Maslow, Abraham (1943): "A Theory of Human Motivation" in Psychological Review #50

Nursing Times (1952): "Visits to Children in Hospital" (15 March)

Rice, Keith E (2007a): "21st Century Group: a Tribute to a 'World-beating' Business Network' http://www.integratedsociopsychology. net/21st_c_g.html (Accessed: 01/01/14)

Rice, Keith E (2007b): "HemsMESH: a Tribute to a Pioneering MeshWORK Project" http://www.integratedsociopsychology.net/hemsmesh.html (Accessed: 01/01/14)

Steed, Nicholas (1967): "The Theory that Explains Everything" in Maclean's Magazine (October)

Trauel, N N (1961): 'The Effects of Perceptual Isolation on Introverts and Extraverts' (unpublished PhD thesis, Washington State University)

Waynforth, David & Robin Dunbar (1995): "Conditional Mate Choice Strategies in Humans: evidence from Lonely Hearts Advertisements" in Behaviour #132

THE SPIRAL OF INTIMACY

By Rafael Nasser

Evolutionary Intimacy

Two pairs of eyes connect across the spirited room and share a timeless moment. A loud blur holding a beer bottle breaks their line of sight and the connection is broken. But magnetized by the exchange, their paths weave through the ambient crowd and converge by the bar. Under the guise of some trivial pretense, a conversation ensues. Numbers are exchanged and texts are traded the next day. He proposes dinner Saturday night, French. She replies, yes.

The beaming faces are sipping a fine Merlot. Flirtation, humor, and a general sense of wellbeing flavor the meal. The body language communicates attraction. Each is wearing the mask of courtship, the playful and light hearted persona that arises naturally in the first stage of relationship. The date ends with a kiss and the promise of more to follow. The following week there is another date, and then a few days later, lunch and an impromptu dinner. Later that night, it is raining hard. She invites him in. The muted lightning striates their faces and the thunderclap renders words superfluous. Clothes fall away to the sound of the torrent rapping the window. The silhouettes draw near and melt through the darkness into the sheets.

I heard a story once about an indigenous tribe that pitched a tent in the middle of the village where potential life mates would spend the night. The following morning, the tribe would gather round and the couple would proclaim to their kinsmen whether or not they were of the same song. Those words don't require translation.

Back to our couple. Daylight is peering through the curtains. Limbs entwined, the sheets stir. One and then the other awakens. Over breakfast their eyes meet again, and this time a warm and tender feeling swells in the area behind their breastbones. While no villagers are gathered around the kitchen awaiting a proclamation, the realization arises without fanfare that they are of the same song. Welcome to the realm of intimacy.

Words can be made to stretch various directions and encompass different meanings. For our purposes, intimacy implies relationship space that embraces both sexuality and love. Experientially, an intimate bond blends the sexual attraction and the heart. Poetically, intimacy is the passionate connection that forms between soulmates. But strip away the romantic gloss associated with that word, soulmate, and dive deep into the psychological dimension of a soul-centered connection. Soulmates have their fingers on our button while our fingers are on their button. As the soul-mating process unfolds, sooner or later, the closet door opens and the skeletons begin their parade.

Six blissful weeks have passed. Our couple is perfectly content. Their hearts are wide open vessels with love pouring between them. But one day, unexpectedly, she raises an issue that troubles her. Her words sting like a scorpion tail. He withdraws guardedly. When their eyes meet again, the love is still present, but now there is a narrow chasm. A critical moment arises as they stand at a fork in the road. Will they manage to address the issue and close the distance that separates them or will the chasm grow and undermine the relationship? Let's envision both scenarios.

In the first scenario, they follow the path of evolutionary intimacy. Evolutionary intimacy manifests in a relationship that recognizes that a core issue dredged up by a loving partner represents an opportunity to develop and grow as a human being. She loves him and is pointing a concerned finger at a legitimate issue. Outside the relationship he might ignore that issue, but from within the relationship he chooses to listen and through the alchemy of sex, love, and conscious engagement in the face of adversity, his awareness grows. After a deep process of soul searching, he rises to the occasion, willingly undergoes a life altering transformation, and becomes a more complete human being. The chasm disappears. Their bond deepens and their love grows. The butterfly is a symbol that captures the essence of transformation: A wormy aspect of the psyche dies and you are reborn a more beautiful creature. Evolutionary intimacy leads to relationship space that is filled with butterflies.

In the second scenario, he lacks the capacity to transform. As the charged issue arises in the relationship, ancient wounds and deep unconscious projections are drawn into the process. Not everyone is prepared to "die" in the name of growth, and the instinct to preserve the status quo sabotages the process of development. Down this way lies repression, depression, blame, denial, betrayal, and pain, as the unconscious grabs the steering wheel and drives the couple to Shadowland, a dark relationship space filled with stinging scorpions.

Which path do our soulmates choose, the way of the scorpion or the way of the butterfly? That depends on two factors; first, the level of development of both partners. Evolutionary intimacy requires two souls that have independently reached a high level of development. Unless both partners embody evolutionary values and are willing to undergo the ordeal of transformation, then intimacy is likely to become a complicated drama dominated by shadow play. If only one partner possesses the capacity for evolutionary intimacy, the relationship oscillates between light and shadow. One individual transforms while the other remains stuck in darkness. Eventually, the relationship becomes painful and unfulfilling and a bittersweet breakup ensues.

Only when both partners enter into relationship with evolutionary intent does the relationship become a cauldron of transformation and a generator of a greater kind of love. But this can only happen - and this is the critical point - after specific evolutionary structures are embodied by each soulmate and incorporated into the relationship.

These structures are described by Spiral Dynamics Integral (SDi), a conceptual framework developed by Dr. Don Beck. SDi is a system that tracks human emergence across eight levels of development represented by a sequence of colors: Beige, Purple, Red, Blue, Orange, Green, Yellow and Turquoise. The system is open-ended suggesting that higher evolutionary possibilities exist beyond the current horizon of human development.

According to SDi, each color represents a set of Life Conditions or existential challenges and the lifeway that emerges to resolve those challenges. A lifeway is a perspective that constellates biological, psychological, cultural, and social systems around a common theme such as safety, power, or order. When Life Conditions change, new more complex existential problems may arise which the current lifeway is unable to manage, and the status quo becomes unsustainable. Eventually a new lifeway emerges and resolves the new existential challenges and a new color is born.

LEVEL	AS LOVER	BOND OF INTIMACY	LEAVES BEHIND	CARRIES FORWARD
Beige	*Sensual Lover*	*Bond of Pleasure*	*Loneliness, Celibacy*	*Sensuality, Juicy Pleasure*
Purple	*Dreamy Lover*	*Bond of Magic*	*Romantic Fantasies*	*Loyalty, Safety, Familiarity*
Red	*Confident Lover*	*Bond of Joy*	*Selfishness, Power Plays*	*Power, Fun, Playfulness*
Blue	*Trustworthy Lover*	*Bond of Commitment*	*Rigidity, Heartless Obedience*	*Commitment, Discipline, Trust*
Orange	*Individuated Lover*	*Bond of Authenticity*	*Alienation, Disconnection*	*Authenticity, Freedom*
Green	*Sensitive Lover*	*Bond of Understanding*	*Hypersensitivity, Self-absorption*	*Consideration, Sensitivity*
Yellow	*Evolutionary Lover*	*Bond of Transformation*	*Turbulence, Intensity*	*Evolutionary Intent, Proactive Emergence*
Turquoise	*Mystical Lover*	*Bond of Harmony*	*Yet to be determined*	*Harmony, Symphonic Coherence*

According to SDi, eight distinct lifeways emerged cross-culturally over the 200,000 year old lifespan of our species, and each lifeway is represented by one of the colors of the Spiral. The relationship between the colors can be understood through the metaphor of mathematics. Some problems can be solved using simple arithmetic. But some problems are more complex and require a more complex form of mathematics, like algebra. And there are some problems that are too complex for algebra and require calculus.

Question, which is better? Arithmetic, algebra, or calculus? Clearly, we can't make a value judgment between these three forms of mathematics since they represent a holarchy, a nested hierarchy. Arithmetic is intrinsic to algebra, and algebra is intrinsic to calculus. Each is equally vital in the context of the whole. The progression from arithmetic to calculus merely represents a progressing along levels of complexity. Similarly, the colors of the Spiral represent a nested hierarchy of lifeways, values, and coping capacities that emerged over time to address existential problems of increasing degrees of complexity. Like mathematics, SDi can be applied to solve problems across different orders of magnitude, the species-wide level, the corporate level, the individual level, or even at the level of an intimate relationship. And like mathematics, SDi can be applied to various fields such as politics, economics, and even relationships.

More concretely: Beige emerged as the lifeway designed to address Beige existential problems. But at some stage of human history, a new challenge emerged that Beige was unable to resolve. Life became complicated. People felt trapped, stuck, frustrated, and some of them lost hope. At this point, facing an existential threat and utter despair, the human spirit introduced creativity into the mix and a novel and more complex vision of life evolved. As a critical mass embraced that vision, a new lifeway emerged. A new color emerged, Purple.

But eventually, Life Conditions changed anew as another existential problem developed that Purple couldn't manage. Life became complicated again. Some lost hope but another vision emerged that gave birth to Red, and a new wave of human emergence ensued. This dialectical process repeated and new colors emerged: Blue, Orange, Green, Yellow, and finally Turquoise, where the leading edge of human emergence is currently unfolding.

A noteworthy theoretical aspect of SDi relates to the alternation between warm colors (Beige, Red, Orange, and Yellow) and cool colors (Purple, Blue, Green, and Turquoise). The warm colors orient lifeways around agentic values that focus on projecting the individual will out into the world, while the cool colors orient lifeways around communal values that encourage a consideration of other people's will and fosters compromise, collaboration, and the subjugation of the individual for the sake of the group. The oscillation between agentic and communal values reflects the evolutionary drive to restore equilibrium whenever a perspective stagnates or reaches an extreme.

The following primer explores the eight colors of SDi in the context of love and sex. What are the Life Conditions and the coping capacities that emerge at each level? How does each color get expressed in a healthy and unhealthy way? What kind of lover emerges at each level of the Spiral?

What kind of relationship bond emerges at each level? Which aspects of a lower level are carried forward and which are left behind as the evolution of intimacy advances?

Our imaginary soulmates are still standing at a fork in the road, their relationship fate undecided. But they are not standing alone. A huge crowd is forming. If you are motivated by the evolutionary impulse and are in an intimate relationship or desire to be in one, you are standing there too. The following primer on the Spiral of Intimacy is meant as a guide for all who dare to evolve in love, including you.

Beige

Beige in History: (Middle Paleolithic, 200,000–50,000 years ago.) Anatomically modern humans appear in the fossil record around 200,000 years ago. For the first 150,000 years, our ancestors utilized tools and exhibited behavioral patterns similar to those of humans dating back a million years. These pre-cultural humans lived like sophisticated animals. They relied on strength, agility, instincts, and reflexes to adapt to the dangers posed by predators roaming the immediate environment. They gathered in loose bands and, although they did not display signs of culture, religion, music or art, had the same potential for intelligence as we have and had mastered fire. The theme that organizes the Beige lifeway is SURVIVAL.

Intimate Beige: You meet a stranger and experience instant attraction. You don't know her name or anything about her. She is an attractive female animal and the male animal in you responds. Your proverbial loins stir. You are experiencing Beige sexual desire.

Beige centers on the theme of survival, and at the level of relationship, Beige centers on the theme of sexual reproduction. Sexual vitality favors the perpetuation of the species and nature uses the power of physical attraction to magnetize potential mates. But human reproduction requires a long-term commitment on the part of both partners. A female is especially vulnerable while she is pregnant and then while tending to her helpless infant. She needs support from a mate who can hunt and provide sustenance for her and the child. To ensure the survival of the species, nature also predisposed mates to love each other. Love is the glue that bonds a sexual relationship that survives over the long term. Intimacy is nature's ways of ensuring the survival of the next generation.

At the ground level of the Spiral of Intimacy we encounter the raw ingredients of intimacy, sex and love, in their pure state. Beige intimacy includes the carnal aspects of love and sex. The joy of touching, hearing, seeing, smelling and tasting your lover are an expression of Beige. Caressing, holding hands, kissing, teasing, grunting, biting, scratching, screaming, and other animal sounds related to lovemaking also fall under that category.

In its healthy expression, Beige intimacy stimulates the senses and awakens sensuality. A heathy Beige relationship feels juicy. A healthy Beige partner personifies the SENSUAL LOVER who exudes animal magnetism. Popular icons like movie stars and athletes with a strong power of attraction embody this quality. The intimate bond formed at Beige is the BOND OF PLEASURE. We enjoy good food at any age and in a vital Beige relationship, we enjoy sensual lovemaking at any age as well.

Unhealthy Beige intimacy occurs when sexual desire wanes and love atrophies in the context of a relationship. Pathological Beige manifests when a partner rejects eroticism and shuts the heart to love. When we stop touching, kissing, and sexual contact becomes unwelcome or repulsive; when we stop caring and dry up, emotionally and physically, Beige intimacy disintegrates.

The delight derived from the physicality of a soulmate forms the base for all the subsequent levels of intimacy and while more complex and meaningful forms of intimacy emerge at higher levels of the Spiral, without healthy Beige sensuality, the process stalls.

But eventually, complications arise in a relationship that even healthy Beige intimacy can't resolve. As emotional needs are revealed and vulnerabilities are exposed, pressure mounts on the couple to develop new coping capacities and for the relationship to evolve. Beige is a warm color that focuses on agentic values and self-expression characteristic of the courtship stage. At Purple, the second level of the Spiral, the focus shifts to the emergence of communal values that emphasize the safety needs of the other and loyalty to the partnership. The shift that accompanies Beige to Purple in relationship reflects the broader historical shift that occurred about 50,000 years ago as Life Conditions changed resulting in new existential problems that transcended the coping capacities of Beige and inspired the emergence of a new Lifeway.

Purple

Purple in History: (Lower Paleolithic, 50,000-12,000 years ago). Around 50,000 years ago, temperatures plummeted, and ice sheets advanced robbing the air of moisture. Life Conditions worsened. A small band of humans coped with this existential challenge by developing symbolic thinking and language, and used those cognitive tools to invent culture. They created complex tools that leveraged the resources of their diminishing habitat and ensured the welfare and safety of the clan or tribe. (Geneticists believe that every human alive today descends from this ancestral group.) Culture lifted consciousness from its identification with the physical environment that defined Beige, and projected reality into symbolic realms vested with symbolic meaning. Myth, religion, art, music, and a magical worldview emerged from this imaginal wellspring and these cultural artifacts instilled a sense of existential wellbeing. The theme that organized the Purple lifeway was SAFETY.

Purple Intimacy: As intimacy spirals into Purple, it carries forward Beige sensuality into the realm of symbolism and the imagination. The root symbol of our identity is our name, and we usually enter the Purple aspect of relationship by asking someone we find attractive, what is your name?

Language generates symbolic universes filled with meaning and each intimate relationship is a private linguistic world made up of particular words. As a relationship develops, nicknames and secret code words are created. A linguistic boundary marks personal relationship space apart from the mainstream. Within this boundary, the couple enters Purple relationship space, where they develop familiarity and deepen their bond.

Imagine that a person of interest didn't speak your native tongue. An intimate relationship lacking of language would be severely limited. Or imagine a relationship in which conversations lack familiarity and sound like a generic technical manual. Both of these scenarios point to a deficiency of Purple.

Rituals and habits form another expression of Purple. Cooking together on weekends, morning nature walks, meditating together every day, celebrating birthdays and anniversaries, and any other way in which a couple routinely carves out chunks of space and time belongs to this level. The rituals of a relationship reinforce common interests such as music, religion, spirituality, and recreation, and reinforce the bond of kinship between two individuals.

The theme of vulnerability, safety, and protection dominates Purple. At the level of intimacy, cultivating the feeling of safety allows for the expression of deeper emotions. Imagine a woman becoming sick and incapacitated with a bad case of the flu that lasts ten days. With healthy Purple, her partner makes himself available and tends to her needs. He cooks her meals, makes her soup, and he runs errands for her. At a time of vulnerability, he nurtures and stands by her side. As this process unfolds, she realizes that her mate truly cares and their relationship space expands to include the quality of loyalty. Perhaps, some day in the future, a serious disease will befall a partner that requires the significant support of the other. Without healthy Purple, the instinct would be to run away. But with healthy Purple the feeling of family arises as does the desire to help unconditionally.

The woman is feeling better now and the couple is making love for the first time in two weeks. She stops midway, smiles, and kisses him on the cheek, "What is that for?" he asks. "For being such a wonderful mother," she replies. Purple intimacy deepens the heart.

Purple intimacy is also characterized by its magical quality. You might not notice the full moon tonight, but if you are in a Purple state of mind and sharing the moment with your partner, that moon is going to tap your shoulder and whisper words of love. As two people fall in Purple love, they enter an otherworldly realm. The world becomes an enchanted paradise. Purple love colors the world pink. Are those angels in the clouds? Are those fairies in the rosebushes? Under the spell of Purple love, you hear the music in the traffic and the rustling leaves reciting poetry.

As Purple grabs a foothold on the heart, romance develops. For one couple, romance might include an evening sipping wine while staring at the fireplace. For another couple, wild dancing in a crowded club. But picture the same proverbial violins playing above the vignettes and those two souls as they experience each other with the vividness of a waking dream. Healthy Purple carries the couple into spellbinding space and time. With healthy Purple, lovers establish a BOND OF MAGIC with a DREAMY LOVER.

Deficient Purple dissociates the imaginative realm from intimacy. Without magic, rituals, and familiarity, a relationship becomes a collection of dull routines. Without moments of dreamtime punctuating drudgery, love and sex lose their charm. As the magical bond of purple weakens, the relationship becomes less hospitable. Without magical Purple, you awaken one morning wondering who this stranger is snoring beside you in bed.

Heathy Purple imbues relationship space with safety, loyalty, and enchantment. But at a certain point, as boundaries are tested, issues arise that require one or both partners to assert their will within the context of the encroaching familiarity. Complications arise that require expanding relationship space to incorporate new values and qualities to address issues related to honoring boundaries and personal space. At Red, the third level of the Spiral, the focus shifts to the emergence of agentic values, self-expression, and the cultivation of power and confidence. The shift that accompanies Purple to Red in relationship reflects the broader historical shift that occurred about 14,000 years ago as new existential problems developed that led to the emergence of a new Lifeway.

Red

Red in History: (The Neolithic Age and the Bronze Age, 12,000–2,500 years ago) About 12,000 years ago, the Ice Age ended and Life Conditions improved. Temperate weather and abundant food transformed nature into paradise. Populations grew and settlements formed. To sustain the swelling populations, horticulture and animal husbandry developed. Populations continued to grow, and as resources became scarce again, metallurgy was invented. Metal plows increased agriculture yields dramatically and populations grew even larger. Cities developed and eventually the great river valley civilizations emerged. Granaries were built to store surplus goods and metal was forged into weapons to protect walled cities and food supplies. Armed and well stocked, collective consciousness experienced confidence for the first time in the history of cultured humans.

The transformation of consciousness that accompanied these developments was the emergence of the ego. An attitude of power, confidence, and strength displaced the sense of vulnerability that had dominated human consciousness during the Upper Paleolithic. POWER subverted safety as the dominant theme. Kingship, institutionalized egoism, emerged as a social institution, as well as the warrior caste and the cult of hero worship. As Red constellated power, honor, glory, majesty, heroism, kingship, and the confident ego into a new lifeway, the Spiral emerged its newest form.

Red Intimacy: From the bedrock of the Purple imagination arises a new structure of consciousness, the ego. Cast aside the slurs heaped on the ego by other levels of development. At Red, the ego refers to your capacity to project your will into the world. The imagination envisions dreams, the ego manifests them. If Purple is the receptive moon, then Red is the beaming sun, and indeed the shift between Purple and Red was a historical shift between lunar and solar consciousness.

You hear a creak at night in the woods. Is it a dangerous animal, an axe murderer, a ghost? In the face of the unknown, the wild imagination makes us feel two inches tall. Fear negates the ego. The same noise in the daytime is shrugged off. While night introverts imaginatively, day extraverts egoically. Day illuminates the external world and our senses expand into that landscape with self-assurance. The high expression of Red embodies the qualities of the sun. Like the sun, a healthy ego radiates light and warmth into the world. At this rung of the Spiral, the archetype of the Hero awakens, that aspect of our identity willing to take on challenges that defy the odds.

Red intimacy strengthens the ego of the partners. A sense of power surges into relationship space and builds confidence. Each member of the relationship develops courage that can be deployed within the relationship to assert rights and also in relationship with the world. A heathy Red relationship empowers an individual to forge ahead and conquer the world.

When both partners embody healthy Red, their combined self-confidence skyrockets. Each member of the relationship can draw on this energy to push beyond his or her limits in pursuit of some personal ambition, or they can join forces to enforce a mutual agenda. At Red, the relationship brims with revitalizing fun and intimacy is awash in creativity, playfulness, and the spirit of adventure. The lover that emerges at Red is the CONFIDENT LOVER and the bond that emerges is the BOND OF JOY.

Imagine a career opportunity manifesting for him: He can quit his safe corporate job and assume a high position at a startup with potential. Purple says: "No, don't do it." There is hesitation to depart from the more secure path, but her healthy Red says, "Go for it, my love, I know that you will succeed." Confidence is often the determining factor between success and failure, and heroic accomplishments often bear the hallmark of a soulmate motivating and inspiring courage. Her bold confidence feeds his Red and he takes the job with vibrant confidence. Move ahead a few years, an IPO is issued, and overnight, they become multi-millionaires. With her encouragement, he has conquered the world. In bed, that evening, he offers her a ribbon-wrapped box. "What is this for?" she asks. "The gift of courage," he replies. Minutes later, she is wearing a sparkling diamond necklace as they make passionate love, both faces beaming Red joy and undulating their victory dance.

In some traditional cultures a woman is conditioned to assume a Purple pre-egoic role in relationship. She is taught to identify with her husband's ego and to subsume her perspective to his will. Without a healthy ego, we cannot escape the gravitational pull of our inwardness and we lead a hidden existence. A partner arrested at Purple is unable to express personal desires or ambitions clearly, especially when the other partner is expressing an opposing point of view. Deficient Red renders an intimate partner into a disempowered puppet and robs intimacy of fun.

Another version of unhealthy Red manifests in a relationship between two partners with excessive Red tendencies. A characteristic typical of Red intimacy is playfulness, and a couple with strong healthy Red enjoy playing competitive games. Red loves to win. But when Red is unhealthy, the games persist without the fun. They degenerate into power plays and destructive modes of behavior intended to subjugate the other partner. When the warmth of two playful egos is transformed into scorching arrogance and selfishness, a relationship becomes abusive and in extreme cases intimacy turns violent.

Heathy Red endows relationship space with playfulness and power. But eventually, new issues emerge that neither Red, Purple, nor Beige can resolve, as each member of the relationship must be prepared to make a long term commitment for the relationship to grow any further. As soon as the element of time is invoked in the context of intimacy, the mood turns serious and we enter novel evolutionary space.

Blue, the fourth level of the Spiral, is a cool color that emphasizes communal values, self sacrifice, and the cultivation of discipline and trust which enable a relationship to thrive over the long term. The shift that accompanies Red to Blue reflects the broader historical shift that occurred about 4500 years ago as new Life Conditions developed that led to the emergence of a new Lifeway.

Blue

Blue in History: (Classical Greece, Antiquity, and the Middle Ages, 2,500–400 years ago.) Red societies centered on the person of the king whose destiny determined the fate of the people. Teams of priests scrutinized omens and signs which were interpreted as messages from a pantheon of powerful sky gods. In the Near East, these gods played a particularly important role in religion and the movement of the celestial bodies was examined carefully. Any irregular activity in the sky became a cause for concern. Eclipses were viewed as especially virulent omens and were especially feared.

Thales of Miletus is known as the father of philosophy. He earned this moniker for predicting the solar eclipse of May 28, 585 BCE. This prediction was a significant event that heralded the emergence of the next whirl of the Spiral, Blue. Thales' prediction proved that the seemingly omnipotent sky gods were subject to a higher power that maintained an orderly and predictable kosmos. A singular omnipotent deity was conceived, God or the Logos, who was supremely logical, rational, and moral. The notion developed that human beings, created in the image of God, possessed a rational soul and the capacity for logic and reason.

With the emergence of Blue, ORDER displaced power as the topmost value. Philosophers and theologians reasoned that humans could discern God's will through the application of reason: Truth could be ascertained through logic, the Good through rationality, and Beauty through justice. As this worldview spread, societies emulated the kosmic order by rationalizing all aspects of daily life including law, ethics, warfare, architecture, art, history, cosmology, religion, and education.

Blue Intimacy: When a relationship is confronted by a demanding long-term challenge that requires strategic thinking, the mood shifts from fun to serious and the Spiral shifts gears from Red to Blue. Consider a child born to a set of young and inexperienced parents used to partying and to having a good time. New coping capacities have to develop in order to sustain the relationship and to preserve the bond of intimacy in the context of the ongoing hardship of child rearing.

The coping capacities that emerge at Blue include discipline, commitment, accountability, trust, and responsibility. These characteristics manifest naturally in the service of some common "higher purpose" or goal that requires restraining the instant gratification and short-term thinking that characterizes Red.

When raw power is unable to achieve a goal, structured discipline is needed. At Blue, a strategic goal emerges like an imposing mountain whose ascent to the peak requires organization, patience, hard work. In a phrase, orderly self-sacrifice over time.

If Beige and Purple correspond to the Id in the Freudian hierarchy, and Red corresponds to the Ego, then Blue corresponds to the Superego, the parental voice of authority that subjugates personal instinct and desire in the name of order and responsibility. When that authoritative voice articulates an objective, duty and obedience emerge as novel coping capacities.

Committing to a shared goal that inspires higher purpose is the keystone of Blue in relationship and chief among Blue goals that arise between intimate partners is the creation of a family. Family is the great work that justifies the abdication of personal desire in the name of a greater good. A father and mother each working two menial jobs to put their daughter through medical school embrace hardship as their loyal duty. Without an inspiring higher purpose, Blue self-sacrifice becomes oppressive punishment. Just imagine that same couple working two jobs to pay off a gambling debt.

Marriage is the rite of passage that ushers an intimate couple into Blue. Marriage vows are a litany of absolutist and uncompromising commitments and the declaration of undying loyalty between two souls. A groom whose development is arrested at Red would squirm under the chuppah envisioning the joys and pleasures asked to be surrendered under oath. But the rationale for self-sacrifice is the emergence of a greater joy that stems from the accomplishment of a great work, building a family.

To be sure, there exist other worthy superordinate goals that unite intimate couples who choose not to raise a family, but those goals are going to plug into the same circuitry as parenthood. Picture a young ambitious couple growing a business together. Or a retired couple tending to their vegetable garden with uncompromising devotion. Any shared responsibility that requires discipline and feeds a sense of lasting accomplishment generates healthy Blue.

A healthy Blue relationship is a robust and resilient partnership that overcomes ongoing hardship with steely determination. When both partners sacrifice personal desire for the sake of the relationship those partners develop trust. A Blue lover is a TRUSTWORTHY LOVER and the bond that emerges at Blue is the BOND OF COMMITMENT.

Envision that hard working husband and wife on the day that their daughter becomes a doctor. That evening, they are lying in bed brimming with pride of accomplishment and recollect the long and arduous sacrifices that enabled them to reach this moment. Silvery moonlight suffuses the bedroom. Their eyes meet and she sheds a tear. He takes her weathered hand and kisses it. She strokes his face and says, "I love you." He wipes away a tear and kisses her mouth. She surrenders to his touch and that evening they celebrate their accomplishment by making unforgettable love. Blue intimacy.

There are several ways a deficiency of Blue undermines intimate relationship. First, one of the partners lacks the capacity to develop healthy Blue qualities and ends up shirking responsibility. Mastering Blue requires sobering maturity and unrelenting discipline. If a member of the couple remains an eternal youth chasing after juvenile interests, the bond of commitment never develops. Alternatively, one lover can undermine the mutual respect that keeps Blue healthy by betraying the trust. Without trust, the relationship may continue to march towards a common goal, but the journey of hardship unfolds under a starless and unloving sky.

An excess of Blue stultifies intimate relationship. Life under rigid Blue becomes too orderly, boring, and predictable. The juicy grape of passion desiccates into a raisin. An overly controlling partner can breach mutual respect, dictate the rules, and become a Blue tyrant. Under fanatical Blue, relationship space hardens, punishment turns the heart to stone, and the bed, the altar on which passion is consecrated, takes on the appeal of a concrete mattress.

Healthy Blue textures relationship space with trust and discipline aimed towards achieving a goal that will benefit a couple or a family over the long term. But at some point, especially after the children are gown up and their security is no longer an issue, new complications may arise. Stereotypically, a midlife crisis initiates the process of questioning the rules and regulations that limit personal freedom. This process can develop at any time in a relationship, but only after Blue has been established, since the need for autonomy inevitably arises from the constraints of commitment. Orange, the fifth level of the Spiral, is a warm color that emphasizes agentic values and self expression in the form of authenticity and autonomy in the context of the positive qualities developed at Blue, Red, Purple, and Beige. The shift that accompanies Blue to Orange reflects the broader historical shift that occurred about 400 years ago as a new set of Life Conditions developed that inspired the emergence of a new Lifeway.

Orange

Orange in History: (The Modern Age, 1600 CE to the present.) Aristotle (d. 323 BCE) was the genius that developed the laws of logic that formalized the rational Blue worldview. His works were revered by Jewish, Christian and Muslim sages. Learned men of all three faiths referred to him as, "The Philosopher." His philosophy formed the backbone of monotheistic theology and religions invested heavily in the cosmological model his work inspired which depicted the universe as a series of concentric etheric heavenly spheres that housed and moved the planets. The imperfect Earth formed the lowest point of creation and was subject to a different set of laws than the eternal heavens. God resided in the Empyrean, the topmost of the Heavenly spheres above the fixed stars. According to this cosmological paradigm, the universe was geocentric, closed, and finite.

About 400 years ago, a series of astronomical observations began to undermine that cosmological vision. Copernicus developed a sun centered model of the universe that was a better predictor of planetary motion. Galileo pointed a telescope at Jupiter and noticed moons in orbit around the giant planet, an observation that contradicted orthodox religious dogma. Newton's discovery that the same mathematical formulas could be used to describe movement across the heavens and on earth shattered the belief that these two realms were categorically distinct.

The new cosmology inspired a new breed of thinkers who championed empirical knowledge over reasoned truth and privileged the insights of empirical science over logic. The Orange worldview that emerged stressed that learned men should rely on scientific innovation and technology to advance humanity and innovate a better future, not religion. As the modern worldview gained traction, God's central role in the affairs of the world moved to the periphery and some thinkers began to question his existence altogether.

The Parisian salons of the 18th Century cultured a progressive vision of autonomy and freedom that inspired social transformation as scientific breakthroughs resulted in new innovative technologies that transformed cities into industrial centers. The Industrial Revolution, the American Revolution, and the French Revolution represent the popular out picturing of the spirit of Orange. With Orange the theme of PROGRESS replaced order as the topmost value and with that switch, the Modern Age was born.

Orange Intimacy: The conventional models of sexuality and relationship that we internalize during our formative years reflect values that may or may not be relevant to our personal development. Consider a lesbian born into a conservative family that expects her to follow the traditional path of a youthful marriage and children. If she followed the footsteps laid down for her before she was even born, she would lose her core identity and lead a miserable existence. When tradition presses down on the heart like a heavy weight and the urge to push convention aside arises, Orange emerges.

At Orange, the process of individuation unfolds as we develop the audacity to break with convention and honor our individuality, even at the cost of disappointing those who love us the most. The liberal values that emerge at Orange inspire an unorthodox journey that leads to greater freedom and individuality.

In a relationship, Orange manifests when two partners honor their authenticity while continuing to honor the Bond of Commitment that emerges at Blue. With healthy Orange, each partner can express his or her authentic identity without the fear of being shamed or made to feel guilty by the other. When the process of individuation is lovingly supported by a partner, Orange intimacy thrives.

In an Orange relationship, progressive and innovative relationships emerge. Perhaps he stays home taking care of the children while she builds a successful career. Or she spends her vacation in India at an ashram while he treks the Appalachian Trail with his best friend. Orange intimacy establishes freedom within the relationship as well as outside the bounds of the partnership. A couple decides that monogamy doesn't suit their sexual needs and they may agree to an open relationship while remaining fully committed to loving each other. While a monogamous couple decides to honor their need for privacy by living in separate homes.

The journey at Orange leads from convention, through individuation, to authenticity. The autonomy sanctioned by Orange values enable individuals to chart their own destiny. A man born to five generations of lawyers becomes an archeologist. A high school dropout becomes an entrepreneurial billionaire. A transgender artist can become a worldwide sensation. If you are past the Red fundamentals of ego development, and leaving the accommodation demands of Blue, and moving against the grain and generating opposition as you express your authentic self, you are moving through Orange.

An Orange relationship inspires innovative ideas that support the journey that leads to authentic success. Imagine a conventional doctor who changes careers in midlife to become a painter. Her peers are startled by her unorthodox decision and try to convince her to change her mind. But with the full support of her husband, she moves ahead with her plan. The first exhibit receives rave reviews and her authentic self is deeply satisfied with her result. That night in bed she reads him a glowing review by a noted critic. "Thank you for supporting my authentic self," she says. "Your authentic self is sexier," he replies. They make love and as he peers into her gaze, he catches the ineffable glint of immeasurable gratitude emanating from her soul. With individuation, love flowers into authentic love.

The unconventional relationship space that emerges at Orange enables a more emancipated form of intimacy to arise. The INDIVIDUATED LOVER that emerges at Orange is able to love her partner more fully and the couple's connection is strengthened by the BOND OF AUTHENTICITY that develops at this level.

Despite the virtue of authenticity, the freedom of Orange can undermine relationship. Individuation is a solitary process and in the process of individuating, the couple can grow apart. If one partner awakens Orange while the other does not, the partners become alienated and begin to feel like strangers. Excessive autonomy on the part of both partners can erode the boundaries of relationship as individual paths diverge to the point where the couple lacks common ground.

Healthy Orange establishes authenticity and autonomy in a committed relationship. But these attributes, taken to an extreme, create new complications. The sense of alienation and disconnection that arise at Orange endanger the viability of the relationship. As the couple grows apart, the desire develops for a deeper form of interpersonal connection, one that includes authenticity and yet transcends the distance created by personal freedom. Green, the sixth level of the Spiral, is a cool color that emphasizes communal values and the cultivation of a refined sensitivity able to reveal the psychological and spiritual dynamics that overshadow the illusion of personal freedom. The shift that accompanies Orange to Green reflects the broader historical shift that occurred about 250 years ago as new Life Conditions developed that led to the emergence of a new Lifeway.

Green

Green in History: (The Postmodern Age - starting about 250 years ago.) Modernity substituted the religious belief in a glorious afterlife with the promise of liberty and material rewards in the present one. But the French Revolution which was inspired by the ideals of modernity was an ugly, bloody affair that ended in the coronation of Napoleon, and the Industrial Revolution which was inspired by modern technology drew millions to urban centers from the pastoral hinterlands to work in overcrowded factories under miserable conditions.

When it became clear that the optimistic promise of Modernity would not materialize, a dark cloud settled over collective consciousness. Green, a new worldview emerged around the need to communicate the misery of the urban masses who labored hopelessly in mills and factories under back-breaking conditions, while a handful of industrial magnates became staggeringly rich.

Artists, writers, and philosophers painted wretched portraits of scientific progress and industrialism. Mary Shelley's book, Frankenstein, was a social critique penned in Green ink about the monstrous creations of modernity that terrorized the common people. Charles Dickens rendered the hellish condition of life in England during the Industrial Revolution in lurid detail. A new sensibility emerged at Green that emphasized a return to nature and the need for social reform. Romanticism, transcendentalism, idealism, naturalism, socialism, and spiritualism were some of the 19th century movements that emerged to bring back dignity and meaning to the human condition.

Under Green, activities unfolding at the level of subjective inner experience became the focus of emergence. Art and spirituality became two popular ways to bring a modicum of beauty and goodness back into existence. Culturally, the focus of existence shifted from exploiting material reality to exploring interiority. Writers described the condition of inner lives through a new medium, the novel. Stories of private lives that were vastly different objectively proved to be strikingly similar subjectively. Green made it possible to identify with anyone, regardless of differences in gender, race, or nationality.

New modes of storytelling emerged, such as photography, cinema, television which brought the unseen inner worlds of more individuals into visibility. The notion developed through the lens of interiority that we are all equal and new movements emerged that embraced an egalitarian ideal such as post-colonialism, multiculturalism, and postmodernism. Interiority became global as news stories captured human experience in real time and dramatically underscored the notion that the suffering of any one individual belongs to the world. In a nutshell, Green replaced the theme of progress with a new theme, SENSITIVITY.

Green Intimacy: The relationship space that emerges at ambitious Orange feels shallow and stifling at egalitarian Green. At Green, the realization dawns that beyond external freedom lies inner meaning and beyond autonomy lies spiritual union. Green seeks a deeper, more mature, and meaningful kind of relationship than Orange is capable of actualizing.

While Orange seeks to expand identity outward and measures success by external criteria such as success and achievement in the world, Green measures success by the easing of psychological suffering, the refinement of consciousness, and expansion of the inner world. While Orange scales heights, Green plumbs the depth.

Green is fascinated by the movements of the psyche and especially the dynamics of the unconscious mind, the vast and invisible realm of darkness and light that includes repressed psychological material as well as a bevy of spiritual treasures waiting to be discovered. Picture an iceberg. The twenty percent rising above the surface represents the aspect of your identity that is visible and consciously integrated into your identity. As the mind navigates this aspect of consciousness it uses perception, reason, and logic to establish the facts of reality. Until Green, the unconscious underbelly of the mind remains invisible, unconscious, and irrelevant. Although the monolithic unconscious dominates our actions and perspectives, it is largely ignored. As Green awakens in a relationship, the unconscious becomes the predominant structure of consciousness that occupies the attention of the couple.

Can you be authentically successful by Orange criteria and still be depressed, or angry? Of course, and no amount of outer development will resolve unmet psychological needs or repressed childhood wounds. At any level of the Spiral, one might make unhealthy accommodations or establish unhealthy forms of expression. Green possesses the broad cognitive complexity and refined sensitivity to hone in on the sources of limitation that could not be revealed previously by less complex perspectives. Green embodies the capacity to perceive those invisible aspects of the psyche that are wounded, unconscious, and hold unhealthy patterns of behavior in place.

A Green partner helps us identify the unconscious traumas that distort our worldviews and behaviors that cause us or others anguish and pain. In the light of a non-judgmental and compassionate Green partner, we feel safe enough to become transparent and reveal our wounds. Together, intimate partners enter the shadow world of the unconscious and diminish suffering with the healing balm of mutual understanding.

Imagine a woman repeatedly betrayed in previous relationships. As a protective measure, she hardens and becomes unconsciously controlling and mistrustful of men. Despite her good intentions, she projects into the world a negative view of men and she attracts into her life partners that confirm her distorted worldview. She concludes that men can't be trusted and enters into relationship with that attitude shaping her behavior and beliefs.

Until Green, the wound remains invisible and dismissible. But at Green, as the underbelly of the psyche becomes the locus of relationship, that distorting wound becomes a central focus. Until Green emerges, there is no space in the relationship for delving consciously into the invisible dark places in the psyche, and any attempt to explore a buried wound is met with denial, impatience, irritation, and defensive posturing. Until Green emerges, the psyche relies on reason, logic, and external criteria to establish a worldview and any insight that does not conform to those parameters is dismissed. Since the unconscious is irrational by definition, it is disregarded.

Until Green, one partner might be dismissive of the other partner's concerns about unconscious patterns of behavior: "Mind your own business," "Don't sweat the small stuff," "You're draining me," "I don't have time for this now." But at Green, mutuality arises. Mutuality is sharing listening with your partner and understanding each other's perspectives without judging or rejecting them. With mutuality and sensitivity, wounds can be healed.

In a healthy Green relationship, both partners are constantly probing each other's psychological state. Why are you feeling sad? Does your sadness trigger a memory? Heathy Green explores psychological space with refined sensitivity and in the process, awareness is raised and eventually, healing occurs.

The underbelly of the psyche is where we store unprocessed wounds but it is also where we store spiritual gifts. While the psychological side of Green focuses on the shadow, the spiritual side of Green focuses on the light. The psyche is a vast realm that holds unimagined possibilities in the context of intimacy. Through spiritual practice, the energies of divine love and ecstatic bliss can be channeled into an intimate relationship.

Imagine a couple attending a heart opening workshop in the mountains. After a week of deep meditation, each partner has unraveled a deeper strata of the heart. Saturated in this energy, they each perceive divine light permeating every blade of grass and each grain of sand. She looks into his eyes and recognizes him as a god. He looks into her eyes and recognizes her as a goddess. He bows to the ground and kisses her foot. Energy from his lips runs up her leg and illuminates her heart. She directs that radiance down her arm and beams it into the top of his head as she strokes his hair. He feels a current of sweet bliss flow down from her fingertips and flood every subtle passage of his being. Saturated with her essence, his lips on her arch, they merge with love.

At Green we encounter the SENSITIVE LOVER who possesses the capacity for contextual thinking and the compassion required to navigate the world of inner darkness and light. When two human beings come together in that space in the spirit of openness and transparency, the BOND OF UNDERSTANDING develops and intimacy flowers in the deepest reaches of the heart.

Despite the beautiful human bond that emerges at Green, a relationship can lose itself in the fathomless ocean of the psyche. If one partner is too eager to delve into the shadow before the other is ready, inner demons can be awakened that are impossible to contain, and instead of healing, more wounds are created. While deficient Green leaves the relationship paddling shallow waters, excessive Green can overwhelm a relationship like a tsunami. Until a partner is ripe for green transformation, too much psychology and spirituality have a destructive effect on intimacy.

Healthy Green sensitizes relationship space by drawing attention towards increasingly refined layers of subjectivity. But in the process of diving deeper into interiority, Green can loose sight of surface manifestations and become detached from outer reality. By privileging subjectivity and discounting objectivity, wholeness is often neglected, and despite good intentions, common sense is lost to abstraction and new complications arise. As Green reaches its natural limit, frustration grows and the developmental need arises for the emergence of a more complex perspective. Yellow, the seventh level of the Spiral, arises in relation to the problems that emerge at Green.

This warm color emphasizes agentic values and a transformative mode of self-expression that embodies of the entire Spiral of human emergence.

Professor Clare Graves, whose research inspired Spiral Dynamics, described the transition from Green to Yellow as a "momentous leap" in human history. He distinguished this pivotal evolutionary shift from the pervious ones based on data that indicated a dramatic increase in complexity and a quantum leap in the coping capacities that emerge next.

The Momentous Leap

As Green matures, a far-reaching global perspective emerges as well as an overwhelming awareness of the monumental chaos facing humanity. With a sensitive eye and an empathic heart, Green recoils as it observes: The exploitation of the biosphere by profit driven Orange industrialists; Blue ideologues motivated by apocalyptic visions developing weapons of mass destruction; Red dictators bloodying their lands to solidify their hold on power; Purple indigenous tribes machete in hand violating and perpetrating genocide.

The swirl of suffering befalling our species crystallizes a vision of our planet rushing towards a precipitous fall. The sense of urgency intensifies with the realization that none of the previous coping strategies are capable of effectively addressing the tangled mess of global problems that threaten our existence on the planet: Orange technocrats can't manage the complexity with spreadsheets; a Blue mythic God isn't going to miraculously heal the planet; Red activists can't redress the swirling mess by venting more outrage; and Purple artists can't dream their way to a viable solution.

Well-intentioned Green attempts to rectify global suffering by raising awareness of the issues and instituting liberal policies to ease suffering such as opening up borders and promoting initiatives to bring about peace and to ease global injustice. But handouts to hordes of beleaguered immigrants and politically correct goodwill initiatives lack the complexity to unsnarl the hyperlinked mess that arises in the postmodern, digital, Yellow world. And often, the good intentions of Green backfire, and the strife worsens.

Mature Green stands at the edge of its worldview and stares down at the abyss. The planet is streaming towards an unsustainable future. Darkness floods awareness. Are we doomed? Maybe. But one possibility remains: Human emergence. Do you dare to step off the edge of Green into the unknown for the sake of the planet? Are you prepared to leap into the void for the welfare of humanity? If you have already taken that leap, then welcome to Yellow, the first color of the next tranche of human emergence, known as Second Tier.

Yellow

Yellow in History: (The Evolutionary Age, starting about 200 years ago.) The early 19th Century German philosopher Georg W.F. Hegel proposed that the tension generated between two opposing forces was the engine of progress. In his view, seemingly irreconcilable contradictions ultimately united and integrated into a higher order reality that included and transcended the lower order polarity. He termed this evolutionary process, dialectics. Hegel used dialectics to describe the developmental arc of spirit or mind expressing itself throughout human history. Hegel's philosophy rejected fixed categories of "being" common to philosophy at the time and inspired a philosophy of "becoming."

Dialectical thinking transformed the horizontal vector of human history by contributing a vertical axis of complexity that developed over time. Under this paradigm, humanity developed from stages of lower complexity to stages of higher complexity as a consequence of conflict and adversity, and in the process, new qualities, capacities, modes of thinking, and values emerged. Hegel inspired many thinkers who applied dialectics to describe emergence in various fields, most notably, Karl Marx developed a theory of dialectical materialism which inspired communism.

The philosophy of becoming inspired by Hegel resonated with the theme of Charles Darwin's masterpiece, On the Origin of the Species, published in 1859. The British biologist took an Abrahamic sledgehammer to the view that species were permanent and fixed and advanced the theory that species had evolved by adapting to changing conditions. Hegel and Darwin's theories envisioned the same process of developmental pressure leading to higher order emergence. While Hegel focused on evolution in the domain of Spirit, Darwin focused on evolution in the domain of nature.

In 1929, astronomer Edwin Hubble presented evidence that substantiated the theory of the Big Bang. Contrary to popular belief that the kosmos was unchanging and fixed, Hubble proposed that the universe had an originating center and was continually expanding. Based on this theory, a cosmological paradigm appeared that described matter as an emergent substance that developed over time as cosmological conditions changed.

Hegel, Darwin, and Hubble each contributed a piece to the puzzle of evolution in the domains of philosophy, biology, and cosmology. Spirit, life, and matter, every strand of existence, was apparently rooted to a beginning and a part of an unfolding evolutionary story.

Over the course of the 20th Century, the evolutionary paradigm spread to every domain of knowledge. About a hundred years ago, psychology Professor James Mark Baldwin proposed that consciousness evolved cross-culturally along stages of development. A few decades later, the psychologist Jean Piaget mapped out in detail the stages of child development. A few decades later, Harvard Professor Lawrence Kohlberg described the stages of moral development in his groundbreaking works. The Jesuit Priest Pierre Teilhard De Chardin's book, *The Phenomenon of Man,* described teleological evolution leading from matter to humanity which continues to evolve on its way to an eventual reunion with the source of all creation, God.

In 1974, Clare Graves, a professor of psychology at Union College presented his theory of the development of the mature adult personality in an article titled, "Humanity Prepares for a Momentous Leap". The theory described eight levels of human existence, each determined by Life Conditions and the values (or vMemes) that emerged to manage the problems of existence at each respective level. The research of Dr. Graves formed the ground for the subsequent development of Spiral Dynamics by his students Dr. Don Beck and Chris Cowen. Dr. Beck went on to form the Center for Human Emergence and refined the theory renaming it Spiral Dynamics Integral (SDi) in deference to the integral vision of philosopher-sage Ken Wilber.

According to Dr. Beck, a pivotal moment arises in human emergence when Green perceives the cacophony of global chaos as the dance of evolution. Through that realization, Green becomes Yellow. Yellow understands that the kaleidoscope of chaos unfolding throughout the planet represents multiple systems simultaneously undergoing transformation and emergence at different levels of the Spiral.

In SDi jargon, the shift from Green to Yellow represents the "momentous leap" to Second Tier described by Graves. The novel coping capacities that emerge at Yellow include a vertical orientation to problem solving, a mastery of the structures that emerged at the previous six levels of the Spiral (First Tier), and the ability to leverage the Spiral proactively to further human emergence.

The most significant difference between First Tier and Second Tier is that at First Tier evolution is reactive while at Second Tier evolution is a proactive phenomenon. A Spiral Wizard is a Yellow chameleon who anticipates evolutionary needs and changes colors at will to accommodate the evolutionary demands of the given moment, a transformation engineer.

Yellow Intimacy: There exist petrifying moments when life rears its Medusa head, the ground breaks open under our feet, and we are swallowed by the yawning mouth of chaos through darkness into the unknown. At Yellow, we develop the coping skills to manage this intensely chaotic side of life, consciously and with evolutionary intent. At this stage of the Spiral, tension that otherwise cripples and paralyzes becomes transformational superfood.

At other levels of the Spiral of Intimacy, we avoid, repress, deny, argue, and rationalize our way around charged issues that stir up mayhem. At Yellow, developmental pressure generates a buoyancy of spirit as a consequence of the understanding that developmental pressure precipitates transformation, emergence, synergy, and integration; in a word, evolution.

The evolutionary journey at Yellow can unfold alone, in a group setting, or more significantly, in the context of an intimate relationship. If two evolutionary minded souls are fortunate enough to fall in love, the potential for deep transformation arises. But the couple will have to consciously and intentionally incorporate the themes that define all the prior levels of the Spiral, i.e. passion, safety, power, trust, autonomy, and sensitivity, into their relationship space before they are ready to manage the process of conscious transformation and leverage complications into higher-order complexity.

At Yellow, a couple measures the success of a relationship by the degree of evolutionary growth that unfolds under its umbrella. Consequently, an evolutionary relationship repeatedly dies and rises from its own ashes like the fabled Phoenix. At each iteration of the process, the relationship becomes more expansive, inclusive, and resilient. As evolutionary growth becomes a steady feature of relationship, the anxiety generally associated with transformation drops away and each partner develops at an accelerated rate.

After soulmates master the art of evolutionary intimacy, the relationship itself becomes a catalyst for transformation that inspires emergence in the lives of other individuals undergoing evolutionary growth. Imagine a couple that practices evolutionary intimacy becoming foster parents. They view each child brought into their home as a universe of possibilities awaiting development. An eight year old boy arrives. His father abused him physically and his mother abused him emotionally. The boy is emotionally repressed, dour faced, and subject to fits of rage. The couple deploys all the colors of the Spiral to inspire a transformation. They bring him Beige pleasure in the form of cookies and a wholesome environment, Purple safety and magic by reading mind-bending fairy tales that capture his imagination, Red fun adventures like a visit to a petting zoo and paddling a canoe in the local river, Blue discipline by enlisting him in the Boy Scouts, Orange independence by encouraging him to indulge in his passion for collecting baseball cards, and Green sensitivity by inspiring him to express his feelings through drawings.

Those drawings begin as dark and unhappy scribbles, but over time the shapes soften and the colors brighten. One day, at dinner this boy breaks into a fit of radiant laughter and unexpectedly tells his foster parents that he loves them. Later that night, the couple lies in bed reveling in the afterglow of the boy's transformation. A dollop of evolutionary intelligence informed their success. Myriad variables might have derailed the process, but the couple tamed the dragon of transformation with exquisite sensibility. As bliss springs from their heart, their limbs brush unintentionally. That spark ignites a wildfire of gentle passion, and before long, they are drawn into a rapture inspired by evolutionary grace. Yellow intimacy.

A Yellow couple flex-flows up and down the Spiral with evolutionary awareness. The EVOLUTIONARY LOVER that emerges at Yellow embodies all the prior lovers and the BOND OF EMERGENCE that develops at this level includes all the other bonds. A Yellow intimate relationship embraces the rainbow of qualities that defines the entire Spiral of Intimacy.

A Yellow relationship becomes unhealthy when it obsesses with transformation and becomes overwhelmed by the desire for incessant change while denying itself the time needed to integrate the changes it inspires. It takes time to integrate transformation and to incorporate an emergent quality. It takes time for the body to adapt to the biology of transformation and for the brain to adapt to the neurology of transformation.

The relentless pursuit of higher consciousness typified by excessive Yellow can frazzle a relationship. A mind laden with knowledge it can't assimilate does not possess the wisdom to embody the wellspring of information it stores. When evolution supersedes integration, a relationship becomes as unstable as an experimental rocket whose structural integrity can't sustain the G-force.

As Yellow matures, it envisions each human being as an evolutionary process of self-actualization. Consequently, Yellow begins to relate to a mate, family members, a circle of friends, and even the rest of the world with evolutionary sensibility. But eventually, even healthy Yellow, endowed with multiple intelligences and manifold capacities, becomes overwhelmed at the prospect of juggling an ever-expanding array of evolutionary challenges, a task that requires the dexterity of a thousand-armed deity. As Yellow reaches its natural limit, the Spiral stirs anew and the need arises for the emergence of a broader perspective able to manage the higher-order complexity.

Turquoise, the eighth level of the Spiral, is a cool color that emphasizes communal values and the cultivation of a perspective that recognizes the unity that underlies the bramble of evolutionary diversity. The shift that accompanies Yellow to Turquoise in relationship reflects the historical shift that occurred about forty years ago as our species began to explore the outer reaches of evolutionary growth defined by this stage of human development.

Turquoise

Turquoise in History: (Forty years ago to present.) The iconic picture of our beloved earth floating silently in space, snapped in 1972, triggered a shift in collective consciousness: We are one family sharing a frail home planet suspended in a dark and mysterious kosmos. The colorful mandala of earth in space also underscored the mystery of the human condition. Where did the evolving kosmos come from? And how do evolving humans beings fit into the kosmic scheme?

Standing at the edge of immense knowledge and considering the unknowable mystery that lies at the center of all evolution, we awaken Turquoise. As we trace back the steps of the evolution of the kosmos to the moment of inception, a question arises: What came before? And as you trace back your own consciousness to your birth, the same question arises. What came before? No one has yet been able to answer these questions objectively. Turquoise revels in the ever-present mystery of being that lies at the root of becoming. But some insights have come out of science about the mysterious nature of being.

Quantum physics confounded conventional science by proposing that the mystery of matter and the mystery of the mind are interlinked and exhibit bi-directional causality at the nano level. And recent scientific evidence suggests that the quantum effect also manifests at the macro level. William Tiller, professor emeritus and former head of the Department of

Material Science at Stanford University devoted his career to exploring the impact of intention on material systems. The numerous studies he conducted concluded that focused consciousness has the power to affect material, biological, and human systems. For instance, a group of seasoned meditators were able to control the pH of a water solution—raising or lowering it—through their intention.

Tiller's work and many other similar experiments suggest that the mystery that underlies origin of matter and the mystery that underlies the origin of the mind is one and the same since mind and matter influence each other intimately. At Turquoise, the realization dawns that there exists just one mystery underlying all evolutionary processes, and that as humans we gain direct access to that mystery through the agency of consciousness.

As humanity further develops the capacity to leverage conscious intention, a Turquoise worldview will solidify and give rise to new values and lifeways. But there are ways to envision some possibilities even at this early stage of development. Imagine a group of meditators directing their intention to facilitate the transformation of an economic crisis or a political impasse in the same way that saints used prayer to effect miracle cures on the sick and suffering. At Turquoise, we develop into collectives of Wizards shaping the future with the hands of the mind.

At Turquoise, the notion also arises that the unconscious mind is a formidable generator of intention, though not always intention with a positive impetus. The repressed unconscious and the suppressed subconscious have the power to manifest malicious intentions like a sorcerer conjuring dark spells in his sleep. Turquoise ethics require us to assume responsibility for our conscious and our unconscious intentions. As a result, Turquoise growth implies a deep and thorough purification of the soul.

A lucid being grounded in a purified soul possesses the capacity to spread coherence to other beings like a resonant tuning fork. Consequently, the theme that emerges at Turquoise is HARMONY, the condition that arises when a pure-hearted soul entrains symphonically with other souls in the service of becoming.

Turquoise Intimacy: Through Turquoise eyes, we recognize oneness harmonizing evolutionary diversity across the kosmic holarchy. Turquoise perceives the wholeness of creation growing like a tree with branches spreading at various levels, the entire structure evolving holistically towards the sun. Through the big picture view that arises at Turquoise, we perceive the kosmos as an indivisible evolutionary wholeness harmonized by an unknowable mystery that lies at the center of every perspective.

Centered in being, an individual at Turquoise releases the overwhelming intensity that emerges at Yellow and places her faith that the mystery of consciousness, properly leveraged, will support the evolutionary Meshwork of becoming. Just as the sun will rise and set tomorrow, and spring and fall will move together in flawless synchrony, so will the messy process of global emergence unfold harmoniously with symphonic coherence.

Turquoise understands that complex events are shaped by synchronicities, meaningful coincidences that from the perspective of Turquoise are orchestrated by the intersection of being and intention. At Turquoise, the notion arises that when an intention arises from within the mystery of being, synchronicities are provoked that harmonize the flow of life. The power to provoke a synchronicity is an emergent phenomenon that arises at Turquoise and an individual grounded at this level is like the musical director of a symphony that harmonizes the instruments and brings coherence by waving his wand. With Turquoise, that wand is conscious intention.

A Turquoise couple embodies the mystery of being and uses the power of their shared intention to harmonize evolution. Turquoise relationship space is a harmonious field that provokes synchronicities. If you encountered a Turquoise couple and stepped into their relationship space, you would experience coherence and mysterious coincidences would follow. Perhaps you have reached a point in your life where you desire evolutionary intimacy but are unable to manifest the right partner. You encounter a Turquoise couple and they instantly grasp that evolutionary urge for intimacy arising from your soul. With Turquoise delicacy, they coordinate their intention and dispose reality to favor the realization of your desire.

Before long, a series of odd synchronicities take place. The couple introduces you to a friend who invites you to a lounge one night with a group of other friends. There you are sitting among the group when you inadvertently look up. You notice a pair of eyes across the spirited room and you share a timeless moment. A loud blur holding a beer bottle breaks your line of sight and the connection is broken. But magnetized by the exchange, your path weaves through the ambient crowd and you both converge by the bar. Under the guise of some trivial pretense, a conversation ensues. Numbers are exchanged and texts are traded the next day. Saturday night, French…

Turquoise serves the Spiral of Intimacy by synchronistically provoking the mystery of love. A Turquoise partner embodies the MYSTICAL LOVER who abides in the great mystery of being, is a generator of synchronicities, and whose mere presence harmonizes the landscape of intimacy. The bond that arises at Turquoise is the BOND OF HARMONY, a deep lyrical connection that arises from the sonorous silence that binds eternity to infinity.

Eventually, a couple at Turquoise is bound to run up against its own limitations and the Spiral of Intimacy will spin its arm once more in search of a higher expression of intimacy. I don't have a clue about the issues that will precipitate the need for emergence beyond Turquoise. But I am confident that the expression of love will grow beyond Turquoise. And although the next stage remains a veiled enigma, SDi has already created a placeholder to secure the next position on the Spiral, Coral.

Bibliography

Beck, D., & Cowan, C. (1996). *Spiral Dynamics: Mastering values, leadership, and change: Exploring the new science of memetics.* Cambridge, Mass., USA: Blackwell Business.

Duska, R., & Whelan, M. (1975). *Moral development: A guide to Piaget and Kohlberg.* New York: Paulist Press.

Graves, Clare, W. (1974). Human Nature Prepares for a Momentous Leap. The Futurist, 72-87.

Tiller, W., & Dibble, W. (2001). *Conscious acts of creation: The emergence of a new physics.* Walnut Creek, Calif.: Pavior Pub.

AUTHORS

Author Contact Information

Bruno-Magdich, Tom

United Kingdom. English.

tom@4dhumanbeing.com
+44(0)7583446075
Skype: online4dhumanbeing
LinkedIn: Tom Bruno-Magdich
www.4dhumanbeing.com

Focus: Integral based personal and professional development through communication skills coaching and training; working with individuals, teams, businesses and organizations.

Christensen, Tom. M.A.

Madison, Wisconsin, USA. English.

tomc@centralmadison.com
608-255-4242
Skype: tomc1243
Facebook: Tom Christensen
LinkedIn: Tom Christensen
www.tomclight.com
www.centralmadison.com

Focus: Gravesian education, oil paintings, real estate investments.

Dickson, John. Ph.D.

Edmonton, Alberta, Canada. English, Spanish, French.

jndickson54@gmail.com
780-431-0908
Skype: jndickson1
LinkedIn: Dr. John Dickson
www.albertabusinesscoach.com

Professional Focus: Executive coaching and organizational development, working with managers, entrepreneurs, and family businesses when in Canada. Overseas, design and implementation of economic development programmes.

Dupuy, John. M.A.

Teasdale, Utah, USA. English. Spanish. German.

435-691-1193
johndupuy@gmail.com
Skype: johndupuy
Facebook: john.dupuy.12
LinkedIn: John Dupuy, M.A.
www.integralrecovery.com
www.iawaketechnologies.com
www.integralrecoveryinstitute.com

Focus: Applying SDi in Integral Recovery with alcoholics and addicts and with iAwake Technologies, an Integral Practice addressing body, mind, spirit and emotions.

Freeman, Jon. M.A.

Salisbury, UK. English. French. German.

jon@spiralworld.net
Skype: jonfreeman2910
Facebook: Jon Freeman
LinkedIn: Jon Freeman
www.spiralfutures.com
www.scienceofpossibility.net

Focus: Organizational development, Culture Scan, certification trainings, public speaking, facilitation, coaching, with special emphasis on organizations and finance.

Hordijk, Ard. MSc

Netherlands. Dutch, English, Spanish.

ard@synnervate.nl
+31613635562
LinkedIn: Ard Hordijk
www.synnervate.nl
www.hordijkconsulting.nl

Focus: Multi-stakeholder collaboration, integral systems analysis, systemic change, sustainable supply chains, biodiversity and ecosystems, corporate sustainability, food and agrisector business.

Laura Frey Horn, Ed.D.

Middleburg, VA. USA. English. French.

540-454-2648
lfheureka@gmail.com
Skype: lfeurika
Facebook: Laura Frey Horn
LinkedIn: Dr. Laura Frey Horn

Focus: Whole systems, Gravesian based, organizational consulting to support and develop healthy organizations which thrive effectively in their environments. Actively engaged in organizational and academic research, writing, and teaching on leadership and organizational development using the Gravesian and whole systems frameworks.

Keller, Michael G. M.A.

Victoria, BC, Canada. English.

michaelkeller@shaw.ca
250-592-6818
Skype: mkellervictoria
LinkedIn: Michael Keller
www.ecologyofdesigninhumansystems.com

Focus: Holistic designing of designers for engaging complexity in human systems...building capacity for capacity-builders.

Kilmartin, Joyce. Ph.D.

Barrington, RI, USA. English, Italian.

jkilmartin@cox.net
401-247-0172
Skype: joyce.kilmartin
LinkedIn: Joyce Kilmartin

Focus: Transpersonal counseling for individuals and organizations.

Merry, Peter. MSc, Ph.D. (candidate)

The Netherlands. English, Dutch, French, German

petermerry@ubiquityuniversity.org
Facebook: www.facebook.com/peterdacremerry
LinkedIn: Peter Merry
ubiquityuniversity.org
petermerry.org
volutiontheory.net

Focus: Education. Leadership and organizational development.

McKinnon, Dan. Ph.D.

Calgary, Alberta, Canada. English

dr.dan@calgarypsychology.com
403-371-5323
Skype: dr.dan.mckinnon
LinkedIn: Dr. Dan McKinnon
www.albertabusinesscoach.com
www.calgarypsychology.com

Focus: Business coaching, counselling and organizational development consulting for individuals, executives, entrepreneurs and small-medium-sized businesses.

Nasser, Rafael

New York, NY, USA. English, French, Hebrew, Spanish.

rafinasser@gmail.com
Skype: RafaelNasser001
LinkedIn: Rafael Nasser
www.RafaelNasser.com

Focus: Applying the wisdom of SDi to leverage human emergence with massage therapy, Qigong, meditation, writing and teaching.

Rice, Keith E. Grad. Cert. Ed.

Bradford, United Kingdom. English.

keith@integratedsociopsychology.net
(44) 01274 975667
Skype: keith.e.rice
Facebook: Keith E. Rice.
www.integratedsociopsychology.net

Focus: To create a rigorous academic framework based on SDi and 4Q/8L around which all the behavioural sciences can be aligned and integrated.

Sanders, Beth. MCIP, RPP

Edmonton, Alberta, Canada. English, French.

beth@populus.ca
780-886-0354
Skype: bethpopulus
Facebook: beth0sanders
LinkedIn: Beth Sanders
Twitter: @bethsanders
www.populus.ca/plan

Focus: Registered Professional Planner. Canadian SDi Trainer with Center for Human Emergence – Canada.

Villemot-Kienzle, Claudia

Germany. French, German, English.

claudine.villemot-kienzle@humanemergence.de
+49 8104 66 64 66
Skype: claudinevillemot
Facebook: Claudine Villemot-Kienzle
LinkedIn: Claudine Villemot-Kienzle
www.claudinevillemot.de
www.humanemergence.de

Focus: Adult education, intercultural design, leadership, through seminars, coaching, social architecture and organizational development.

Waller, Philippa. M.A.

United Kingdom. English, French.

philippa@4dhumanbeing.com
+44(0)7958316227
Skype: online4dhumanbeing
LinkedIn: Phillipa Waller
www.4dhumanbeing.com

Focus: Integral based Personal and Professional Development through communication skills coaching and training. Provided to individuals, teams, businesses and organizations.

Webne-Behrman, Harry M. M.S.

Madison, WI, USA. English.

hwebnebehrman@ohr.wisc.edu
608-262-9934
LinkedIn: Harry Webne-Behrman
www.cultureofgenerosity.org

Focus: Facilitation, mediation, education, and consulting. Helping individuals and groups navigate complex, often conflictive challenges in their work and in their lives.

Wilkie, Rosemary

Kent, England. English, French.

rw@rosemarywilkie.co.uk
Skype: Rosemary Wilkie
LinkedIn: Rosemary Wilkie

Focus: SDi introductory talks and workshops. Heart Awakening, individual sessions.

GRAVES-CONTEXTUALIZATIONS

Barrett, Richard. *Building a Values-Driven Organization: A Whole System Approach to Cultural Transformation.* (2006) Routledge, NYC, USA.

Barrett, Richard. *Evolutionary Coaching: A Values-Based Approach to Unleashing Human Potential.* (2014) Lulu Publishing Services.

Beck, Don & Linscott, Graham. *The Crucible: Forging South Africa's Future. In Search of a Template for the World.* (1991) New Paradigm Press, Johannesburg, South Africa

Beecroft, Nicholas. *Analyze West: A Psychiatrist Takes Western Civilization on a Journey of Transformation.* (2014) Nicholas Beecroft, UK.

Beecroft, Nicholas. *New Magna Carta: A Psychiatrist's Prescription for Western Civilization.* (2015). Nicholas Beecroft, UK.

Chabreuil, Fabien; Chabreuil, Patricia. *La Spirale Dynamique.* 2012. ISBN-13: 978-2729612085. Title in English: The Dynamic Spiral.

Dawlabani, Said E. *MEMEnomics: The Next-Generation Economic System.* (2013) Select Books, Inc. NYC, USA

Dupuy, John. *Integral Recovery: A Revolutionary Approach to the Treatment of Alcoholism and Addiction.* (2013). SUNY Press, NYC.

Freeman, Jon. *The Science of Possibility: Patterns of Connected Consciousness.* (2008) SpiralWorld, Ferndown, UK.

Hamilton, Marilyn. *Integral City: Evolutionary Intelligences for the Human Hive.* (2008) New Society Publishers, Gabriola Island, BC, Canada.

Krumm, Reiner. *Werteorientiertes Führen.* Gabal. 2014. ISBN-13: 978-3869366050. Title in English: *Values Based Leadership.*

Krumm, Reiner. *Clare W. Graves: Sien Leben, Sein Werk: Die Theorie Menschlicher Entwicklung.* Werdewelt Verlags- und Medienhaus, 2014. ISBN-13: 978-3981531886. English translation: *Clare W. Graves: His Life, His Work – The Theory of Human Development.*

Küstenmacher, Marion; Haberer, Tilmann; Küstenmacher, Werner Tiki. *Gott 9.0: Wohin Unsere Gesellschaft Spirituell Wachsen Wird.* Gütersloher Verlagshaus, 2010. ISBN-13: 978-3579065465. Title in English: *God 9.0: The Goal of Our Society's Spiritual Growth.*

Laubscher, LI. *Human Niches: Spiral Dynamics for Africa* (2013) Unpublished PhD thesis from the Da Vinci Institute for Innovation and Technology. Modderfontein: South Africa. http://www.mandalaconsulting.co.za/Documents/Thesis%20-%20Loraine%20Laubscher.pdf

Laloux, Frederic. *Reinventing Organizations: A Guide to Creating Organizations Inspired by the Next State of Human Consciousness.* (2014) Nelson Parker, Brussels, Belgium.

Lessem R., Abouleish I., Pocagnik M. and Herman L. *Integral Polity: Aligning Nature, Culture, Society and Economy.* (2015) Gower. Farnham, UK.

Maalouf, Elza S. *Emerge! The Rise of Functional Democracy and the Future of the Middle East.* (2014) Select Books, Inc. NYC, USA.

Mackey, John & Sisodia, Rajendra. *Conscious Capitalism: Liberating the Heroic Spirit of Business.* (2014) Harvard Business School Publishing, Boston, Massachusetts, USA.

Macleod, Jordan. *New Currency: How Money Changes the World as we Know it.* (2009) Integral Publishers, Pacific Grove, CA, USA.

Merry, Peter. *Evolutionary Leadership: Integral Leadership for an Increasingly Complex World.* (2009) Integral Publishers, Pacific Grove, California, USA.

Nasr, Amir Ahmad. My Islam: *How Fundamentalism Stole My Mind –And Doubt Freed My Soul.* (2013) St. Martin's Press. NYC, USA.

Rice, Keith E. *Knowing Me, Knowing You: An Integrated SocioPsychology Guide to Personal Fulfilment & Better Relationships.* (2006) Trafford Publishing, Victoria, B.C., Canada.

Spiller C. & Wolfgramm R. (Eds.) (2015, in-press). *Indigenous Spiritualties at Work: Transforming the Spirit of Business Enterprise.* Information Age Publishing. Charlotte, NC.

Stamper, Gary. *Awakening the new Masculine: The Path of The Integral Warrior.* (2012) iUniverse, Bloomington, Indiana, USA.

van Leijden, Wilbert & Zuiker, Paul. *Nederland op Doorbreken: een Vernieuwend Perspectief voor een Land in Crisis.* (2007) Emergent Publishing, NL Title in English: *The Netherlands on the Verge of a Breakthrough: an Innovative Perspective for a Country in Crisis.*

Viljoen R. (2015) *Inclusive Organisational Transformation: An African Perspective on Human Niches and Diversity of Thought.* Gower. Farnham, UK.

Viljoen R. *Organisational Change and Development: an African Perspective.* (2015). Knowledge Resources. Braynston. South Africa.

Wade, Jenny. *Changes of Mind: A Holonomic Theory of the Evolution of Consciousness.* (1996) State University of New York, Press. Albany, NY, USA.

Waller, Philippa. *Spiral Into Love: How to Stop Falling in Love with the Wrong Ones and Stay in Love with the Right Ones.* (2012) FeedARead. com Publishing, UK.

Wilkie, Rosemary. *Emergence: Vol 1 - Introduction.* (2013) Rosemary Wilkie, UK.

Wilkie, Rosemary. *Émergence Vol 1.* Édition Française (2013) Rosemary Wilkie, UK

Primary Resources for Graves and Beck Material

Beck, Don & Cowan, Christopher. *Spiral Dynamics: Mastering Values, Leadership and Change.* (1996) Blackwell Publishing, Malden, MA, USA.

Cowan, Christopher and Todorovic, Natasha. *The Never Ending Quest: Clare W. Graves Explores Human Nature.* (2005) ECLET Publishing, Santa Barbara, CA, USA.

Lee, William R. Ed. *Clare W. Graves: Levels of Human Existence.* (2002) ECLET Publishing, Santa Barbara, CA, USA.

THE BOOKS SPEAK

Editor: Dear Books. What do you want to be?

Voice of Vol 1 and 2: I am a cognitive virus, a meme. I intend to propagate into a critical mass of human beings, such that the tipping point is reached after which the pattern entailed in these books becomes a common resource for patterning of human thought. This is, of course, not my only effort to achieve this end. I have been busy in many narratives, and some work is still left to do before the tipping point occurs.

This pattern of thought, this meme, is best named "a developmental schema". With this pattern instantiated in a mind all matters of interest are described in terms of what they were, what they are, and what they will be. The schema of Aristotelian definition is included and transcended with this broader, more complex, assessment that adds a consideration of change to the identity of interest. What did it change from? What is its potential for change in its present form? What is it likely to change to?

In these books I am instantiating this template for thought with the use of the Gravesian body of distinctions. There is nothing sacred about this body of information. The reader is encouraged to use any model of development, model of change, that they wish to. I am present in all of them. But, to move humanity to a more comprehensive, and thus more integrated and healthy, way of knowing its reality, some developmental framework must be internalized and put to use. The Gravesian instance of a developmental model works very well in training the mind to view the world in a developmental schema. Since the opportunity to infect humanity with the developmental meme, thru the Gravesian material, was available, I took this opportunity. Had there been a better opportunity available I would have taken it, and when it does show up, I will take it. Eventually a critical mass of minds will naturally perceive developmental trajectories in all things. When this time comes it will be as natural for most humans to place an identity within a flow of change as it is natural to put subjects before verbs.

This report on what I, the books, am really up to, will not be of interest to most readers. So, dear editor, please place this info in an Appendix. Those who wish to see the workings I am up to, will find me there.

INDEX

mind 2, 29, 39–40, 48, 53, 55, 68, 72, 79–81, 84, 94, 96, 98, 106, 109, 112, 115, 122, 126, 141, 144, 156, 163, 172, 182, 190, 193, 196, 198, 203–204, 214–215, 220–221, 229, 232, 251, 260, 262–263, 266, 268–271, 276, 286, 288–289

momentous leap 65, 123, 158, 265, 267, 273

multidisciplinary 60

myth 94, 150, 158–159, 162, 250, 265

N

narrative 69–71, 169, 238, 288

Natural Designs 32, 34, 208

needs 11–12, 17, 20–24, 37, 40, 42, 44, 51, 54, 59–60, 75, 78–80, 82, 87, 92, 101, 103, 125, 128, 131, 133–136, 138–142, 149, 156, 161, 167, 170–171, 173–174, 195–196, 199–200, 210, 220, 223, 232–233, 239, 248–249, 251, 259, 262, 268

Needs 39

O

objective 66, 100, 126, 142, 174–175, 184, 189–191, 236, 238, 256, 261, 270

objectivity 67, 126, 151, 264

omega point 69

open 3, 6, 16–18, 20–21, 26–27, 62–63, 67, 77, 97, 103, 126, 135, 138, 141, 145, 166, 172, 180, 190, 194, 196–198, 200–201, 204–205, 212, 234, 241, 244–245, 259, 264–265, 268

Orange 20, 22–26, 29–30, 32, 39, 60–65, 76, 94–99, 102–107, 113, 123, 125, 130, 134, 138–139, 141–142, 146, 150–153, 156–158, 162, 166–167, 169, 178–182, 185–187, 211–224, 236–237, 245–247, 257–260, 262, 265, 269

Orange/Green 138, 141, 218, 220–224

organization 2, 5–6, 9, 32–36, 61–63, 89, 104, 159, 162, 173, 175, 182–183, 207, 209, 218, 221, 223, 255, 274–276, 277–279, 281–282, 284–285

P

paradigm 44–46, 141, 158, 173, 188–190, 193–194, 225, 258, 266–267, 284

participation 62, 168

passion 62–64, 132, 141, 163, 211, 214, 232, 244, 254, 257, 268–269

past 3, 5, 9, 24, 28, 37, 55, 59, 69, 77–79, 89, 122, 127, 131, 145, 152, 168, 185, 187, 189, 192, 195, 201, 215, 223, 234, 239, 240, 259

pathologies 160

personality 48, 56–57, 78, 80–81, 87–88, 179–180, 241, 267

perspective 2, 12, 27–28, 57, 62, 66–68, 70–71, 80, 86, 90, 96–97, 99–100, 102–106, 118, 125–127, 131, 136–137, 139–144, 147, 150–153, 157–159, 161, 166–167, 169, 171, 180, 189–191, 193, 195–196, 204–205, 235–237, 245, 247, 254, 262–265, 270, 272, 286

planning 60–61, 64, 95, 103

policy 97, 167, 182

politics 78, 94, 178–179, 183, 222, 247

poverty 66, 78, 238

power 3, 11, 20, 22, 24, 26, 37, 39, 42, 46, 51, 54, 62–63, 75, 77, 80, 85, 87, 89–92, 101–102, 105, 111, 117, 120, 127–128, 130, 142, 146–147, 149–151, 156, 158–159, 172–173, 178, 184, 196, 200–201, 220, 225, 229, 232, 245–246, 248–249, 252–255, 265, 268, 271–272

practice 1, 29–30, 33–37, 50, 52, 59, 61–64, 78, 88, 117, 126, 132, 134, 136, 150–152, 157, 161–162, 164, 169–173, 180, 189–191, 194, 198, 200, 209–211, 214–215, 217–219, 221, 223, 264, 268, 276

present 13, 16, 28, 31, 39, 43, 59, 69, 71, 81, 94, 107, 127, 132, 136, 140, 144, 146, 152, 157, 159–160, 166–168, 170, 172, 179–180, 187, 191, 199, 201–203, 205–206, 209, 211, 217, 222, 235, 244, 258, 261, 266–267, 270, 288

process 1–3, 24, 27, 35, 46, 57, 68, 75, 82, 85, 88, 122–123, 128, 131–132, 134–135, 139–140, 142, 146, 149, 154–155, 159, 161, 163, 166–169, 171–172, 175, 182, 191–194, 197, 202, 204, 211, 214, 235, 239, 241, 244, 247, 249, 251, 257, 259–260, 263–264, 266, 268–269, 271–272 psychological 1, 6, 89, 118–122, 126, 128, 210, 214, 226, 239–240, 242, 244–245, 260, 262–263

psychologically 51

Purple 13, 20, 22–23, 26, 29, 39–40, 42, 46–51, 54–55, 59, 62, 64–65, 77, 79, 88–91, 94, 99–100, 105–108, 119, 121, 127, 134–135, 138–139, 142, 146, 169–170, 178–181, 184–187, 210, 212–213, 215–218, 220, 222, 224, 227–233, 235–236, 238, 245–247, 249–254, 256–257, 265, 269

Purple/Red 29, 77, 220, 222, 224

purpose 11–12, 15, 22, 31, 49, 62, 69, 75–76, 78–79, 92, 133–135, 137, 139–140, 142, 146, 149, 166, 169, 190, 202, 209, 212, 215, 221, 223–224, 244, 255–256

Q

quadrant 13, 59, 78, 128, 145, 156, 161–162, 167

quality 38, 88, 136–137, 171, 182, 197, 201–205, 220, 236–237, 249, 251, 269

R

rational 79, 89, 92, 94–95, 98, 100, 122, 150, 153, 157–158, 160, 189, 190, 196, 204, 255–256, 258, 268

readiness 214

Red 13, 20, 22, 29, 39–40, 42, 46–53, 55, 59, 61–65, 77, 90–95, 97, 99, 102–103, 105–107, 110, 120–122, 127, 134–136, 138–139, 142, 146–150, 156–159, 178–187, 211–214, 216–224, 226, 229–230, 232–234, 236, 240, 245–247, 252–257, 259, 265, 269

Red/Blue 29, 211, 219–220, 222, 224, 229

resilience 226

responsibility 17, 23, 80, 91, 103, 135–136, 143, 169, 199, 214, 221, 223–224, 255–257, 271

rights 61, 77, 97, 116, 150–151, 158, 253

risk 25, 94, 96, 114, 122, 212–214, 216–217, 227–228, 232

role 2, 7, 39, 46, 53, 61, 117, 122, 134–137, 142, 148, 156, 164, 166, 168, 172, 174, 185, 187, 202, 210, 214, 230, 254–255, 258

S

safety 21–22, 25, 39, 42, 89, 119, 146, 231–233, 245, 246, 249–252, 268–269

scale 13, 37, 122, 157, 262

science 2, 38, 40, 72, 75, 76, 84, 96, 128, 151, 157–158, 162, 173, 189, 212, 226, 228, 235–236, 239–241, 258, 270–271, 273, 276, 280, 285

scope 2, 68–69, 189

sdi 56

SDi 13, 15–16, 19–21, 23–24, 28, 32–40, 42–43, 47–50, 53, 59, 64, 72, 74, 76–79, 81–82, 84, 86–88, 99, 117–119, 122–123, 127, 130–131, 133, 138–139, 144–145, 154, 156, 161, 165–167, 171, 173, 177, 187–188, 194, 208–210, 225–226, 228, 231–240, 245, 247, 267, 273, 276, 280–283

Second Tier 13, 26–27, 65, 79, 81, 99, 123–126, 128, 130–131, 133, 140–143, 152–159, 161, 171–173, 233, 235, 266–268

security 22, 89, 94, 99, 103, 134, 180, 218, 233, 257

self-actualization 269

self-confidence 96, 121

self-esteem 29, 48, 50, 52–54

self-worth 52, 121

sensing 176, 188, 192, 194

shadow 128, 213, 219, 245, 263–264

soul 56, 80–81, 83–85, 122, 156, 165, 198, 204, 214, 244, 251, 255–256, 260, 268, 271–272, 286

Spiral 10, 13, 16, 20–22, 24–28, 37, 40, 42, 56, 59, 62–64, 72, 75, 78–80, 82, 86–88, 97–101, 107, 117, 123–127, 130–133, 139, 141–142, 145–147, 149–153, 155–156, 158, 163, 165, 169, 171, 177, 179, 181, 187–188, 205, 209–210, 216, 224–225, 228, 235, 239–241, 243, 245, 247–249,

W

Y

CPSIA information can be obtained
at www.ICGtesting.com
Printed in the USA
LVOW01s0709011115

460593LV00032B/562/P